M000119652

THE RISE AND FALL OF CLASSICAL LEGAL THOUGHT

The *Rise & Fall* of *Classical Legal Thought*

WITH A NEW PREFACE BY THE AUTHOR,
"Thirty Years Later"

❧ ❧

DUNCAN KENNEDY

❧ ❧

1975
AFAR
Cambridge
2006

BeardBooks
Washington, D.C.

ISBN - 13: 978-1-58798-278-1
ISBN - 10: 1-58798-278-1

A version of Chapter 1 was published in
Research in Law and Sociology
(JAI Press, 1980), p. 3-24.

Printed in the United States of America

❧ CONTENTS ❧

PREFACE   *Thirty Years Later*   vii

CHAPTER 1   *Legal Consciousness*   1

CHAPTER 2   *Pre-Classical Public Law*   31

CHAPTER 3   *Pre-Classical Private Law: Property*   93

CHAPTER 4   *Pre-Classical Private Law:*
                   The Transformation of Contract   157

CHAPTER 5   *The Integration of Classical Legal Thought*   242

BIBLIOGRAPHY   265

INDEX   271

Thirty Years Later

THE RISE AND FALL OF CLASSICAL LEGAL THOUGHT is the first draft of the first half of a book about the history of American legal thought from the early nineteenth century to World War II. I researched and wrote it between September 1973 and September 1975, when I submitted it to the Appointments Committee at Harvard Law School as the principal element in my tenure file. At the time, I saw the manuscript as the "rise" part, and planned to write the second or "fall" part to make a big book.

I kept working on the project until 1979, and then abandoned it. In 1980, Steve Spitzer published the first chapter, under the title "Toward an Historical Understanding of Legal Consciousness: The Case of Classical Legal Thought in America: 1850-1940," in volume three of Current Research in Law and Sociology. In 1998, Patricia Fazzone word-processed Cynthia Vergados' 1975 typescript of chapters two through five, and Lisa Clark reformatted the whole manuscript as it appears here (I corrected a few errors of spelling and—horrors—grammar in the process). For this edition, I've added this preface, a bibliography and a rudimentary index.

Through the late seventies and the eighties, *The Rise and Fall* cir-

---

* Thanks to Lama Abu-Odeh, Chris Desan, Janet Halley, David Kennedy, Karl Klare, Talha Syed and Laura Trachtman. Errors are mine alone.

culated widely in its original typescript form among the younger generation of American legal historians. It was a well known and controversial part of the rejuvenation of American legal history that occurred during this period and, at the same time, one of the several documents that defined a current within the critical legal studies movement of the late seventies through the early nineties. The published first chapter is still cited, typically as part of the "revisionist" scholarship that replaced the condemnatory progressive historiography of the Lochner era with a more nuanced picture.

The Rise and Fall was intended as an intervention in the contemporary debate about how to understand late nineteenth century American law. In this respect, it did indeed involve a sharp "revision" of the picture presented by the progressive historians who condemned the Lochner era as simultaneously reactionary in politics and formalist in legal theory. But the manuscript had a more ambitious agenda. It aimed to be the first structuralist narrative of the path of emergence of the "legal objects," private rights and public powers, that are the building blocks with which modern law is made. It was supposed to be what Foucault called, following Nietzsche, a "genealogy,"[1] in this case, of American law understood as a discourse rather than as a body of rules.

The first narrative claim was that private rights and public powers received their characteristic modern form, the form in which they became the universal building blocks, only in the late nineteenth century. Rights and powers, as we understand them today, are a very recent invention. The second claim was that the jurists who did the work of construction were engaged in an ambitious rationalization project that paradoxically ended in loss of faith both in the coherence of their conceptual scheme and in the existence of a distinctive legal reason. The third was that this outcome left us in "a post-classical age of disintegration," with multiple reconstruction projects, bearing only an oblique resemblance to the legal thought of the pre-Civil War period.

1. Michel Foucault, "Nietzsche, Genealogy, History," in *Language, Countermemory, Practice: Selected Essays and Interviews* (D. Bouchard ed.; D. Bouchard & S. Simon, trans., 1977).

The Rise and Fall was supposed to be an intervention in legal theory as much as in legal history. The goal, shared with, among others, Alan Freeman, Peter Gabel, Al Katz, Karl Klare and Roberto Unger, was to introduce critical theory and structuralism, including the Frankfurt School and (in my case) the work of Claude Levi-Strauss and Jean Piaget, into American jurisprudence and legal sociology.

This Preface discusses the ideas in the manuscript that seem to me still of interest, the context for the writing of it, and its fate. My hope is that the ideas will get a second chance at life through this first formal publication, but even if nothing like that were to happen it is a pleasure to make the work available as an archival item for legal historiographers.

I. A history of American legal thought

The Rise and Fall was to be a history of American legal thought. I thought of such a history as distinct from a history of the doctrines of American law, from an historical sociology of the impact of law in America, and, less obviously, from a history of professional reflection on the nature of law by American lawyers (their philosophy of law or jurisprudence).

Legal thought, for the purposes of *The Rise and Fall*, is the conceptual apparatus, the reasoning techniques, the legal ideals and the key images that the elite bar, including judges, treatise writers and important lawyers, deploy when they make legal arguments or give opinions or declarations about what the law "is" or ought to be. There were two models for the project, each an intimidating masterpiece: Pollock and Maitland's *History of English Law Before the Time of Edward I*, and Rudolph von Jhering's *The Spirit of Roman Law*.[3]

---

2. Frederick Pollock & William Maitland, *The History of English Law Before the Time of Edward I* (2nd ed., S.F.C. Milsom, ed., Cambridge: Cambridge Univ. Press, 1968).

3. Rudolph von Jhering, *Geist des Romischen Rechts* (Leipzig: Breitkopf und Hartel, 1852-1865), French translation: *L'Esprit du Droit Romain* (O. de Meulenaire, trans., Paris: Chevalier-Maresq, 1887).

Legal thought, in this tradition, is distinguishable from other bodies of thought, say economic and political and social and religious thought, and also "relatively autonomous" from the interests, material and ideal, that impel social actors to take positions about what the law in particular cases is or ought to be. The notion of a history of legal thought is that the conceptual apparatus, reasoning techniques, legal ideals and key images have changed over time in ways that are important for our understanding of our current legal practices.

A. Classical Legal Thought

The approach of *The Rise and Fall* posits that the thought of a period has a certain kind of unity. This is not the unity of a "spirit" of the period, nor the unity produced by the working out of a master idea (we called that approach "idealism"). It is rather the unity that comes from the existence, within the overall consciousness of a period, of a dominant doctrinal "subsystem," within which concepts, reasoning techniques, ideals and images are analogous across legal domains.

The ambition of the book was to discover these analogies in the periods of American legal thought by the close reading and comparison of legal treatises, leading cases, and the reported arguments in leading cases. The claim that there was this peculiar kind of unity by analogy put me in the position of wanting to say something about the conceptual ordering of legal doctrine in all of the areas of law conventionally recognized in a given period (both public law and private law, etc.).

The periodization I adopted was the conventional one for describing three overlapping "Ages of American Law:" the period from the Revolution to the Civil War (pre-Classical legal thought); the late nineteenth and early twentieth century (Classical Legal Thought or CLT); and the "modern" period beginning before WWI and lasting to the present of 1975. But I proposed a new understanding of the periods and their relationship to one another.

According to *The Rise and Fall*, Classical Legal Thought (CLT) differed radically, discontinuously, from the model that dominated up to the Civil War, but was conceptually similar to the one we employed in 1975. Pre-Classical legal thought got its unity-by-analogy through the ideal of "liberality" (in opposition to "technicality"), the manipulation of a tension between morality and "policy," reasoning to results through the "implication" of a fictitious intent, the right/remedy and vested/unvested distinctions, and the notion of a "relation" as the basis for legal rules in a private law system understood as primarily contractual.

My claim was that, in the second half of the nineteenth century, legal actors dramatically revised the conceptual apparatus, reasoning techniques, ideals and images that had dominated in the pre-Classical period. The Classical subsystem built all legal rules out of a will theory using strictly analogous conceptions of state and federal power and private right. Private law rules were elaborately divided and subdivided around the public/private distinction *within private law*. The preferred reasoning technique was induction/deduction, the ideal was the deployment of democratically validated public power as the framework for private freedom, and the key image was of powers and rights that were "absolute within their spheres."

There were three major changes in the modern period. First, the boundaries between conceptual domains (public law and private law, contract and tort, etc.) were blurred or collapsed. Second, actors within modern legal thought experienced their ideals as contradictory, rather than as diverse but harmoniously distributed across subject matters. Third, there was a dramatic transformation in the dominant technique of legal reasoning, from induction/deduction to balancing.

1. CONSTITUTIONAL LAW

According to the argument, modern constitutional law thinking is organized into the three domains of the separation of powers, individual rights against the state and federalism. The areas have a deep level of analogy because in each there is the notion that the constitution itself establishes opposing entities—judicial, legislative and executive powers, federal vs. state powers, and state powers vs. individual rights—that are intrinsically in conflict or "contradictory" if taken at face value. It is these that the moderns have to balance in order to resolve the conflict in particular cases of judicial lawmaking.

A thesis of *The Rise and Fall* was that this situation came about through the "disintegration" of CLT, which had developed over time this very underlying structure of powers and rights, but whose practitioners had believed that it was possible to resolve conflicts (do judicial lawmaking) by distributing questions according to the firm categorical scheme established in the federal constitution and then inducing/deducing the solution from that scheme. The solutions got their analogical character from their deployment, across the domains of constitutional law, of the image of "powers absolute within their spheres," with the sphere of the federal judiciary being the neutral policing of all the boundaries, while respecting the will of the relevant power or right holder when operating within its proper domain.

The period before CLT was, according to *The Rise and Fall*, different, first, because there were multiple ways of dealing with judge/legislator, state/federal and right/power conflict (conflicting theories of the nature of the Union in federalism; quasi-justiciable natural rights, vested rights, and implied limitations for right/power conflict). Judicial reasoning techniques were correspondingly diverse.

"Powers absolute within their spheres," combined with induction/deduction, were an element of the pre-Classical way of thinking only in the Marshallian theory of federalism. After the Civil War, this way of thinking about federalism won out, and then colonized public law as a whole. The "powers absolute" notion was able to win out in the law of rights against the state only because private law thinking had undergone an evolution analogous to that of the law of federalism.

2. PRIVATE LAW

According to *The Rise and Fall*, the classics operated just as dramatic a transformation of private law as of constitutional law. In

the early nineteenth century, legal thinkers lumped most private
law rules under the category of property; by mid-century, they
had reconceived the system as primarily contractual. The Classics
reorganized it yet again, into the modern fields of contract, quasi-
contract, tort, trusts, constructive trusts, and the law of status,
which included family law. They marginalized property and got
rid of the remaining traces of the writ system, of the pre-Classical
discourse of liberality versus technicality, morality versus policy,
right versus remedy and vested versus unvested, and of "implication" as a reasoning technique.

The transformation of private law thinking was accomplished
by the iteration and re-iteration of the public/private distinction
to differentiate fields within the private domain, and then to further internally differentiate each field. The upshot was a "will theory" within private law, with the will being either the will of the
parties or the will of the state.

There was a strong analogy to the "powers absolute" conception in constitutional law. This analogy permitted the final crucial conceptual development within CLT. The shift from vested
rights to substantive due process became possible through the
conceptual equation of the rights of individuals vis a vis one
another, as defined by the common law, with the constitutional
rights of individuals, guaranteed against legislative infringe-
ment.

According to the argument of the manuscript, modern thinking about private law is both organized and disintegrated in the
same way as thinking about constitutional law. The opposing elements are not explicit constitutional mandates establishing judicial, legislative, state and federal powers, and individual rights.
Rather they are opposing orientations to how to deal with a small
number of perennial conflicts (formality vs. informality, community vs. autonomy, paternalism vs. self-determination, and regulation vs. facilitation). As in constitutional law, the Classical mode
of categorically separating questions and then resolving them
inductively/deductively has succumbed to the blurring of boundaries, and the moderns have defaulted to more or less ad hoc balancing from situation to situation.

B. Structuralism and critical theory

The Rise and Fall was an intervention in legal theory as well as in legal history. It aimed to demonstrate that the modes of thought called structuralism and critical theory could be adapted and used in the analysis of law, both law as a technical discourse and law as an element in the social thought of a period.

The point here was not to convert the reader to belief in a theory called structuralism, as one might be converted to orthodox Marxism or to the Freudian psychoanalytic view of the world. Rather it was to take very specific ideas from the literatures of structuralism and critical theory, revise them as seemed appropriate, and use them to illuminate, hopefully, specific aspects of legal discourse.

In other words, the point was to add structuralist and critical techniques to the repertoire available for understanding law as a phenomenon too large and messy and complex to be fully grasped within any one theoretical frame. Of course, there was also the fantasy that these adaptations would be contributions to the literatures proper to structuralism and critical theory, and prove useful in similar endeavors in other fields. In retrospect, there seem to me to have been five distinct ideas in the manuscript that fit this description. Because they are if anything even more exotic today than they were in 1975, I present them here in some detail.

1. LEGAL CONSCIOUSNESS

The structuralist element in the notion of legal consciousness is that of a "subsystem," within consciousness broadly understood. A subsystem is distinct from the larger entity, utilizing a small set of conceptual building blocks, along with a small set of typical arguments as to how the concepts should be applied, to produce results that seem to the jurists involved to have a high level of coherence within and across legal fields. The argument of *The Rise and Fall* was that there was a Classical subsystem within late nineteenth century legal thought that cohered through the notion of powers absolute, the will theory, the iteration and re-iteration of the public/private distinction, and the inductive/deductive method.

CLT was not "the" legal consciousness of the Classical period, but the dominant subsystem within it. The subsystem was not a theory, explicit or implicit, that Classical thinkers consciously or even unconsciously put into effect. The subsystem came into existence as legal actors applied, to one legal issue after another, a vague general or ideal orientation and a set of evolving tools used when "doing" law.

The subsystem expanded from small beginnings during the pre-Classical period to become dominant after 1870. It did this by what we might call "reworking" of doctrine using the tools at hand. Instead of change mirroring transformations in the "material base" (e.g., from competitive to monopoly capitalism), change was driven by the efforts of litigants representing conflicting interests to restate the law to favor their side, under the supervision of courts with a role commitment to deciding according to rational and universalizable criteria. The model for this process was *bricolage* as described in the first chapter of Claude Levi-Strauss' *The Savage Mind*,[4] a book I read and was blown away by in law school.

Today it seems to me that one of the most interesting aspects of this theory was that the concepts that were used over and over to construct the subsystem changed each time they were extended to a new sub-sub-system. "Judicial interpretation of the law," "a power absolute within its sphere," the "will" of a power or right "holder," "contract," and so forth, started with what I called "core" meanings as applied in narrow areas. Each time they were used in a new area, they changed the way the legal elite understood that new area.

At the same time, the concepts themselves came to mean something different when they were used both in the core and in the peripheral area. This idea was an adaptation of Jean Piaget's concepts of "assimilation" and "accommodation" in his masterpiece, *Play, Dreams and Imitation in Childhood*,[5] which I read as a new

---

4. Claude Levi-Strauss, *The Savage Mind* (Chicago: Univ. of Chicago Press, 1966).

5. Jean Piaget, Play, *Dreams and Imitation in Childhood* (C. Gattegno & F. Hodgson, trans., New York: Norton, 1962).

parent law student in 1969. This approach to thinking about legal thought seems to me useful in understanding the contemporary global phenomena of juridification, rights consciousness, and economic analysis of law.

Starting around 1900, CLT as a subsystem didn't so much shrink as disintegrate, likewise through reworking piece by piece, morphing little by little into modern legal thought. The legal consciousness of 1945 contained residual elements of pre-Classical legal thought and residual elements of classicism, as islands in a modernist sea. In social theoretical terms, perhaps we could say it had undergone "derationalization," by analogy to Freudian desublimation, leading to what I saw as a pervasive sense that the system was loaded with contradictions, from the most abstract level down to the micro-level, of, say, the law of offer and acceptance.

It was an important aspect of this narrative that it provided no explanation of why one subsystem triumphed over the others. The goal was to provide a description of transformations that had been ignored, along with a mechanics of transformation. I thought that recognition of what changed would be an interesting and important event, even if I had nothing to contribute to the quest for larger causes. I was happy to concede that the agents of transformation had "bad" motives, so long as it was admitted that they permanently changed the way we think now. [6]

Just before I started writing *The Rise and Fall*, I read, at Roberto Unger's and Karl Klare's suggestion, Georg Lukacs'

---

6. This agnostic aspect of the project was sharply criticized by Mort Horwitz, among others, as both politically and methodologically retrograde. The restriction of ambition was implicit in *The Rise and Fall*, but explicit in "The Structure of Blackstone's Commentaries," 28 *Buff. L. Rev.* 205, 220 (1979): "My focus on interpreting the larger framework ... means that what I have to say is descriptive and descriptive only of thought. It means ignoring the question of what brings a legal consciousness into being, what causes it to change, and what effect it has on the actions of those who live it. My only justification for these omissions is that we need to understand far more than we now do about the content and the internal structure of legal thought before we can hope to link it in any convincing way to other aspects of social, political, or economic life. There are dangers to deferring the task, but I think them well worth risking." See note 19 infra.

"Reification and the Consciousness of the Proletariat,"[7] and found it highly suggestive. Lukacs showed analogies across the whole range of "bourgeois thought," from physics to law to politics to economics to art. *The Rise and Fall* tried to show a similar analogical pattern within "bourgeois legal thought."

But the general conception was quite different from his, and cannibalized other theorists along with Lukacs. To begin with, what emerged through this semi-conscious process was most definitely not the Lukacsian conception of a "legal form" whose logic derived from and mirrored the logic of the commodity form, understood to be the essence of capitalist relations of production. CLT was always "emergent" and "relatively autonomous" from other domains.

As in Lukacs and in Herbert Marcuse's *Reason and Revolution: Hegel and the Rise of Social Theory*,[8] another big influence, there were "contradictions." In my conception, consciousness functioned to "mediate the contradictions of experience," rather than, as in the neo-Marxist formulation, to mask the internal contradictions of the capitalist mode of production. In other words, my approach was modernist rather than Marxist in that as in many other respects.

2. THE PHENOMENOLOGICAL APPROACH TO LEGAL REASONING, BY
ANALOGY AND BY DEDUCTION, TO PRODUCE A CONCEPTION OF THE
"MODE OF INTEGRATION" OF A SUBSYSTEM.

The Rise and Fall adopted a phenomenological approach to reasoning by analogy, through the notion of "horizontal integration," which refers to the extent to which legal thinkers *experience* results within one doctrinal complex as relevant to results in another. What makes this approach phenomenological is that it is not about whether there really "is" an analogy, but only about whether a legal reasoner "feels" or "sees" or "intuits" that there is one. What makes a doctrine part of a sub-system is that it is

---

7. Georg Lukacs, "Reification and the Consciousness of the Proletariat," in *History and Class Consciousness: Studies in Marxist Dialectics* (R. Livingston, trans., Cambridge: MIT Press, 1971).

8. Herbert Marcuse, *Reason and Revolution: Hegel and the Rise of Social Theory* (Boston: Beacon Press, 1968).

experienced as close enough to the other members so that one moves easily by analogy from it to the others and back again.

The phenomenological approach to deduction was a much more innovative idea, because it involved getting rid of the concept of legal "formalism" that had dominated discussions of late nineteenth century legal thought since Roscoe Pound wrote "Mechanical Jurisprudence"[9] in 1908. The idea of the blocking level in Chapter 1 and Chapter 5 of *The Rise and Fall* is that all thought deploys concepts that are understood to permit deduction, and other concepts that are meaningful but too vague or abstract to permit anything like that kind of logical rigor. The blocking level is the level of abstraction below which concepts have felt deductive "operativeness," and above which they are experienced as no more than indicators, or just as convenient labels for items without intrinsic logical connection.

The blocking level can vary over time within a given discourse, so that one period's "deduction" is another period's "abuse of deduction" or "formalism." In the phenomenological approach, there is *no outside perspective* from which to judge that a period experiences operativeness in concepts that are "really" so vague or incoherent as to be useless, or, conversely, that a period failed to grasp the "underlying logic" of legal relations.

The move to operativeness and the blocking level turns "formalism" into a relative term. In other words, in the traditional mode, most extremely stated by Felix Cohen in "Transcendental Nonsense and the Functional Approach,"[10] there is an objective criterion for deciding when there has been an abuse of deduction. The vice of CLT, according to Cohen, was that virtually all its concepts were *in fact* meaningless. In my version, all systems are deductive but they vary in the level of abstraction at which deduction is experienced as convincing. This is a phenomenological criterion because we distinguish systems according to how the participants experience them rather than according to whether they really are or are not using deduction correctly.

9. Roscoe Pound, "Mechanical Jurisprudence," 8 *Colum. L. Rev.* 605 (1908).

10. Felix Cohen, "Transcendental Nonsense and the Functional Approach," 1935 *Colum. L. Rev.* 809 (1935).

The combination of felt horizontal integration, through the experience of analogy across legal fields, with felt vertical integration, when very abstract concepts were understood as governing large numbers of doctrines within fields, produced the broad and tight "integration" of CLT. The "disintegration" of CLT occurred in the vertical dimension. In other words, the abstractions, which had allowed Classical thinkers to place cases firmly within spheres and then to reason deductively about the consequences, lost their operative power. Everything was still analogous to everything else, but the analogies no longer led to necessary conclusions. What was left was balancing.

In retrospect, 1975 may have been the year when this claim achieved its maximum plausibility. Starting at some point in the nineteen sixties, the blocking level in American legal thought seems to have begun to "go back up." The first indication was in some Warren Court opinions, but the most striking change occurred in the nineteen seventies in the Burger Court's federalism decisions, and then spread everywhere. As a child of postrealism, I find both the deductive civil libertarianism of the Warren Court and the deductive federalism of the Burger and Rehnquist Courts absurd. But I don't doubt that the writers experienced the concepts that seem to me mere invitations to balancing to be fully operative. I have the same reaction to our contemporary legal version of international human rights discourse.

In private law, the right wing reconstruction projects of law and economics and libertarianism are self-consciously deductive. As Jay Feinman[11] has pointed out, we may now be entering a phase of reintegration of the schema as a whole, as conservatives put together individualist private law with takings and due process jurisprudence in a kind of "second time as farce" revival of CLT.

I see the conception of the mode of integration of a legal consciousness as a contribution to the critical theory enterprise that might be called "modeling the organic." In other words, it is supposed to let us think a body of thought as indeed a "body" or "whole," by virtue of analogies among the parts, along with expe-

11. Jay Fineman, "Un-making Law: The Classical Revival in the Common Law," 28 *Seattle Univ. L. Rev.* 1 (2004).

rienced horizontal and vertical integration, ideals, and a tool kit for new cases. The idea is to explain, without departing from Weberian methodological individualism, how a subsystem can be a unity without anyone having designed it.

I can't remember where I got the idea of a phenomenological turn, but the later chapters of *The Savage Mind* clearly influenced the picture of continuity and change of a structure over time, and my understanding of phenomenology was wholly derived from *Reason and Revolution*.

3. The notion of "nesting"

As I've already mentioned, *The Rise and Fall* depicts the emergence of a new organization of private law through the iteration and reiteration of the public/private distinction *within the private*. So contracts and trusts are private vis a vis torts, quasi-contract, constructive trust and status. But within contract, the consideration doctrine is public, offer and acceptance private. In family law, the decision to marry is a contract, and so private, but its terms are fixed by the state, and so public. Within tort law, the fault principle is private; strict liability represents the will of the state.

The plausibility of this picture of the dynamic of Classical private law was recently confirmed for me by Stephen Siegel's study[12] of John Chipman Gray's treatises on perpetuities and restraints on alienation. Gray reorganized the chaotic masses of real property law around a simple opposition between the will of the parties and the policy-driven will of the state, represented by the rules against perpetuities and restraints on alienation. (See p. 148-52 below.)

"Nesting" is a name for this phenomenon: the system is organized around an opposition (here, public vs. private); the opposition then reappears within one or both terms of the initial ordering (here, e.g., contract vs. tort). The notion of a fractile order is analogous, as is the move in Classical rhetoric called "chiasmus," but I encountered this way of understanding a socially constructed order in the later chapters of *The Savage Mind*, in which Levi-

---

12. Stephen Siegel, "John Chipman Gray and the Moral Basis of Classical Legal Thought," 86 *Iowa L. Rev.* 1513 (2001).

Strauss applied it to the kinship and plant classification systems
beloved of anthropologists. In later work, I've applied it to patterns of legal argument as well as of legal classification.[13]

Once one discerns a nesting pattern within an aspect of a body of thought (for example, classification or argument), it appears dramatically more integrated than it would if classification or argument were ad hoc adaptations to the "reality" of what was being classified or disputed. Finding a nesting pattern, like identifying the felt sense of analogy across domains or the felt sense of compulsion through deductive argument, allows one to model a giant mass of rules as organic without making it in any sense transpersonal.

4. The Ontology of Rights and Powers

The most exotic of the ideas in *The Rise and Fall*, and perhaps for that reason the idea that has had least resonance, is that of the *construction of the legal object*. *The Rise and Fall* argues that the judicial, legislative, commerce and police powers, and individual rights, all changed their nature after the Civil War, because they became "multi-dimensional" entities. The state police power was understood as "essentially" the same thing in relation to the federal commerce power that it was in relation to the individual right of property. An individual's right of property, in turn, was the same thing in relation to legislative power that it was in relation to the property right of another individual. The judicial power was the same whether adjudicating federal vs. state power, legislative power vs. individual right, or individual right vs. individual right.

The Rise and Fall claimed that, before the Civil War, each of these relations was understood as distinct from all the others. It was not that pre-Classical thought was less organized, just that its elements were embedded in the pre-Classical whole according to its distinct organizational mode, rather than in the Classical mode.

---

13. Duncan Kennedy, "A Semiotics of Legal Argument," 42 *Syracuse L. Rev.* 75 (1991) (same article with European Introduction: 3 *Collected Courses of the Academy of European Law*, Book 2, 309-365 (Amsterdam: Kluwer Academic Publishers, 1994)); see also, Jack Balkin, "Nested Oppositions," 99 *Yale L.J.* 1669 (1990).

Once the process of unification of the power or right in all its external relations had occurred, CLT was dramatically more integrated than it had been. Conclusions about the nature of the commerce power reached in a commerce power vs. police power case could be deployed, mutatis mutandis, in a case pitting the commerce power against freedom of contract.

As throughout *The Rise and Fall*, this point is phenomenological rather than logical. The Classics brought about this particular ontology of rights and powers through their working and reworking of the materials, and then experienced it as a truth about rights and powers. The manuscript takes no position about these truth claims. It simply asserts that modern "sophisticated" legal thinkers no longer experience them in that way. The "we" the book addresses sees strong analogies between a given right/power conflict and a conflict between that power and some other power. But "we" feel no necessity flowing from the treatment of the power in its encounter with the other power to its treatment in the encounter with the right.

This idea is an adaptation of Piaget's theory, in *Six Psychological Studies*[14] (another book for young parent law students), of the developing infant's "construction of the object" by unifying the data obtained through sight, touch, smell, sound, etc. The "aha" moment is when the infant grasps all the data as pertaining to a single "thing." Whereas Piaget was a "genetic epistemologist," i.e., believed that the infant got it right as to the truth of the object, *The Rise and Fall* was persistently phenomenological. In other words, the truth of the object for CLT was no longer its truth for the moderns. The idea of an ontology of rights and powers seems to me still very useful in understanding phenomena like the emergence of European quasi-federalism.

5. REASON DIES WHILE GIVING BIRTH TO LIBERALISM

In its last chapter, *The Rise and Fall* presented an interpretation of the significance for legal thought of the narrative as a whole. Here it is:

14. Jean Piaget, *Six Psychological Studies* (A. Tenzer & D. Elkin, trans., New York: Random House, 1967).

The irony was that the very success of the enterprise of subsuming all legal relationships under a single small set of concepts
eventually destroyed belief that it was the concepts themselves
that determined the outcomes of their application. When the
abstractions had performed their task of integrating legal thought,
it became apparent that while pre-Classical particularity had been
irrational, the new unity was merely linguistic—a verbal trick—
rather than a substantive reconstruction. We came gradually to see
that there were an infinity of possible results that might all plausibly find expression in the new conceptual language, and, what was
worse, might all claim to be derivations of the abstract governing
principles. The concepts, then, could be nothing more than a
vocabulary for categorizing, describing and comparing, rather
than the elements in a method for deriving outcomes. The famous
principles, taken together, appeared either self-contradictory or so
vague as to be worthless as guides to particular decisions.

It was only for a relatively brief moment, that during which
the process of abstraction and unification was proceeding apace
but had not yet achieved its disillusioning total triumph, that it
was possible to believe in the objectivity of the new method. But
it does not follow that the emergence of the new language was
without long range influence on results. The work of destruction
was in itself of massive impact on what could be thought about
the legal order. Because the old way of thought was swallowed
whole and digested by Classicism, we are without anything more
than an indirect, quasi-antiquarian access to it. We attempt the
construction of operative categories and integrating schemes in a
world dominated by the death of the Classical organism, rather
than in the naively pluralist world in which Classicism itself arose.
(p. 251)

The manuscript contained no attempt to tie its claims into a yet
grander narrative transcending legal theory. But there was an
implicit conception, worked out explicitly in the next phase of the
project, in an article entitled "The Structure of Blackstone's
Commentaries."[15] The story, which still seems right to me, was

15. Supra note 6.

that "reason dies while giving birth to Liberalism." The way we think about justice in a system with a state has a particular form, which we can call Liberalism with a capital L, to indicate that it includes both the typical liberal and the typical conservative ideas of the time. The article proposed that the crucial features of this very general structure within which we think about justice and the state are the organization of rights and powers in the integrated whole of CLT, and the idea that there is a sharp distinction between legal reasoning and general political discourse.[16]

The Rise and Fall was supposed to be a history of the last stages of the emergence of this way of thinking, that is, the stage at which the various relatively inchoate approaches typical of seventeenth and eighteenth century Liberalism got organized into a tight and coherent ordering of the legal universe. Each of the steps in the evolution of the modern structure required a vast labor of critique of previous solutions, and the proposal of new ones. According to the manuscript, we should understand it as an epochal accomplishment of jurists working on the project of determining justice through reason. Nothing could be wronger than to dismiss CLT as just right wing self interest combined with the jurisprudential error of "formalism."

According to the larger theory, we should also see the Liberal way of thinking as contingent, in the sense that it is only one possible way of ordering experience so as to address the problem of justice in the state, and there is no warrant that the concepts and operations we deploy from within Liberalism are true mirrors of the intrinsic properties of the elements of the problem. This was the point of applying phenomenological and Piagetian structuralist ideas to concepts like induction/deduction, police power or contract.

That the Liberal ordering is "socially constructed" is not to say that we can change it by recognizing it as such. *The Rise and Fall's*

16. The structure of rights and powers represented majority rule (the legislature), individual rights (constitutional guarantees) and the rule of law (the separation of powers) in a context that constitutionalized both national and local self-government (federal and state powers). See Duncan Kennedy, *A Critique of Adjudication* [fin de siecle] (Cambridge: Harvard Univ. Press, 1997) Chs. 2 & 3, for an elaboration of this understanding of Liberalism.

"death of reason" narrative is that "our" modern situation is one in which we no longer believe that the structure mirrors reality, and have concluded that from within it the best one can do is balance conflicting considerations that reflect our contradictory ideas and emotions. This outcome is the result of the work of mutual destruction carried on by Liberal legal thinkers of all political persuasions as they "cleared the ground" of their rivals before proposing their own versions of the project.

In the modernist view (in opposition to the Marxist view), the critical project *within Liberalism itself* has led us to lose any hope of an "outside" to which we could resort in order to have a better way of doing official justice through reason. Reason is *felo da se,* dead by its own hand ... meaning dead as a way to solve the problem of justice in the state, not, of course, dead, as a way to critique attempts to solve the problem through reason, or as a way to figure out the situation within which we have to decide politically, or as a way balance one's checkbook.

I didn't come across the death of reason slogan until the appearance of *The Essential Frankfurt School Reader*[17] in 1978. I am quite sure that the notion got a great deal of its power for me from its resonance with the particular kind of post-realism that characterized the senior members of the Harvard Law School faculty I most respected. I had known three of them somewhat as a child—Mark Howe, Louis Jaffe and Ben Kaplan—and got to know Jack Dawson when I returned to Cambridge as an Assistant Professor.

They had no interest in critical theory or structuralism, and certainly didn't think that either Liberalism or reason was dead. But they were producers of the very wide web of analogy, combined with the disintegration of deductive structure into mere balancing, that I saw as the defining characteristic of modern legal thought. *The Rise and Fall* was in a sense an attempt to theorize them, and thereby escape them into a different kind of political/intellectual engagement (or *engagement)*.

For this reason, perhaps ... but, an interruption: This whole

---

17. *The Essential Frankfurt School Reader* (A. Arato & S. Piccone, eds., New York: Urizen Books, 1978).

enterprise of "reading" the manuscript as its imputed author feels fishy to me even as I carry it out, because the text says, often, things I don't remember it saying, and which I certainly wouldn't say today. For example, there is a nostalgia for reason in politics very reminiscent of the Frankfurt School in *The Rise and Fall*'s introductory section. The study of legal consciousness might help us understand judicial activism, and we should care about activism because judges doing it "are carriers of the notion that the ideal of justice is accessible to the reason of people acting in the real situations of political and economic life." (p. 4)

The implication is that we should want "human reason [to be] something more than an instrumental mechanism for the execution of collective or individual decisions reached through the clash of interests, passions or appetites." There is no suggestion that reason is or will soon become any such thing. I think I meant this hedged formula as defining a modernist position in dialogue with Roberto Unger's far more serious demand, "Speak God," at the end of *Knowledge and Politics*.[18]

II. Some Context

The Rise and Fall was to be part of a larger leftist political/intellectual attack on the status quo in American legal scholarship generally. I set out with that agenda, over-confident and irrationally exuberant, without any formal training at all in legal history or in the general techniques of historical scholarship as it is done today. As I mentioned above, my heroes and models were Maitland and Jhering. I read a good deal of the available literature on the history of American law after the Revolution, but by no means all. I hadn't yet read the Commonwealth school, for example, and concentrated on the New Deal era constitutional historians Haines and Corwin, some Dawson, Howe and Milsom, some Pound and some Llewellyn, some Hurst and Lawrence Friedman, the populists Twiss and Jacobs, Fairman, McCloskey and Gilmore, and my contempo-

---

18. Roberto Unger, *Knowledge and Politics* (New York: Free Press, 1975).

raries, particularly Morton Horwitz, who was, at the time, leading
the movement toward a sophisticated politicization of the field.

For me, the great accomplishment of his *The Transformation of American Law* was that it was the first historical work to identify a politics of private law on a par with the by then well recognized politics of constitutional law. *The Rise and Fall* was written in dialogue with this project, but it was quite different. I think I would have said that Horwitz, no less than the progressive historians of constitutional law, tended to fluctuate between too much "instrumentalism," i.e., reducing law to extra-legal material interests (the mercantile interest, the requirements of capitalist economic development), and too much idealism, i.e., treating the law of the period as the working out of an extra- or supra-legal theory (laissez-faire, natural rights, utilitarianism, Classical liberalism, positivism, formalism, etc.).[19] What lost out was legal thought understood, in its own right, as an important form of political/social thought whose development and disintegration speak directly to our current situation.

I was even more out of touch with the general ethos of academic history than I was with the field of legal history. I'd barely taken a course or two in college, and in so much as I was aware of them at all, I was instinctively antagonistic to such ideas as the foreignness of the past, that history is a craft somehow beyond theory, that the archive is the indispensable field work of the historian, and that present-orientedness is an unforgivable professional sin. I was aware that young leftist historians had begun to do "history from the bottom up," and that social history was in vogue. I thought that was an interesting development, but a form of self-marginalization, if you were interested in attacking the

19. By 1979, our positions had begun to converge on the study of legal consciousness and the notion of contradictions, but were more divergent on the causation issue. In "The Structure of Blackstone's Commentaries," supra note 6, at 363, n. 56, I summed up my critique of the progressivist economic causation claims as follows: "It is idealism masquerading as materialism to substitute 'commodities' for 'rights,' and 'development' for 'social policy,' and then play the liberal game of deriving the actual rules of the legal system as necessary consequences." This cryptic idea is unpacked in *A Critique of Adjudication* [fin de siecle], supra note 16, Ch. 11. For an interesting discussion of some of these issues, see Louis Wolcher, "The Many Meanings of 'Wherefore' in Legal History," 68 *Wash. L. Rev.* 559 (1993).

way people at the top used law to support the status quo. Not that we were any more successful in avoiding marginalization.

While I was writing *The Rise and Fall* I happened to have a conversation with an acquaintance who was a senior member of the Harvard History Department. He told me that the department was considering making an offer to Michel Foucault, but had more or less decided not to because he was "a bad historian." I had read a good bit of his *Histoire de la folie a l'age classique*.[20] My glimpse into the Harvard historical mind made me want to laugh, because Foucault seemed to me to vastly transcend the wrongness of any of his particular claims, but also sent shudders up my untenured spine. Eventually I came to see my historical method, such as it was, as close to identical to that Foucault outlined in *Nietzsche, Genealogy, History*[21]. It was also quite close to the Louis Hartz of *Economic Policy and Democratic Thought: Pennsylvania, 1776-1860*.[22]

By 1975, the American liberalism that had dominated the upper end of American culture and politics since WWII was beginning to lose ground, just how rapidly no one could yet see, not to the small but growing radical minority but to resurgent American conservatism, which already subtly mixed free marketism with social authoritarianism. The sixties would turn out to have polarized the baby boomers, with many of them hating the whole thing as much as the cultural and political radicals had loved it.

Those of us who polarized to the left were just coming to realize to what an extent liberal hegemony had marginalized or invisibilized the literatures of Marxism, structuralism and critical theory generally. Among the people I had read only a little or not at all in 1975 were Hegel, Marx, Gramsci, Althusser, E.P Thompson, Husserl, Heidegger, Benjamin, Schmitt, Horkheimer, Sartre, Saussure, Lacan, Foucault, Derrida, Rorty, Habermas, Bourdieu. I hadn't even *heard* of many of them and to this day haven't fully caught up with all the stuff mainstream college educators thought not worth teaching us.

20. Michel Foucault, *Histoire de la folie a l'age classique* (Paris: Gallimard, 1972), later translated as *Madness and Civilization: A History of Insanity in the Age of Reason* (R. Howard, trans., London: Routledge, 2001).

21. Michel Foucault, "Nietzsche, Genealogy, History," supra note 1.

22. Louis Hartz, *Economic Policy and Democratic Thought: Pennsylvania, 1776-1860* (Cambridge: Harvard Univ. Press, 1948).

Those of us who thought of ourselves as doing a radical theory project were discovering and sharing these books, starting them, sometimes finishing them, often getting inspiration and even insight from passages we didn't understand very well at all. We made up what Diego Lopez calls a "hermeneutically impoverished context of reception."[23] We took in books by famous living and dead Europeans in an ahistorical jumble rather than as part of a sequence within which there were traditions of interpretation and critique developed in loosely linked milieux at each step along the way. And we "applied" them to our own national situation in ways that would often have astonished their authors.

The Rise and Fall was completely conventional in form, but its ambition was to be not just original, but also legally avant-garde, both politically and intellectually, by combining advanced European "theory" with advanced American jurisprudence. In retrospect, it is striking that all of us took it for granted that there was no European legal theory worthy of the name. *The Rise and Fall* is blind to the extent to which the United States of CLT and sociological jurisprudence was tightly linked to Western Europe, not as an influence but as an influencee. The phrase "powers absolute within their spheres," for example, is a strange translation to public law of a Kantian and Savignian slogan about private law.

In 1975, there were four discernible currents of legal academic politics, each with a characteristic approach to legal theory. These were the legal process school, liberal constitutionalism, law and economics, and a little radicalism. The legal process was into post-realist, centrist "reasoned elaboration;" the liberal constitutionalists were into legal "right answers" that made the Constitution a left liberal document. The newly emergent law and economics scholars were hyper-realist about doctrine (simply dismissing it) and naively deductivist about efficiency. The radicals saw law either as the instrument of dominant interests or as determined by the economy, although sufficiently autonomous to be sometimes available for radical defense or offense.

The Rise and Fall drew on each, but was also incompatible with

23. Diego Lopez Medina, *Teoría impura del derecho, la transformación de la cultura jurídica latinoamericana* (Bogota: Legis, 2004).

each. Reason had died while giving birth to Liberalism and we lived in a "post-Classical age of disintegration," prey to contradiction with no basis for action but a balancing technique that was ultimately arational. *The Rise and Fall* wasn't supposed to be political in the sense that the above schools were. Its view that modernism was synonymous with the sense of internal contradiction was supposed to be the registering of a fact of "our situation." But that said, if you accepted it, then you had to decide on your own which way to move politically within the contradictory legal field.

One had to do this without the guidance of a theory of law that would reinforce one's normative orientation and at the same time guide the articulation of the ideal into the legal. Nonetheless, the legal had to be acknowledged as a relatively autonomous resistant medium, whatever one's orientation toward operating within it. The implications were antinomian, or anarchist, or "decisonist," by contrast to the legalism of legal process and liberal constitutionalism, and the rationalism (instrumentalist or idealist), of the legal economists and the radicals.

The Rise and Fall treated the willingness of judges to defy legislative majorities and the balance of private power as a valuable, odd aspect of the American political tradition. It rejected the attempt to distinguish the Lochner Court from the Warren Court in a way that would make the first wrong and the second right. They were both "activist;" the difference was which side they were on. In other words, the ms. accepted the analysis of Learned Hand,[24] McCloskey[25] and Bickel,[26] but turned it on its head by celebrating rather than bemoaning counter-majoritarian aggression. (The trouble with the Warren Court was that it didn't go far enough.)

I was concerned that my colleagues' dislike of my New Leftish radical reform activities at Harvard Law School would cause them to deny me tenure. Not that they would have consciously done

---

24. Learned Hand, *The Bill of Rights* (New York: Atheneum, 1958).

25. Robert McCloskey, "Economic Due Process and the Supreme Court: An Exhumation and Reburial," 1962 *Sup. Ct. Rev.* 34.

26. Alexander Bickel, *The Least Dangerous Branch: The Supreme Court at the Bar of Politics* (Indianapolis: Bobbs-Merrill, 1962).

that; just that it was plausible that they would be unconsciously xxxi
motivated to manipulate the vague meritocratic standard to do me
in. The first draft of the first half of the book was not supposed
to be the whole story by any means. There would be plenty of
space, and plenty of post-tenure freedom, to develop the political
implications in the "fall" part. But I couldn't resist a sally, at the
very end of the manuscript. Reading it today, it may seem so
oblique that no one was likely to notice it, but I'll bet that those
members of the Appointments Committee who managed to slog
through all the way to the very end didn't fail to.

The middle aged generation of legal academics in power in
elite law schools in the seventies were overwhelmingly liberals or
moderates, but also overwhelmingly disenchanted pragmatists,
skeptical of any attempt at grand theory of either a descriptive or
a normative kind, at the same time that they were very compla-
cent, to my mind, about the basic goodness of elite legal academia
and its benign role in American life. The late nineteen sixties were
a disaster, in their experience, not just in national politics but also
in the academic politics of law schools "assaulted" by the student
movement.

The last paragraph of *The Rise and Fall* alluded to "the ironies
of generational conflict." It then quoted from Henry James on the
consequences of the Civil War for the liberal leaders of the pre-
War generation: "their illusions were rudely dispelled, and they
saw the best of all possible republics given over to fratricidal car-
nage. This affair had no place in their scheme, and nothing was
left for them but to hang their heads and close their eyes." (p. 264)
The first idea was to suggest that CLT was part of the generational reaction James described. But the second implication, which
I remember intending, was a parallel between the pre-Civil War
and the pre-Vietnam liberals.

III. Contrast with current modes

The Rise and Fall launched two floating signifiers, "Classical legal
thought" and "legal consciousness" that to this day bob up and
down on the waves of legal discourse. However, the intense inter-

est in all the variants of critical theory that characterized the mid nineteen seventies didn't last long. As for structuralism, it was out of fashion before most of its potential audience had even heard of it. The turn away from critical theory was partly caused by the shift to the right of the whole culture that accelerated after 1980. As in the thirties, it had been briefly possible to study and use Marxism without academic career danger, then the window closed. But two other factors were probably just as important in the particular world of the legal academy.

The first of these was the rise of feminist legal theory and critical race theory. Both pushed hard against the ultra-white-male ethos of the New Left, as well as against the critique of rights we developed in the early eighties. The second was the arrival of post-modernism (also known as post-structuralism), which pushed hard, from the other direction, so to speak, against the super-straightness of that same white male ethos, and against our clinging to structure, as an indispensable moment in critique.

Combining critical theory with structuralism in order to study the evolution of legal doctrine as a species of Liberal theory ran up against the further problem that taking doctrine seriously was reactionary from the point of view not only of feminist legal theory, critical race theory and postmodernism, but also from the point of view of the sociology of law and even of legal realism. The death of reason was not a lot more popular with a left nostalgic for the good old days of the Warren Court and now barely hanging on to a place in the national debate between retreating liberals and steadily advancing right wingers. It wasn't surprising that quite different approaches to Classical Legal Thought emerged and mainstreamed.

A: Langdell's Orthodoxy

Thomas Grey's famous article "Langdell's Orthodoxy"[27] can serve as a useful point of comparison between the methodology of *The Rise and Fall* and the more typical approach to intellectual

---

27. Thomas Grey, "Langdell's Orthodoxy," 45 *U. Pitt. L. Rev.* 1 (1983).

history of liberal post-realist legal scholars. Grey presents the orthodoxy using different descriptive words, calling it sometimes a "system of legal thought," or a "discursive structure," and a "kind of legal thinking," but more often a "legal theory." It is his "rational reconstruction" (presented with minimal textual evidence) of the theory supposedly held by Langdell and his Harvard-based law professor followers, who were the leading Classical private law doctrinalists.

The core of the theory, according to Grey, was the idea that (private) law is a science, whose goal is to develop legal rules from the inside in the correct way. The correct way is to work to make the system "doubly formal." It should and could consist of a small set of consistent high level principles covering the whole domain of private law, derived inductively from the cases and capable of deductive elaboration into new rules that can be applied deductively to new cases. Grey shows that Langdell restricted the theory to private law, and that he and his followers disapproved of the development of the Classical jurisprudence of contract and property rights against the state.

In my reading, Grey construct is not "a system of legal thought," a "discursive structure," or a "kind of legal thinking." I would describe it as a quite brilliantly developed Weberian ideal type of common law gapless conceptual jurisprudence, differing from Weber's "logically formal legal rationality" because the data used in induction are cases rather than code provisions. Supposing that it was indeed the implicit legal theory of the authors he is describing, it is helpful in understanding what I am calling the legal consciousness of the period, but in a quite limited way.

To the extent we believe that leading Classical privatists held the theory, we can understand better the actual development of the private law part of the Classical subsystem. Under the influence of this ideal, they would have tended to construct concepts (contract, tort, quasi-contract, offer, consideration) intended to be operative at a higher level of abstraction than had characterized pre-Classical legal thought. In other words, Grey's ideal type fits quite well into the structural/phenomenological approach of *The Rise and Fall.* It is a tool to describe an ideal image of "legal science" that guided some of the professors who did the concrete doctrinal work that transformed the conceptual ordering of private law. But here is where the limitations come in.

The orthodoxy is not a description of how contract law, for example, changed in the Classical period. Many of the jurists who developed it had nothing to do with the Harvard school, and it is hard to see how the theory could have been responsible in any direct way for the actual transformations of private law. The "orthodoxy" is about the method the scientist was supposed to follow, not about what the conceptual elements in private law were or ought to be (these were the findings of the science). Even if we were to verify that most jurists held to the orthodoxy in theory and practiced private law as it suggested they ought to, we still wouldn't know anything about the body of rules and the conceptual building blocks they were made from.

The approach of *The Rise and Fall* is in almost every respect the exact opposite of Grey's. Its goal was to decenter both Langdell, who appears in the manuscript as a minor contract doctrinalist, and the whole issue of formalism as a supposed jurisprudential theory, in favor of the narrative of conceptual construction and disintegration. It started not with one of the contending legal theories of the time, but with the contrasting conceptual architectures of pre-Classical and Classical legal thought. The legal consciousness approach set out to trace the felt relationship between concepts at different levels of abstraction, by contrast with the "top down" approach of the idealist historians who saw late nineteenth century legal thought as the instantiation of an abstraction (i.e. "formalism").

It argued that the substantive changes in the arrangement of the concepts and in the mode of resolving the contradictions among the elements allowed the classics in the end to put all the elements into a new unified structure, dramatically different from that of the pre-Civil War period, but identical to our own. The unity was phenomenologically compelling, and pre-theoretical. It came into existence through *bricolage*, the step by step reworking of the earlier system. When it disintegrated, a lot more was lost than the jurisprudential theory of a leading light of the period.

The jurisprudential theory of the Langdellians was a production within the legal consciousness of the period, rather than its
roadmap. Jurisprudence was one textual site among many for the
manifestation of the structural traits of the consciousness, and not
privileged, as a site, over statements in arguments, opinions and
treatises. The jurisprudential theory did not produce the structural transformation of CLT. It would be more accurate to say that it
was a partial theorization of what some of the jurists involved
were doing in their doctrinal practice, a theory that coexisted with
very different ideas about "scientific" method held by other jurists
equally important in the construction of CLT.

B. Contrast with "Revisionism"

It may also be useful to contrast *The Rise and Fall* with the "revision"
of the history of late nineteenth century American law of which it is
often considered a part.[28] The revision is, as is the manuscript, a
reevaluation of the period that rejects the progressive historiography,
according to which it was reactionary and formalist, adopting a bad
legal theory that permitted the "abuse of deduction" for nefarious
ends. By now, the literature of the revision is large, and it has permanently changed the way those of us who are interested see late nineteenth century legal thought. Though *The Rise and Fall* figures in its
genealogy, the approaches of the revision exist on a different plane,
so to speak.

The approach of the manuscript was that the consciousness of the
period, equally manifested in the majority and dissenting opinions in
Lochner, was something deeper and broader than any of the political
tendencies of the time. *The Rise and Fall* is supposed to be a genealogy of Liberalism, within which liberalisms and conservatisms quar-
relsomely coexist. So it is important to the book that powers are
emerging and transforming along with rights. Substantive due
process in CLT didn't abolish the police power, in spite of progressive rhetoric to that effect, but rather constructed it as a new thing.

28. See generally, Stephen Siegel, "The Revision Thickens," 20 *Law & Hist. Rev.* 631
(2002).

The multi-dimensionality of rights–that they were "the same thing" in public and private law–did not mean that the legislature couldn't change the common law, but rather that the rights, in the conflict of rights and powers, were the same as the rights in the conflict of right and right, and had to be accommodated using the same judicial techniques. There had to be an explanation of apparent inconsistencies between the private law rule and the constitutional requirement.

Specific doctrines resolved the conflicts in ways that favored the right or the left, without thereby making the underlying structure right or left. In *The Rise and Fall*, the "bias" involved in this process comes in because the structure was open, rather than because it was closed. It seemed obvious to me that if you were a Progressive you correctly viewed the U.S. Supreme Court as more often than not your political enemy because the judges were more often than not your political enemies. This was true even if they didn't strike down any more than a large minority of the measures you managed to push through the state legislatures.

Of course, sometimes there were no obvious political stakes, or mixed stakes, so the legal process seemed and seems highly autonomous. And sometimes the positions of the Progressives look much worse from the point of view of today's leftism or radicalism than those of the conservatives, whether "old" or "new." This seemed to be one of the lessons of *Yick Wo v. Hopkins*. [29]

In private law, it was the same. The splitting of contract as will of the parties from quasi-contract as will of the state was followed by the splitting of offer and acceptance as will of the parties from consideration doctrine as will of the state. The regulatory side of private law was formally acknowledged for the first time, rather than denied. The source of "bias" was that the conceptual structure of private law made the will of the parties the core and the will of the state the periphery, as illustrated by the nifty diagram at the end of Chapter 4 (p. 241).

---

29. 118 U.S. 356 (1886) (holding that a local "health regulation" aimed to shut down Chinese owned laundries in San Francisco violated the equal protection clause).

In *The Rise and Fall*, this was all part of the death of reason narrative. The biases of the public and private law outcomes produced a partly politically motivated assault on the vertical dimension of CLT, combined with a radicalization of the process of analogizing across fields, ultimately leading to disintegration into modern legal consciousness. Just as there is no sense, for me, in denying the conservatism of the authors of CLT, while admiring their tranformative accomplishment, there is none in denying the political progressivism of the attackers who brought us to the next stage of policy analysis and balancing. But the point is derationalization by stages, rather than that the actors had political motives.

The two modes of revision that contrast with *The Rise and Fall* are, first, the search for the true legal principles of the *Lochner* era constitutional cases, and, second, the enrichment of our understanding of the diverse factors, other than the supposed Langdellian orthodoxy, that went into the thought of the leading figures of the period. In the first mode, it indeed appears that there were a variety of threads of principle running through the cases. There were far too many cases that upheld what look to us like unmistakable interferences with freedom of contract, and far too much tolerated interference with laissez-faire, for us to be able to reduce the law as a whole to these slogans.

There is something rather Langdellian about the attempt to sort this chaos by finding a few strong abstract principles, like a ban on "class legislation," for example, or "equal rights." From the point of view of *The Rise and Fall*, the contradictory character of the Classical discourse, the ultimate weakness of its mediating devices, makes the quest seem quixotic, just as attempts to do the same sort of thing for the law of our time seem quixotic. It would seem to me more promising to use the rich new mine of data to investigate the mechanisms by which political conflict is uneasily and inconsistently translated into legal argument. But I recognize that this is far from the tenor of this branch of the revision.

The other approach has been to turn the stick figures of the progressive historiography into convincingly complex characters. They emerge as representatives of the various social, cul-

xxxviii tural, regional, political, philosophical, religious and legal theoretical currents of their time. The vicissitudes of their personal
lives, their mental illnesses, family crises, personal animosities
and love affairs get their due as causative in their work. As they
should.

In *The Rise and Fall*, CLT appeared to its practitioners "to have
synthesized successfully the positivist science of law, natural
rights constitutionalism, and classical economics." (p. 9) As for
the disintegration of CLT, it occurred "regardless of one's choices between or within the traditions of natural rights/morality and
social welfare maximization." (p. 251)[30] For *The Rise and Fall*,
nothing turned on whether or not you were an historical school
person, a utilitarian, a Kantian, or whatever. Nothing, that is, so
long as all one cared about was the emergence of the structure that
"rules us from the grave."[31]

In other words, the manuscript aimed at changes understood to
be independent of the legal philosophies the individual Classical
thinkers held. Field, Bradley, Cooley, James Coolidge Carter,
Bishop, Gray, Wigmore and the rest, including Englishmen like
Austin, Pollock, Markby and Holland, could be lumped together
with Langdell and Beale, not because they were all "formalists,"
not at all. Rather, they all worked on different bits of the transformation of the larger structure toward rights and powers absolute
within their spheres. In retrospect, their contributions still seem to
me quite completely independent of their individual placement in
the fascinating grids the revision has developed for understanding
them as historical figures.

30. I was influenced in this view by Pound's amazing article of 1917, "The End of Law
as Developed in Juristic Thought: II. The Nineteenth Century." 30 *Harv. L. Rev.* 201
(1917). In it, he argued that all the schools of nineteenth century legal theory, meaning the
historical school, Kantianism, utilitarianism and social Darwinism had turned out to have
the same basic idea about modern law: it had evolved from feudalism to the will theory! My
revision was to argue that it had evolved to the structure in which private opposed public
will. This formulation dispensed with Pound's claim that the nineteenth century evolution
had been Romanist and individualist, and therefore maladapted to the socialization of society at the turn of the century.

31. See also "The Structure of Blackstone's Commentaries," supra note 6, at 362, n. 56.

IV. Fate of *The Rise and Fall*　　　xxxix

The Rise and Fall did get me tenure. The faculty was raising the standard, and the new generation had been told that we had to produce "substantial writing," though without a publication requirement. After I submitted the manuscript to the appointments committee, I spent two months playing solitaire waiting for their decision, and then decided to start work on an article, which became "Form and Substance in Private Law Adjudication,"[32] finished in the spring of 1976. In that article, besides summarizing the manuscript, I lifted, more or less verbatim, the description of the modern way of thinking about private law from the opening section of chapter 3. But "Form and Substance" reconceptualized the larger conflict within private law as individualsim vs. altruism, whereas *The Rise and Fall* spoke of efficiency vs. equity and rights vs. powers.

The Appointments Committee consisted of Al Sacks (the Dean and co-author of the Legal Process Materials), Milton Katz, Paul Bator, James Vorenberg, Arthur Miller, Frank Michelman and Larry Tribe. I had asked the Dean to take Clark Byse off the Committee, because he was openly hostile, and that they poll my students randomly about my teaching rather than consulting the students they happened to know already, which had been the practice up to then.

The semester wore on. After Thanksgiving, Frank Michelman and Larry Tribe said exactly the same thing: "If I were you, I would be worried, but let me tell you, you have nothing to worry about." I am still grateful to them. Then my closest friends on the faculty, Mort Horwitz and Roberto Unger, each of them recently tenured, went separately to tell the Dean that if I was denied they would leave. Not to be forgotten.

The Committee met a final time between Christmas and New Year's and recommended me, and the faculty voted a few weeks later. A senior colleague, not on the Committee, told me there had never been any question, and that it was just wrong to imagine

32. 89 *Harv. L. Rev.* 1689 (1976).

that my case had been controversial in any way, and particularly not in any kind of political way. There was no feedback about the manuscript from Committee members other than Tribe and Michelman, and aside from Horwitz and Unger, the only members of the faculty who seemed to have read it were Abe Chayes, Phil Heymann and Henry Steiner. I was very happy, but also alienated. In that respect, I think my experience was typical of what the tenure process was becoming at all the self-styled elite schools.

The Rise and Fall became the spine of my course, *Legal History: American Legal Thought.* I split it up and distributed it along with two dozen cases and long excerpts from treatises and the like. I kept on writing new pieces, one of them a quite elaborate narrative of the discrediting of CLT as constitutional theory, which I didn't try to integrate into the ms., but just stuck into the course materials at appropriate places, and I developed elaborate outlines of the lectures on federalism before the civil war and corporate law.

It seemed clearer and clearer to me that a serious flaw of the manuscript was that it was written as though we had "always/already" had the public/private distinction, and that what happened in CLT was just a novel and intense deployment of it. "The Structure of Blackstone's Commentaries, "[33] published in 1979, was supposed to be a new first part of a now much larger *The Rise and Fall*, narrating the early stages of reason working to give birth to Liberalism in law, centered on the genealogy of the public/private distinction.

Then, around 1980, I decided I had to work hard and fast on other things, both to "have a career" and to further the critical legal studies project. *The Rise and Fall* was supposed to have a section on the interdependence of late nineteenth century economic and legal thought, and I wrote this as a separate article in 1985.[34] It soon seemed that if I were to publish the manuscript, I would have to completely redo it, and by then I was much more aware than I had been at the outset of the difficulty of the task. It seemed like a life work, and not my life work.

33. Supra note 6.
34. Duncan Kennedy, "The Role of Law in Economic Thought: Essays on the Fetishism of Commodities," 34 *Amer. Univ. L. Rev.* 939 (1985).

An oddity of the situation was that not publishing it did not mean that it disappeared into a desk drawer somewhere. It was read every year by a large class of students, and circulated persistently to law students at other schools. It was cited. The critical legal studies milieu provided an interested audience. The audience it might have reached through a university press was unlikely to be friendly, given its violation of the canons of professional historical scholarship and its structuralist and critical theoretical enthusiasm.

Along with Tom Grey,[35] a number of colleagues, including Mort Horwitz,[36] Bob Gordon,[37] Cass Sunstein,[38] Greg Alexander[39] and Steve Siegel,[40] found the narrative of conceptual transformation useful, though they understood it in various different ways and fitted it into their own diverse undertakings, all quite distinct from the project of the manuscript. The most complex of these adaptations is Horwitz's endlessly fascinating *Transformation II: The Crisis of Legal Orthodoxy*. It melds *The Rise and Fall* seamlessly into a version of the revision of the progressive historiography that aims to retain the element of political/economic "tilt" for CLT, a feat that I would have thought impossible given my effort to make the two incompatible.

Other students and young colleagues entered directly into the effort to reconstruct the structural transformations of legal discourse. In the late nineteen seventies and early nineteen eighties, they wrote and published a set of third year papers, job market

---

35. "Langdell's Orthodoxy," supra note 27.

36. Morton Horwitz, *The Transformation of American Law II, 1870-1960: The Crisis of Legal Orthodoxy* (New York: Oxford Univ. Press, 1992).

37. Robert Gordon, "Legal Thought and Legal Practice in the Age of American Enterprise, 1870-1920," in *Professions and Professional Ideologies in America* (D. Geison, ed., Chapel Hill: Univ. of North Carolina Press, 1983).

38. Cass Sunstein, "Lochner's Legacy," 87 *Colum. L. Rev.* 873 (1987). But see David Bernstein, "Lochner's Legacy's Legacy," 82 *Texas L. Rev.* 1 (2003).

39. Gregory Alexander, *Commodity and Propriety: Competing Visions of Property in American Legal Thought, 1776-1970* (Chicago: Univ. of Chicago Press, 1997).

40. Stephen Siegel, "Understanding the Lochner Era: Lessons from the Controversy over Railroad and Utility Rate Regulation," 70 *Va. L. Rev.* 187 (1984).

xlii offerings and tenure pieces that extend *The Rise and Fall,* elaborate it across new legal domains and in many cases correct it.
These are listed "in the margin," as they used to say.[41] Each has its
own political agenda, and its own slant into the critical theoretical
and structuralist approach. Together they make up a rich genealogy of present day legal thought. I am more proud of my association with the effort of their production than with any other aspect
of my teaching career. The pieces by Karl Klare, Jerry Frug, Fran
Olsen, Joe Singer and David Kennedy seem to me to figure
among the best law review articles of the late last century.

In the last five years, I've gone back to intellectual history,
developing the same old death of reason narrative, concentrating
on the "social" critique of CLT, and on the realists as critics of the
social, on the interdependence of European and American legal
thought, and on the nineteenth and twentieth century globalizations of legal thought in the context of the world system of
Western domination.[42]

Cambridge, Mass., December 2005

41. Ira Nerkin, "A New Deal for the Protection of 14th Amendment Rights: Challenging the Doctrinal Bases of the Civil Rights Cases and State Action Theory," 1 *Harv. CR –CL L. Rev.* 297 (1977); Karl Klare, "The Judicial Deradicalization of the Wagner Act and the Origins of Modern Legal Consciousness, 1937-1941," 62 *Minn. L. Rev.* 265 (1978); Gerald Frug, "The City as a Legal Concept," 93 *Harv. L. Rev.* 1057 (1980); John Nockleby, "Tortious Interference with Contractual Relations in the Nineteenth Century: The Transformation of Property, Contract and Tort," 93 *Harv. L. Rev.* 1510 (1980); Kenneth Vandevelde, "The New Property of the 19th Century," 29 *Buff. L. Rev.* 325 (1980); Elizabeth Mensch, "Freedom of Contract as Ideology," 33 *Stan. L. Rev.* 753 (1981); Elizabeth Mensch, "The Colonial Origins of Liberal Property Rights," 31 *Buff. L. Rev.* 635 (1982); James Kainen, "Nineteenth Century Interpretations of the Federal Contract Clause: The Transformation from Vested to Substantive Rights Against the State," 31 *Buff. L.Rev.* 381 (1982); Kipp Rogers, "The Right of Publicity: Resurgence of Legal Formalism and Judicial Disregard of Policy Issues," 16 *Beverly Hills Bar Assoc. J.* 65 (1982); Joseph Singer, "The Legal Rights Debate in Analytical Jurisprudence, from Bentham to Hohfeld," 1982 *Wisc. L. Rev.* 975; Frances Olsen, "The Family and the Market: A Study of Ideology and Legal Reform," 96 *Harv. L. Rev.* 1497 (1983); Ellen Kelman, "American Labor Law and Legal Formalism: How 'Legal Logic' Shaped and Vitiated the Rights of American Workers," 58 *St. John's L. Rev.* 1 (1983); Gregory Alexander, "The Dead Hand and the Law of Trusts in the 19th Century," 37 *Stan. L. Rev.* 1189 (1985); Hagai Hurvitz, "American Labor Law and the Doctrine of Entrepreneurial Property Rights: Boycotts, Courts and the Juridical Reorientation of 1886-1895," 8 *Ind. Rel. L. J.* 307 (1986); David Kennedy, "Primitive Legal Scholarship," 27 *Harv. Int'l L.J.* 1 (1986); Gregory Alexander, "The Transformation of Trusts as a Legal Category, 1800-1914," 5 *Law & History Rev.* 303 (1987); Mark Hager, "Bodies Politic: The Progressive History of Organizational 'Real Entity' Theory," 50 *U. Pitt. L. Rev.* 575 (1989); Rudoph Peritz, "The 'Rule of Reason' in Antitrust: Property Logic in Restraint of Competition," 40 *Hastings L. Rev.* 285 (1989); Robert Steinfeld, "Property and Suffrage in the Early American Republic," 41 *Stan. L. Rev.* 335 (1989).

42. "From the Will Theory to the Principle of Private Autonomy: Lon Fuller's Consideration and Form," 100 *Colum. L. Rev.* 94 (2000); with Marie-Claire Belleau, "François Gény aux États-Unis," in *François Gény, Mythe et Réalités 1899-1999: Centenaire de Méthode d'Interprétation et Sources en Droit Privé Positif, Essai Critique* (Claude Thomasset, Jacques Vanderlinden & Philippe Jestaz, eds., Montreal: Editions Yvon Blais, 2000); "Two Globalizations of Law and Legal Thought: 1850-1968," 36 *Suffolk Univ. L. Rev.* 631 (2003).

CHAPTER I

Legal Consciousness

∿ 1 ∾

MY SUBJECT is the development and disintegration of a form of American legal thought that emerged between 1850 and 1885 and flourished between 1885 and 1940, allowance made for the spurious precision of dates. Because this way of thinking amounted to a rationalistic ordering of the whole legal universe, I will call it Classical legal thought. For a crucial season, that of the transformation of American economic and social life, the thinking of the legal elite was organized neither around the categories of natural right and utilitarianism, nor in the vaguely instrumentalist or nationalist mode of the "Formative Era." During this period, treatise writers, leaders of the bar, Supreme Court Justices, and the like shared a conception of law that appeared to transcend the old conflicting schools, and to ally the profession with science against both philosophical speculation and the crudities of democratic politics.

That the "real" alliance influencing legal outcomes between 1865 and 1940 was that of the older conservatism of the profession with a class of despoiling entrepreneurs and politicians against the working class, the farmers, and the "public interest" is an article of faith in the liberal historiography of the period. I believe that the preoccupation with validating this vision of the recent past has hindered understanding of the dilemmas of modern legal and political theory. We can understand these only if we recognize and confront the existence of legal consciousness as an entity with a measure of autonomy. It is a set of concepts and intellectual operations that evolves according to a pattern of its own, and exercises an influence on results distinguishable from those of political power and economic interest. The autonomy of legal consciousness is a premise; yet that autonomy is no more than relative. Not only the particular concepts and operations characteristic of a period, but also the entity that they together constitute, are intelligible only in terms of the larger structures of social thought and action.

This approach denies the importance neither of ideologies like laissez-faire, nor of concrete economic interests, nor of the underlying structure of political power. It insists only that legal consciousness, which has its own structure, mediates their influence on particular legal results. The introduction of a third tier between interest or power and outcomes greatly complicates the task of historical exposition. This chapter is devoted to outlining the general conceptual apparatus: the language necessary to describe the form and content of a consciousness. If this is worth the effort, it is because it makes it possible to learn things about our present situation which were obscured by the simpler vision of an unmediated interplay of purposes and outcomes.

Stated in the most general possible way, this is what happened: Before the Civil War, the legal elite conceived the set of legal relationships that together comprise the American legal system—i.e., private citizen to private citizen, private citizen to state, legislature to judiciary, and federal to state government—as qualitatively distinct from one another and as operated legally according to qualitatively distinct analytic principles—i.e., the common law, sovereignty limited by written constitutions, the equilibrium of forces between separate governmental powers, the union of sovereign states.

During the Classical period, the legal elite conceived these four institutional relationships as four particular instances of a single general legal relation: each of them was an example of the delegation of legal powers absolute within their spheres. The role of the judiciary (its sphere of absolute power) was the application of a single, distinctively legal, analytic apparatus to the job of policing the boundaries of these spheres. The legal system appeared to have synthesized successfully the positivist science of law, natural rights constitutionalism, and Classical Economics.

After 1900, this highly-integrated system began a process of further integration that tended toward the reduction of all legal action to the enforcement of intrinsically just ground rules for economic struggle among private actors. The refinements were a response to attacks by liberals and progressives on the political role of the judiciary, but proved ultimately self-destructive. The triumph of a purely formal theory of marginal utility in economics and the appearance of American philosophical pragmatism undermined the analytic apparatus, leading to the dissipation of faith in the intrinsic justice of the rules, and discrediting the notion that they could be objectively developed or applied. The outcome was a disintegration of legal thought into mutually autonomous subcategories different from but somewhat resembling those of the pre-Civil War period, and the recession of the judiciary from the role of guardian of the integrity of fundamental legal relationships.

The rise and fall of Classical legal thought was an integral, necessary event in the current of development within which we live. I reject the conception of "formalism" as an aberrational interlude, marring what would otherwise be a uniform and consistent approach sometimes vaguely denominated "instrumentalism" equally characteristic of the pre-Civil War and post-1937 periods. As I see it, we live not in a time of return to the sound practice of 1830, but in a post-Classical age of disintegration.

My primary purpose is to write a history of the transformations of legal consciousness. I believe that it is possible to isolate and describe the significant dimensions or aspects of the body of ideas through which lawyers experience legal issues. But once legal consciousness begins to take on a certain definition, a whole

4   series of hypotheses suggest themselves concerning the relationship between its form and the behavior of the actors in the legal system.

I am particularly interested in the connection between the forms of legal consciousness and what I will call judicial activism or interventionism. Judicial activism is a relative term indicating an unusually great willingness to treat judicial power as an autonomous, creative factor in the development of economic and political life. In public law, it refers to the judge's willingness to intervene dramatically in political life in a way that appears to flout majority sentiment, as represented by the legislature and executive. In private law, it refers to willingness to change or evolve the law in ways that upset existing patterns of economic and social advantage. As I use it, judicial activism has no inherent political tendency to the right or to the left. The conservative critics of the Warren Court have taught us to see the strong parallel between the right-wing interventionism of the period 1890-1937 (the rights of property and contract) and the left-wing interventionism of 1955-1970 (equality). I take this perspective as a starting point.

The significance of the general phenomenon of activism lies in its premise. It is that human reason is something more than an instrumental mechanism for the execution of collective or individual decisions reached through the clash of interests, passions, or appetites. It is perhaps no more than an accident of our institutional history that we have put judges in the position of being at once enormously powerful and without democratic political legitimation. What is important is that their anomalous position has forced them, generation after generation, to justify their actions in terms that transcend the rhetoric of our political pluralism. They are carriers of the notion that the ideal of justice is accessible to the reason of people acting in the real situations of political and economic life. This is what seems to me valid and worth developing in the theoretical part of our peculiar political/legal tradition. But my sense is that the study of the characteristics of legal consciousness holds the key to a large number of the most puzzling aspects of the intellectual history of law.

~ 2 ~

The notion behind the concept of legal consciousness is that people can have in common something more influential than a checklist of facts, techniques, and opinions. They can share premises about the salient aspects of the legal order that are so basic that actors rarely if ever bring them consciously to mind. Yet everyone, including actors who think they disagree profoundly about the substantive issues that matter, would dismiss without a second thought (perhaps as "not a legal argument" or as "simply missing the point") an approach appearing to deny them.

These underlying premises concern the historical background of the legal process, the institutions involved in it, and the nature of the intellectual constructs which lawyers, judges, and commentators manipulate as they attempt to convince their audiences. Among these premises, there are often links creating subsystems with their own internal organization and rules of operation. These change. For example, they expand and contract to cover or not cover a greater or lesser number of the aspects of legal reality that are within legal consciousness at a given time. Classicism, in its developed form circa 1900, was a particularly powerful subsystem of this kind. My thesis is that by tracing the transformations involved in its emergence, flourishing, and decline, we will find a way to understand the mass of seemingly self-contradictory or plainly mistaken verbiage that makes up the greater part of our legal tradition.

Classical legal thought was a way of understanding the whole American legal system. Its context was the first protracted period in America of the kind of economic and class conflict that had characterized the Western European countries during the period of rapid industrialization. The issues involved were the concentration of industry and finance combined with "cut-throat competition;" the struggle between the farmers and the railroads; the struggle between unions and employers over working conditions and wages; and the relation of state to federal governments in the regulatory process.

The premise of Classicism was that the legal system consisted

6 of a set of institutions, each of which had the traits of a legal actor. Each institution had been delegated by the sovereign people a power to carry out its will, which was absolute within but void outside its sphere. The justification of the judicial role was the existence of a peculiar legal technique rendering the task of policing the boundaries of spheres an objective, quasi-scientific one.

Classicism consisted of two exactly analogous systems whose common link was the judiciary. The two systems evolved in parallel fashion, and it is rarely possible to say with certainty which served as the model for the other. The first system was that of federalism, the participants being Congress, the federal judiciary, and the States. Federal and state governments were seen as exercising "sovereignty," a legal concept formally the same in all cases. The similarity of the respective powers meant that it was equally meaningful to speak of state usurping state; of state usurping federal; and of federal usurping state authority.

The second system consisted of individual property holders, a legislature, and a judiciary. Both the property holders and the legislature were seen as exercising a formally identical absolute dominion over property. The difference as among property holders and between them and the legislature was one of jurisdiction. The physical boundaries between citizens were like those between states. The non-physical division of jurisdiction over a given object between legislature and citizen was like that between state and federal governments. Because all the actors held formally identical powers of absolute dominion, one could speak equally of trespass by neighbor against neighbor, by state against citizen, and by citizen against state.

In this system, the judge was also conceived as the holder of a power, whose nature was identical whether the occasion of its exercise was a quarrel between neighbors, between sovereigns, or between citizen and legislature. Its function was to prevent the various kinds of usurpation already referred to. There was always a danger of the judge, under the cover of performing this function, himself usurping the authority of the legal actors whose spheres he was supposed to be defining, What prevented this was that he acted by elaborating general principles. Whereas the other actors exercised their own wills, he obeyed the will of the people who had set up the whole system in the first place.

Classical legal thought reflected a state of mind deeply preoccupied with an opposition between freedom, conceived as arbitrary and irrational, yet creative and dynamic, and restraint, conceived in similar stark terms, as rigid, principled in an absolutist way, yet necessary as the antidote to freedom. Activity within the spheres of power represented liberty, autonomy, and unbridled mastery for legal actors. By the sharp delineation of boundaries, the virtues of such an unleashing of private energy were to be secured without the dangers of anarchy, and with only that minimum of injustice and immorality that are necessary if there is to be any autonomy at all.

∾ 3 ∾

Classical legal thought was an *ordering*, in the sense that it took a very large number of actual processes and events and asserted that they could be reduced to a much smaller number with a definite pattern. What was ordered was the enormous mass of rules and standards courts applied to different kinds of cases. The particular simplification that developed was influenced by the actual content of the rules it organized and, in turn, constantly influenced them. In other words, there was a reciprocal action between the system of premises and practice. The study of the Classical subsystem within legal consciousness does not aim at a description of what the practices "actually" were, or of their effects on things like the distribution of power and resources within society. It is designed to tell us about the theoretical atmosphere within which practices occurred, and to tell us about the manner in which the theoretical atmosphere influenced particular results.

The basic mode of this influence of theory on results is that the ordering of myriad practices into a systematization occurs through simplifying and generalizing categories, abstractions that become the tools available when the practitioner (judge or advocate) approaches a new problem. These abstractions operate the way a technology operates on the design of physical objects: the

8   concepts impose limits, suggest directions, provide one of the elements of a style, but do not uniquely determine outcomes. In the Classical systematization, the concept that was most significant in this way was that of a constitutionally delegated power absolute within its sphere. As time went on, *all* legally significant action came to be thought of as the exercise or creation of such powers, whether the particular actor was public or private, state or federal, legislative or judicial.

One of the functions of systems of legal thought —one of the reasons for their existence—is the reconciliation of what appear to be conflicts between institutions and contradictions among ideas. In other words, system is necessary not just to permit us to deal in a cognitively effective way with the chaotic mass of rules. It is also necessary because the theorist wishes to show that where many perceive confusion, danger, insecurity, rivalry, and aggressive action, there exists a latent order that has a legitimate claim to our respect. This order, once recognized, is both a reassuring fact and a goal for constructive striving.

Classical legal thought (and in particular the concept of a power absolute within its sphere) appeared to permit the resolution of the basic institutional conflicts between populistic legislatures and private businesses, between legislatures and courts over the legitimacy and extent of judicial review, and between state and federal governments struggling for regulatory jurisdiction. At the level of ideas, it mediated the contradictions between natural rights theories and legal positivism, and between the democratic theory of legislative supremacy and the Classical economic prescriptions about the optimal role of the state in the economy. It placed judges, lawyers, and legal thinkers in the center of the web of government while shielding them from the charge of having usurped the Constitution.

∾ 4 ∾

The extremely abstract propositions of the last few paragraphs may become more intelligible applied to one of the most famous of Classical cases, that of *Lochner v. New York*, decided by the

Supreme Court in 1905. The majority and dissenting opinions of Justices Peckham and Harlan illustrate some of the more striking traits of Classicism. (The dissent by O.W. Holmes, in which he uttered the immortal phrase, "the Constitution does not enact Mr. Herbert Spencer's Social Statics," is a vital document of the attack on Classicism; we will consider it later.)

The issue in *Lochner* was whether a New York statute fixing a ten-hour day for bakers violated the clause of the Fourteenth Amendment forbidding the states to "deprive any person of life, liberty or property without due process of law." Justice Peckham's opinion striking down the law has been a continuing source of outrage, both because of the inhumanity of the result and because it contains language that can be reasonably interpreted as violently hostile to all attempts to use the legal system as a conscious mechanism to redress the bargaining position of workers in their dealings with employers. In modern legal consciousness, the case serves as a horrible reminder of the bad consequences of Supreme Court justices letting their "subjective" and "political" passions draw them into a kind of judicial review that is both anti-democratic and institutionally suicidal. Modern commentators discussing controversial cases habitually club each other with the charge of "Lochnerism."

It seems a good idea to state emphatically at this point that my purpose is neither to add to the debate about the correctness of *Lochner* and cases like it, nor to try to draw conclusions from it about how modern judges should behave. The case provides, in Harlan's dissent as well as in the majority opinion, good evidence about the structure of the legal consciousness of the period. The concept of legal consciousness, and the particular descriptive characterization of Classical legal thought as a subsystem within it, should help in understanding what the justices thought they were doing. They also help in understanding the nature of the conceptual limits within which they worked. Of course, no one case suffices to "prove" anything about a consciousness, and a single case rarely even illustrates more than a few of its aspects. But if the reader will immerse herself in these long quotations, she may come away at least with a sense of the period's style.

10   Peckham frames the issue as involving individual rights and public powers. The court is in a disinterested position with respect to two exactly analogous entities:

> The statute necessarily interferes with the right of contract between the employer and employees, concerning the number of hours in which the latter may labor in the bakery of the employer. The general right to make a contract in relation to his business is part of the liberty of the individual protected by the Fourteenth Amendment of the Federal Constitution. Allgeyer v. Louisiana, 165 U.S. 578. Under that provision no State can deprive any person of life, liberty or property without due process of law. The right to purchase or to sell labor is part of the liberty protected by this amendment, unless there are circumstances which exclude the right. There are, however, certain powers, existing in the sovereignty of each State in the Union, somewhat vaguely termed police powers, the exact description and limitation of which have not been attempted by the courts. Those powers, broadly-stated and without, at present, any attempt at a more specific limitation, relate to the safety, health, morals and general welfare of the public. Both property and liberty are held on such reasonable conditions as may be imposed by the governing power of the State in the exercise of those powers, and with such conditions the Fourteenth Amendment was not designed to interfere. Mugler v. Kansas, 123 U.S. 623; In re Kemmler, 136 U.S. 436; Crowley v. Christensen, 137 U.S. 86; In re Converse, 137 U.S. 624.
>
> The State, therefore, has power to prevent the individual from making certain kinds of contracts, and in regard to them the Federal Constitution offers no protection. If the contract be one which the State, in the legitimate exercise of its police power, has the right to prohibit, it is not prevented from prohibiting it by the Fourteenth Amendment. Contracts in violation of a statute, either of the Federal or state government, or a contract to let one's property for immoral purposes, or to do any other unlawful act, could obtain no protection from the Federal Constitution, as coming under the liberty of person or of free contract. Therefore, when the State, by its legislature, in the assumed exercise of its police powers, has passed an act which seriously limits the right to labor

or the right of contract in regard to their means of livelihood
between persons who are sui juris (both employer and employee),
it becomes of great importance to determine which shall prevail—the right of the individual to labor for such time as he may
choose, or the right of the State to prevent the individual from
laboring or from entering into any contract to labor, beyond a certain time prescribed by the state.

It is worth pausing a moment to dwell on the odd locution by
which Peckham turns the confrontation into one between the
"right of the individual" and the "right of the state." This parallelism of concepts comes up again five pages later: "It is a question of which of two powers or rights shall prevail—the power of
the State or the right of the individual to liberty of person and
freedom of contract." In the second reference, the parallelism is
reinforced by showing that rights can be seen as powers, as well as
vice versa.

It may seem as though there is an asymmetry between rights
and powers implicit in the presentation of the situation as one in
which rights are not "absolute," but rather limited by the police
power. But this is an accident of exposition:

> It must, of course, be conceded that there is a limit to the valid
> exercise of the police power by the State. There is no dispute con-
> cerning this general proposition. Otherwise the Fourteenth
> Amendment would have no efficacy and the legislatures of the
> States would have unbounded power, and it would be enough to
> say that any piece of legislation was enacted to conserve the
> morals, the health or the safety of the people; such legislation
> would be valid, no matter how absolutely without foundation the
> claim might be. The claim of the police power would be a mere
> pretext—become another and delusive name for the supreme sov-
> ereignty of the State to be exercised free from constitutional
> restraint. This is not contended for (*Lochner v. New York*, 1905:
> 56).

Both the right and the power are entitled to protection; each over-
rides and annihilates the other, and is in that sense absolute, but

12   only within a "sphere." The two concepts are mutually limiting. The two categories of right and power could be spatialized as two contiguous areas. They most certainly do not come across as conflicting "interests" to be "balanced" within some imagined field of forces.

The Classical conception of the judicial role is stated by Peckham, in the next sentence after that last quoted, as a deduction from the character of legal rights and powers:

> In every case that comes before the court, therefore, where legislation of this character is concerned and where the protection of the Federal Constitution is sought, the question necessarily arises: Is this a fair, reasonable and appropriate exercise of the police power of the State, or is it an unreasonable, unnecessary and arbitrary interference with the right of the individual to his personal liberty to enter into those contracts in relation to labor which may seem to him appropriate or necessary for the support of himself and his family? (*Lochner v. New York*, 1905: 56).

The notion is that of an objective task of drawing lines or categorizing actions as though they were objects to be located in the spatial map of spheres of power. This task constitutes itself a "power" to be exercised within and only within a limited sphere, as Peckham says in the next paragraph:

> This is not a question of substituting the judgment of the court for that of the legislature. If the act be within the power of the State it is valid, although the judgment of the court might be totally opposed to the enactment of such a law. But the question would still remain: Is it within the police power of the State? and that question must be answered by the court.

There are two important traits of Classical legal thought that are not well illustrated by Peckham's opinion. These are the two large structural traits. First, the identity of private law (individual-individual) rights with constitutional law (individual-state) rights is present only implicitly. Peckham takes it as established that constitutional "liberty" includes "contract"; that everyone agrees that the baker-employer relation is "contract" within the constitution-

al definition; and that the fixing of hours abridges "freedom of
contract." The nature of the triangular individual-individual-state
relation becomes clear only when there is some argument about
the correspondence between constitutional freedom of contract
and common law freedom of contract.

Second, the relation of this triangular structure to that of federalism (state-state-federal government) is missing from the
majority opinion, but suggested in the dissent, as we will see in a
moment.

The main point about Harlan's dissent is that it employs exactly the same conceptual structure as the majority opinion:

> Speaking generally, the State in the exercise of its powers may not
> unduly interfere with the right of the citizen to enter into con-
> tracts that may be necessary and essential in the enjoyment of the
> inherent rights belonging to every one, among which rights is the
> right "to be free in the enjoyment of all his faculties; to be free to
> use them in all lawful ways; to live and work where he will; to earn
> his livelihood by any lawful calling; to pursue any livelihood or
> avocation." This was declared in *Allgeyer v. Louisiana*, 165 U.S.
> 578, 589. But in the same case it was conceded that the right to
> contract in relation to persons and property or to do business,
> within a State, may be "regulated and sometimes prohibited, when
> the contracts or business conflict with the policy of the State as
> contained in its statutes." (*Lochner v. New York*, 1905: 65-66).

Like Peckham, Harlan argues that the Court's function is to carry
out the objective task of classification, and that this judicial power
is strictly limited:

> Whether or not this be wise legislation it is not the province of the
> court to inquire. Under our systems of government the courts are
> not concerned with the wisdom or policy of legislation. So that in
> determining the question of power to interfere with liberty of
> contract, the court may inquire whether the means devised by the
> State are germane to an end which may be lawfully accomplished
> and have a real or substantial relation to the protection of health,
> as involved in the daily work of the persons, male and female,

14   engaged in bakery and confectionery establishment. But when this inquiry is entered upon I find it impossible, in view of common experience, to say that there is here no real or substantial relation between the means employed by the State and the end sought to be accomplished by its legislation. Mugler v. Kansas, supra. Nor can I say that the statute has no appropriate or direct connection with that protection to health which each State owes to her citizens, Patterson v. Kentucky, supra; or that it is not promotive of the health of the employees in question, Holden v. Hardy, Lawton v. Steele, supra; or that the regulation prescribed by the State is utterly unreasonable and extravagant or wholly arbitrary, Gundling v. Chicago, supra. Still less can I say that the statute is, beyond question, a plain palpable invasion of rights secured by the fundamental law. Jacobson v. Massachusetts, supra. Therefore I submit that this court will transcend its functions if it assumes to annul the statute of New York (*Lochner v. New York*, 1905: 69-70).

The justices differed, however, and not just about the application of the rules to the facts of this case. Peckham stated his test for classifying a statute as follows:

Statutes of the nature of that under review, limiting the hours in which grown and intelligent men may labor to earn their living, are mere meddlesome interferences with the rights of the individual, and they are not saved from condemnation by the claim that they are passed in the exercise of the police power and upon the subject of the health of the individual, whose rights are interfered with, unless there be some fair ground, reasonable in and of itself, to say that there is material danger to the public health or to the health of the employees, if the hours of labor are not curtailed. If this be not clearly the case, the individuals, whose rights are thus made the subject of legislative interference, are under the protection of the Federal Constitution regarding their liberty of contract as well as of person; and the legislature of the State has no power to limit their right as proposed in this statute (*Lochner v. New York*, 1905: 61).

Harlan stated the test very differently:

> Granting then that there is a liberty of contract which cannot be violated even under the sanction of direct legislative enactment, but assuming, as according to settled law we may assume, that such liberty of contract is subject to such regulations as the State may reasonably prescribe for the common good and the well-being of society, what are the conditions under which the judiciary may declare such regulations to be in excess of legislative authority and void? Upon this point there is no room for dispute; for, the rule is universal that a legislative enactment, Federal or state, is never to be disregarded or held invalid unless it be, beyond question, plainly and palpably in excess of legislative power.... If there be doubt as to the validity of the statute, that doubt must therefore be resolved in favor of its validity, and the courts must keep their hands off, leaving the legislature to meet the responsibility for unwise legislation. If the end which the legislature seeks to accomplish be one to which its power extends, and if the means employed to that end, although not the wisest or best, are yet not plainly and palpably unauthorized by law, then the court cannot interfere. In other words, when the validity of a statute is questioned, the burden of proof, so to speak, is upon those who assert it to be unconstitutional. McCulloch v. Maryland, 4 Wheat. 316, 421 (*Lochner v. New York*, 1905: 68).

Let me be quick to say that two legal actors can differ about far more than the placing of a burden of proof and still share a legal consciousness. Indeed, Peckham and Harlan share so much that one might argue that there were simply some well-settled legal rules, and a disagreement about burden of proof. Who needs a pretentious concept like consciousness to explain the situation? Alternatively, one can see the similar statements I have quoted from majority and dissenting opinions as a kind of compulsory curtsy to the audience before the "real" battle, which is over whether the judiciary should favor capital or labor in the struggle for social justice. As I said a moment ago, a case "proves" nothing. If proof is to be had, it is in the eating of the later courses.

But note, nonetheless, that at the end of the last passage quot-

16   ed, Harlan cites the case of *McCulloch v. Maryland*. He cites it for
the proposition that "when the validity of a statute is questioned,
the burden of proof, so to speak, is upon those who assert it to be
unconstitutional."

McCulloch was a case about the relation of state to federal powers, decided in 1819. Marshall's opinion for the Court argued that
both state and federal powers are absolute within their spheres,
and that the job of the Court is to employ an objective technique
of constitutional exegesis to draw the line between them. I believe
that at the time *McCulloch v. Maryland* was decided, it would have
seemed, to the overwhelming majority of the legal elite, decided-
ly bizarre to offer the case as authority about the relation between
individual rights and state power, whether one was talking about
federal or state constitutional law. Harlan very Classically assumes that
the concept of a power is essentially the same in the two systems.
The argument is that this kind of change is important.

∾ 5 ∽

The emergence of Classical legal thought was an instance of the
phenomenon of change in the mode of "integration" of consciousness. Integration refers to an aspect of legal consciousness
at a particular moment in time: the manner in which the different
elements that are in it (e.g., the doctrine of consideration and the
rule against perpetuities) fit together into subsystems. The notion
is that we can compare and contrast states of consciousness with
respect to this aspect.

One way to do this is to attempt a kind of map of the subsystems composing a consciousness. We construct a map by asking
whether a legal actor experiences a particular rule or doctrine as a
possibly useful analogy in an argument about some other particular rule or doctrine. When we feel that an argument for X can
draw on the arguments for Y, then, by definition, these two are
parts of a subsystem. If the arguments for Y would never come to
mind or would be dismissed as absurd in the argument for X, then
they are parts of different subsystems. Another way of putting the
same idea is that if your position about X puts a good deal of
moral and intellectual pressure on you to take a particular position

with respect to Y, then the two are part of a subsystem. If you experience no such pressure, they are not.

One can test the manner of integration of the parts of a legal consciousness through the answers to questions like the following: We have to decide whether, in the absence of a relevant statute, the federal government can get an injunction from a federal court against a railroad strike on the ground that the strike has interrupted interstate commerce. First, is it relevant that the courts would grant an injunction against a state statute which discriminated against interstate commerce through unequal taxation? Second, is it relevant that a private party, under the private law of nuisance, can obtain an injunction against a house of prostitution?

Justice Brewer's opinion in the 1895 case of *In re Debs* answers these two questions in ways that seem highly implausible to modern critics, yet were merely "creative," given the legal consciousness of the time. In *Debs*, the initial question was whether the federal government had any business at all protecting the railroads against invasion of private property rights of a type usually regulated by the states. Supposing some basis of federal jurisdiction, it was not clear that the strike leaders had violated any criminal provision of federal law. If they had not, there was no obvious basis for federal action against them; if they had, then the usual notion would have been that equity would not enjoin a crime, especially when the injunction would deprive the accused of the right to a jury trial. The conceptual problems involved in convicting Debs of contempt make the head swim.

As Justice Brewer approached the case, there was a single important fact involved: simply by ordering its members to strike, the union leaders had had the power, as a practical matter, to interrupt interstate commerce by railroad. Given this factual premise, Brewer (*In re Debs*, 1895: 577) posed two questions:

> First. Are the relations of the general government to interstate commerce and the transportation of the mails such as to authorize a direct interference to prevent a forcible obstruction thereof? Second. If authority exists, as authority in governmental affairs implies both power and duty, has a court of equity jurisdiction to issue an injunction in aid of the performance of such duty?

18   His answer to the first question begins by defining the relation
of federal to state power over commerce. It points out that federal power over commerce is absolute within its sphere of subject
matter jurisdiction, so that the federal government acts directly on
the citizen in this regard. The states have their own sphere of
authority, over matters of local police, and "the one does not
exclude the other, except where both cannot be executed at the
same time." Then federal power is supreme. Brewer sets forth the
basic Classical notions about the relation between state and federal powers.

At first blush, it seems that the only relevance of this discussion
is to show federal jurisdiction based on the fact that commerce and
the mails are involved. But Brewer (*In re Debs*, 1895: 581) con-
cludes with the following:

> It is curious to note the fact that in a large proportion of the cases
> in respect to interstate commerce brought to this court the ques-
> tion presented was of the validity of state legislation in its bear-
> ings upon interstate commerce, and the uniform course of deci-
> sion has been to declare that it is not within the competency of a
> State to legislate in such a manner as to obstruct interstate com-
> merce. If a State with its recognized powers of sovereignty is
> impotent to obstruct interstate commerce, can it be that any mere
> voluntary association of individuals within the limits of that State
> has a power which the State itself does not possess?

Brewer here analogizes the exercise of the sovereign legislative
will of a state to the exercise of private will by the citizen and
asserts that the absolute power of the federal government within
its sphere of commerce is the same with respect to each. The
assertion of the identity of the commerce power in the two relations gives it definition, as against individuals, since the Court can
draw on the whole body of case law about federal-state conflicts
over economic regulatory powers. Nothing could be more
Classical than this course of argument. The conclusion from an
analysis wholly in terms of the relation of the federal commerce
power to the state police power is that "the national government
may prevent any unlawful and forcible interference" with inter-

state commerce or the transportation of the mails, whether public or private.

Brewer's second question was whether the federal government, granted a power to remove obstructions to interstate commerce, could proceed by injunction. For contemporaries, the most striking thing about his answer was the assertion that the executive can use the army (and the "militia") to remove a private obstruction without recourse to any judicial process and without statutory authority of any kind. This seemed to some like a stirring reaffirmation of the inherent power of the central government to act quickly and decisively against semi-revolutionary left-wing tactics. To others, it seemed an invitation to shoot first and ask the question of legality afterward. The argument has been with us ever since. For our purposes, it is less important than the next step: Brewer claims that if the government can, in the absence of a statute, act directly to suppress an obstruction, then it should be able, still without a statute, to act by injunction to the same purpose.

The executive may be able simply to act, but a federal court can grant an injunction only according to law. By hypothesis, there is no statute covering the obstruction in hand. So what is the basis of the injunction? In other words, where can the court go for a definition of which private activities are lawful and which are unlawful invasions of the governmental regulatory power?

Brewer's answer was to invoke the law of nuisance. The federal government's entitlement to an injunction was defined by the right of public authorities to abate as public nuisances obstructions to their highways. And in case the reader had doubts about this body of law as a basis for a strike-breaking jurisdiction, Brewer (*In re Debs*, 1895: 592-93) appealed to the body of private law doctrines defining the relations of property holders among themselves:

> The difference between a public nuisance and a private nuisance is that the one affects the people at large and the other simply the individual. The quality of the wrong is the same. and the jurisdiction of the courts over them rests upon the same principles and goes to the same extent. Of course, circumstances may exist in one

case, which do not in another, to induce the courts to interfere or
to refuse to interfere by injunction, but the jurisdiction, the power
to interfere, exists in all cases of nuisance.

Brewer's opinion supplied the total absence of closely analogous
precedents with what he took to be logical inferences from precedents about the relation of federal commerce power to state
police power, about the power of a state to remove physical
obstruction from highways and water-ways, and about the abate-
ment by injunction of nuisances in general. I will argue that his
frame of mind in so arguing was different from that of the judges
of 1870. His analogies almost certainly would not have occurred
to them; but they would have found his assurance of the objective
character of the method of inference quite natural. His approach
was also very different from that of today's Supreme Court.
Modern judges have easy mental access to Brewer's analogies, but
little faith in the possibility of drawing logical inferences from
them.

∾ 6 ∾

As the example suggests, it is often useful to divide the question
of the mode of integration into two more specific subsidiary
questions. First, there is the question of how many of the doctrinal areas or fields within legal consciousness have been assimilated to a particular integrating sub-system or structure that interests
us. In other words, there is a question of horizontal inclusion and
exclusion, of incorporation into a particular schema. Questions
like those just put concerning the *In re Debs* opinion are designed
to measure this aspect, which I will sometimes call the breadth of
integration.

Second, there is the question of the internal structure of items
within a subsystem. Here, the issue is the nature of the relevance
of ideas to one another, given incorporation or assimilation.
There are many possible modes of organization within a subsystem. For example, we may feel that the minute we know that the
states cannot pass laws impeding commerce, it follows "logically,"
"necessarily," "obviously," and as "part of the nature of things"

that the federal government can obtain an injunction against a strike that disrupts interstate rail traffic. Or we might feel that the state-federal cases were useful "by analogy," and then want to say something about their aptness or compellingness as such. Or we might see the two situations as requiring the application of a single principle to quite radically different contexts, with the relevance of the state-federal cases lying in that they establish the principle and illustrate the prudential manner of its application.

Each of these modes of interrelation involves the experience of being bound, to some extent, to do X as an implication of commitment to Y. Within a subsystem, the positions we take can influence each other in this way because they are linked through abstractions. If they are treated as deductions from a single premise, then that premise is the link. If they influence each other "by analogy," then we have managed to disentangle certain key aspects from each for comparison. Over time, there are constant changes in the relationships between the particular, concrete, situationally well-defined rules judges use in real everyday cases and those more abstract, open-ended maxims, principles, doctrinal categories and general legal concepts (e.g., "duty," "power") that tie the rules together. I will refer to this set of relationships as the "vertical" dimension of a subsystem within legal consciousness.

The vertical dimension has the same structure as the horizontal. In each, there is a distinction between two experiences. Horizontally, bodies of doctrine are assimilated to the integrating subsystem, or they are not. In the vertical dimension, there is either a connection between an abstract proposition (contract protects will of the parties) and a particular rule (expectation damages), or there is not. By inquiring about the breadth of inclusion and the degree of abstraction in the different subsystems within a legal consciousness at different times, we can arrive at a history of the experience of judicial boundness. It is this history, as much as that of particular doctrines or philosophies, that powerfully influences the place of law and lawyers in social life.

THE RISE AND FALL OF CLASSICAL LEGAL THOUGHT

The notion of a vertical dimension of a subsystem within legal consciousness may be clarified by a description in those terms of our modern understanding of legal reasoning. We begin with the idea that legal actors enjoy a large number of particular rights and are subject to a large number of particular duties. For example, the law grants me expectation damages for breach of contract. It also grants me an action of trespass for nominal intrusions on my property, and so forth through a list of, say, 300 other particular rules of law of which I am beneficiary or which obligate me.

What do these rules have in common? We organize them for convenience, for reasons of utility into larger categories—e.g., once I have 15 rules that all refer to situations of agreement, I may decide, for some purposes, to refer to them collectively as rules of "contract." The notion of this type of classification is not that the contract category adds or subtracts anything, by itself, to or from the 15 rules I denote by it. If I learn a new rule, I will decide to include it or exclude it by asking whether it is useful to include it. And if my purposes in using the word change, I will feel no hesitation in expelling some of my 15 rules and adding new ones; the fact that I still use the word "contract" to describe my new collection gives me no qualms at all.

If you ask me the basis of one of my rules, I might answer that it is a maximizer of utility. Or I might answer that it protects a natural right, or that it is a binding precedent, or that it is a statute. The one thing that I would not do would be to justify it on the ground that it is "implicit in the institution of contract." This would make no sense, since that concept is no more than my invented category to group some rules that I often want to refer to together. Nothing is included in "contract," except what we have decided to put into it. Nothing is "implicit" in the existence of the category except some purpose making it convenient to refer to the rules together. "Contract" as a category won't be changed if we abolish a particular component, except that it will have 14 instead of 15 members.

In the system I have been describing, the units of thought, the operative wholes, are dozens of very concrete rules; the category of "contract" is non-operative, artificial, composite. But what does "operative" mean? It means that the rule of expectation damages can be used to provide solutions to problems, while the category of contract simply records the outcomes of solutions. For instance, suppose that I believe that it is the rule that I get expectation damages, and I justify this on the ground that such a rule most efficiently promotes reliance on contracts. Now suppose that there is a rule that a seller of a fungible good injured by a buyer's breach on a falling market can collect the difference between contract price and market price. If asked to justify this rule, I might very well state that it was "implicit" in the more general rule about expectation damages. In any case, I would almost certainly acknowledge a much closer relation between this rule and the more general rule of expectation damages than I would acknowledge between the latter rule and the principle that pacta sunt servanda.

It is possible to imagine a very different state of consciousness of the body of rules integrated in the subsystem of contracts. An observer might, and during the Classical period many observers did, see all the rules gathered under the contract rubric as implications of a general principle of freedom of contract, or one might conceive them all as the working out of the social purpose summarized by the notion of contract, or as designed to re-enforce a natural right of contract, or as included in a single composite utilitarian calculation about the enforcement of agreements.

We simply do not understand the system this way. We apply the deductive mode, the style of reasoning from general to particular, from maxim to application, from premises to implications, only from the level, say, of the rule of expectation damages to that of contract price less market price. We see the expectation rule as quite distinct from the rule about duress, and it does not occur to us to propose a more abstract category as providing a single, all-embracing, compulsive rationale. (Contract protects will; in cases of duress, there is no will to protect; in case of breach, the equivalent of the willed performance is expectation damages.) We treat

24   duress rules and damage rules in relation to, say, freedom of contract, the way a Classical observer might have treated contract,
tort, and property in relation to the more abstract category of
"private law."

Within contracts, there are two different modes of reasoning
and argument, reflecting the two different forms of relationship
that may exist between the rules. Sometimes, a lawyer attempts to
show that the correct decision in the case is compelled because the
situation is subsumed by implication within a powerful operative
rule or category. (Because we have adopted the expectation rule,
we have also adopted the contract and market rule.) Sometimes,
the lawyer argues for his proposed solution as resting on its own
bottom, as valid without compulsive assistance from other rules of
the contract subsystem. (He may do this in terms of utilitarian
social maximization, or natural rights, or morality, or statutory
authority.)

The point is that between the operative rule and the more particular subrule, there is structure, direction, influence, finally
compulsion. Between two operative rules each justified in its own
right, or between an operative rule and a passive, non-operative
conventionally defined category ("contract" in the example given
above), there is no nexus except the looser sense that it is convenient (or not) to deal with them together when pursuing some
extrinsically determined set of purposes.

Suppose that for purely utilitarian reasons we adopt a particular operative rule of contract law felt to have many implications.
Now suppose that on examination it appears that one of the
implied subrules costs more than it is worth, taken apart. A utilitarian may argue that he can consistently reject the subrule and
replace it with something else, while accepting the operative rule.
If this is so (i.e., if the rule-maker feels that he can consistently
enforce both the operative rule and the new antagonistic subrule), then the relationship of downward derivation I have been
talking about never existed in the first place. In other words, what
I am referring to is the psychological fact of the feeling of boundness in moving from general to particular, so that rejection of the
particular would be felt inescapably to mean rejection of the gen-

eral and vice versa. If the judge decides that the breaching buyer must pay only one-half the contract price less the market price, we would simply deny that he was enforcing a rule of expectation damages. What is involved here is a distinction between two experiences: that of being bound in all consistency to accept A given B, and that of being able to consider B on its own merits in spite of having accepted A.

It should already be clear that a defining characteristic of Classical legal thought was the assimilation of a great deal of law to a single subsystem dominated by the concept of a power absolute within its judicially delineated sphere. A second defining characteristic of Classicism, in contrast to pre-Classical and modern thinking, was the claim that very abstract propositions were nonetheless operative.

I am speaking of across-the-board changes in the way legal reasoning operated. During the period 1850-1900, as the Classical subsystem expanded, there was a general increase, and since about 1900 we have experienced a general decrease, in the felt operativeness of constitutional and doctrinal principles. With the disintegration of Classicism, there has been something close to a disappearance of an experience that appears to have been common at the turn of the century: that of the compulsion by which an abstraction dictates, objectively, apolitically, in a non-discretionary fashion, a particular result. As a consequence, there are claims to an objective basis for judicial review, and to an objective basis for innovation in private law, that seemed perfectly plausible during the period of the broadening and tightening of the Classical schema, but seem anti-democratic or merely naive in these days of its decadence.

∽ 8 ∾

While the legal elite may have experienced these changes in terms of a radical opposition between full operativeness and complete lack of nexus between abstraction and subrule, it does not follow that the historian should describe legal consciousness in these terms. We know that a rule or doctrine is within a subsystem only

26   by applying some quantitative criterion of relatedness, just as we determine operativeness by looking at a quantitatively variable interaction between abstraction and concrete rule. Wouldn't it be better to say that there is a general equilibrium system of relationships, with every element in legal consciousness related to every other, at least to that minimal degree necessary to lead us to define it as, in fact, "in" rather than out of consciousness?

If my main concern were a static analysis, comparing states of a given system or of different systems frozen at particular moments, then the general equilibrium model might be the best. My purpose, however, is to describe a particular historical process: the emergence, flourishing, and decay of a particular integrating subsystem (Classicism) within a particular historical consciousness (that of the American legal elite between 1850 and 1940). For this purpose, the image of the grid or network of forces is inadequate. The importance of the materials for us is much better conveyed by the image of a microscopic organism that takes to itself and transforms the biologically distinct organisms around it; finds itself transformed by the very process of assimilating those foreign bodies; and finally falls apart into a set of pieces which bear no more than an indirect and subtle resemblance either to their integrating predecessor or to the various weaker organisms the predecessor fed on.

I mean to be vague as to why the Classical subsystem triumphed over its contenders. My focus here is on how it happened, on the series of interactions among ideas within legal consciousness, rather than on the various kinds of energy that impelled the interactions. Given this initial point of view, what is salient is that particular ideas were initially relatively isolated, though within legal consciousness. Then, abruptly or gradually, a distinct, qualitatively new process took hold of them: they were drawn into the integrating subsystem of Classicism. In the process, they changed. In the process of causing those changes in the parts, the integrating subsystem went through its own transformation of internal structure, a tightening in the mode of interrelatedness.

The notion of incorporation or assimilation of elements conveys the transformation of the parts as they came in contact with the Classical subsystem. The notion of change in the level of abstraction at which concepts remain operative conveys the idea that the subsystem evolved as a whole. To some meaningful extent, it changed autonomously from, although in response to, what happened outside of it. The description of the historical process is thus cast in organic terms. We can identify, and follow through time, clusters of ideas that are entities. They develop, evolve, transform themselves, but are nonetheless somehow "the same thing," as opposed to other entities, that they were at the beginning.

A GLOSSARY OF TERMS,
BY WAY OF SUMMARY

Consciousness refers to the total contents of a mind, including images of the external world, images of the self, of emotions, goals and values, and theories about the world and self. I use the term only in this vague, all-inclusive sense. It defines the universe within which are situated the more sharply-delineated concepts that are the vehicles for analysis.

Legal Consciousness is an only slightly more defined notion. It refers to the particular form of consciousness that characterizes the legal profession as a social group, at a particular moment. The main peculiarity of this consciousness is that it contains a vast number of legal rules, arguments, and theories, a great deal of information about the institutional workings of the legal process, and the constellation of ideals and goals current in the profession at a given moment.

A subsystem within legal consciousnesses is a kind of structure; that is, a formal arrangement of some of the elements in consciousness. Subsystems are structures that arrange relatively large numbers of elements; e.g., the Madisonian eqiuilibrium theory of federalism. Any number of subsystems can exist within consciousness at a given moment. Unlike the concept of consciousness, those of structure and subsystem can be given precise meaning. They are tools of analysis.

28   *Classical legal thought, pre-Classical legal thought,* and *modern legal thought*: pre-Classical legal thought flourished between 1800 and 1860 and declined between 1860 and 1885. Classical legal thought emerged between 1850 and 1885, flourished between 1885 and 1935, but was in rapid decline by 1940. Modern legal thought emerged between 1900 and 1930 and survives to this day.

A subsystem *integrates* some number of the elements in a legal consciousness; that is, it includes them in a formal arrangement. Such an arrangement has a horizontal dimension and a vertical dimension. A description of the horizontal dimension tells us how many of all the rules in consciousness are within a particular subsystem, and the manner in which they are related to one another. A description of the vertical dimension tells us how the more and less abstract elements in a doctrinal area are related.

Assimilation refers to the transformation undergone by elements in legal consciousness as they are drawn into a subsystem.

Operativeness is a property of some rules and principles. It is the ability to generate subrules, more concrete prescriptions that are felt to be inescapable once the abstraction is assented   to.

One of the functions of a structure within consciousness, and particularly of a subsystem, is the *mediation of the contradictions of experience.* The sense of contradiction arises from the persistent existence within consciousness of elements which seem mutually exclusive. These can be inconsistent facts, conflicting emotions, or operative abstractions whose implication contradict one another. Mediation is the reduction of the sense of contradiction by an arrangement of the elements that makes the problem less salient.

ACKNOWLEDGMENTS

I am grateful to Morton Horwitz, R.W. Kennedy, Karl Klare, Fred Konefsky, Gerta Prosser, Henry Steiner, Larry Tribe, and Roberto Unger for helpful comments. Cedric Chao and Mark Lauritsen researched expertly.

NOTE

This is a slightly revised version of an essay written in 1975. The works of Ihering (1883), Pollock and Maitland (1968), Levi-Strauss (1966), Piaget (1962), Mannheim (1936), Lukacs (1971), and Marcuse (1941) were the main influences on the conception of legal history put forward. I also profited greatly from reading early drafts of Unger (1975, 1976) and Horwitz (1977). Readers interested in the future development of the ideas outlined here should consult Kennedy (1976, 1979).

REFERENCES

Horwitz, Morton J., The Transformation of American Law, 1780-1860. Cambridge, Mass.: Harvard University Press, 1977.

Ihering, Rudolph von, Der Geist des Romischen Recht. Berlin, 1883.

In Re Debs, 158 U.S. 546 (1895).

Kennedy, Duncan, "Form and Substance in Private Law Adjudication," Harvard Law Review 89 (1976): 1685-1778.

_____, "The Structure of Blackstone's Commentaries," Buffalo Law Review 28 (1979): 205-382.

Levi-Strauss, Claude, The Savage Mind. Chicago, University of Chicago Press, 1966.

Lochner v. New York, 198 U.S. 45 (1905).

Lukacs, Georg, "Reification and the Consciousness of the Proletariat," in History and Class Consciousness, pp. 83-222. Cambridge, Mass.: The MIT Press, 1971.

Mannheim, Karl, Ideology and Utopia. New York: Harcourt, Brace & World, Inc., 1936.

30 Marcuse, Herbert, Reason and Revolution. New York: Oxford University Press, Inc., 1941.

Piaget, Jean, Play, Dreams and Imitation in Childhood. New York: W.W. Norton & Co., Inc., 1962.

Pollock, F., and F.W. Maitland, The History of English Law. (Two Volumes) Cambridge, England: Cambridge University Press, 1968.

Unger, Roberto M., Knowledge and Politics. New York: Free Press, 1975.

_____, Law in Modern Society. New York: Free Press, 1976.

CHAPTER II

Pre-Classical Public Law

∞ 1 ∞

THE PARTICULAR IDEAS that composed Classical legal thought are the familiar elements of American political-legal discourse: federalism, the system of individual rights against the state, the common law, the separation of powers. These had all been important parts of legal thought since 1789, and we can follow their permutations during the period before the Civil War, as they gradually assumed the configuration that would be integrated in Classicism. Conversely, we can trace the system of 1900 back toward 1800, watching its well knit elements gradually drift apart, lose their common physiognomy, become disparate objects no one thought to relate among themselves in what now seem the obvious ways.

The difficulty in such an inquiry is to imagine that the elements, as they appeared in pre-Classical legal thought, were at once heterogeneous, not systematically interrelated at all, if we choose the Classical mode as the criterion of integration, yet perfectly adequately integrated from the perspective of the pre-Classical legal thinkers themselves. It is true that when we look at 1830 in terms of the categories and in terms of the perceived problems of theory that

32   have pre-occupied us since 1885, we discover a state of confusion or
      insouciant unawareness. We are assessing legal thought in terms of
      difficulties they had not thought of or didn't care about. It may well
      be that the typical Supreme Court justice of 1830 felt more confi-
      dence in the way things legal hung together than his equivalent 60
      or 90 years later. When we assess their thought in terms of the con-
      flicts and theoretical contradictions that preoccupied them, we may
      find this appropriate and in no way paradoxical.

      Once we adopt the notion of integrating subsystems within
      consciousness, it is easy to see that there may be more than one
      such structure at work at a given moment of time, and that there
      may be many unintegrated elements or none at all. Consciousness
      as a whole is an enduring unity that evolves through time. Within
      consciousness, different subsystems flourish and decay. Their par-
      ticular histories are only a part of the history of the whole. For
      example, a broadening and tightening of one subsystem may
      coincide with a loosening of the ties within others. Indeed, the
      growth of one may require or cause the disintegration of others.
      The characterization of consciousness as a whole therefore poses
      problems that are quite distinct from those posed by a part. It is
      one thing to inquire into the condition, in 1830, of each of the ele-
      ments that were to be integrated in the Classical subsystem, to ask
      to what extent they had come to be interrelated theoretically in the
      Classical fashion. It is a more difficult task altogether to portray
      the state of the larger pre-Classical consciousness that *actually*
      linked those elements in 1830.

      When the common lawyers theorized about private law, they
      drew on European sources in the tradition of natural rights,
      according to which all of private law was the rational working out
      of immutable, divinely established principles. They thereby creat-
      ed what seems to us a striking incoherence within private law, typ-
      ified by Blackstone's combination of sweeping natural rights gen-
      eralities with meticulous rehashing of the mass of medieval prece-
      dents. To Classical eyes, private law natural rights theorizing fur-
      ther aggravated the split between public and private law, since the
      positivist, legislatively oriented principles of constitutionalism
      would not square with the anti-state, mystically based approach of

the natural lawyers. On the other hand, Classical eyes were blind to elements that may have played an integrating role in the earlier mode of thought, such as the ordering of the social universe according to God's laws, or the notion of the Great Chain of Being, or the use in private law of a utilitarian calculus of social policies not much different in practice from the purposive interpretation of general constitutional provisions.

My purpose in this part is to sketch in the outlines of the legal consciousness of the American legal elite of the year 1870. Classical legal thought was emerging throughout the period between 1850 and 1885. I believe that as a consequence the legal universe was radically different in 1900 from what it had been in 1830. 1870 was a year of transition. This was true both of the theory of federalism and of the theories of rights against the state, private law, and the separation of powers. In this chapter, I will describe the pre-Classical and Classical versions of federalism and rights against the state, with the emphasis on the contrast of ways of thought rather than on the stuff of legal doctrine. We will revert to public law at the end of Book One, when we have the whole of Classical legal thought before us.

∾ 2 ∾

The great accomplishment of the immediate post Civil War period was the firm establishment of the analogy of state-state relations to state-federal relations through the settling of the pre-War disputes about sovereignty and citizenship. Thomas M. Cooley's statement, in his *Treatise on Constitutional Limitations* (1868), was definitive:

> *Sovereignty,* as applied to States, imports the supreme, absolute, uncontrollable power by which any State is governed. . . The sovereignty of a State commonly extends to all the subjects of government within the territorial limits occupied by the associated people who compose it; and. . . the dividing line between sovereignties is usually a territorial line. In American constitutional law, however, there is a division of the powers of sovereignty between the national and state governments by subjects: the former being possessed of

34   supreme, absolute, and uncontrollable power over certain subjects
throughout all the States and territories, while the States have the
like complete power, within their respective territorial limits, over
other subjects.2

Footnote 2: . . . "The powers of the general government and of
the State, although both exist and are exercised within the same
territorial limits, are yet separate and distinct sovereignties, acting
separately and independently of each other within their respective
spheres. And the sphere of action appropriated to the United
States is as far beyond the reach of the judicial process issued by a
State judge of a State court, as if the line of division was traced by
landmarks and monuments visible to the eye." Taney, Ch. J., in
Abelman v. Booth, 21 How. 516.

These statements assert that there is an essential similarity
between the territorial line dividing conventional sovereigns and
the non-material line dividing state and federal jurisdictions. In
one sense, this was a legal commonplace going back to Marshall:
it was expected that in the division of functions the federal government would act on state territory yet with "plenary" power.
But in another sense, the quote had quite a different meaning after
the Civil War than it could have before it. The problem was that,
as Cooley's definition suggested, the idea of sovereignty as developed by the Romans, by Blackstone, and by the Utilitarians, had
in it a notion not only of absoluteness within a sphere, but of
unlimited, absolute absoluteness.

In this conception, it was the "very nature" of sovereignty that
it knew no bounds. As a matter of fact, there might be different
sovereigns with different territorial jurisdictions, but this state of
facts was inherently unstable. There was no way to draw a line
around the ambitions of the rivals; boundaries were simply the
outcome of the struggle for power. It followed that the notion of
boundaries *within* a territorial unit was peculiar to say the least.
Such a line between state and federal could be accepted as the outcome of a struggle between nation and state. It could not be conceived as a meaningful statement about legitimate political power,
since either the state or the federal government must be the *real*

sovereign. If neither was the real sovereign, then the Union was in a state of war. The peaceful coexistence of two *legitimate* sovereigns was "simply incompatible" with the "Idea" of sovereignty.

Although Marshall and Taney represented opposite sides of the controversy between federalism and states rights, they were in full agreement about the formal mode of resolution of this legal dilemma. Only the people were "really" sovereign; the Constitution allocated spheres *within which* state and federal government were sovereign; the role of the federal judiciary was to enforce this allocation. This way of looking at the matter was sometimes acceptable to one side in the states rights conflict, and sometimes to the other, but it was never uncontroversial; and it had to be admitted that it constituted an anomalous body of doctrine, not obviously compatible either with the extreme positivism or the extreme natural rights standpoints prevalent at the time.

The Civil War settled the controversy, but not in the obvious way of asserting that the federal government was the "real" sovereign. Indeed, it might be more accurate to say that the Civil War killed off the states rights party and substantively satisfied (more or less) the extreme federalists, so that the pre-War Supreme Court theory was the victor by default. At any rate, the most controversial propositions of Marshall's theory of federalism came to be among the least controversial premises of Classicism. Chief Justice Chase's conversion from radical Republican to moderate Democrat symbolized the emergence of a new equilibrium on the issue of federalism. In 1866, he cast it in terms that were to acquire a sort of magical incantatory power in later discussions of the subject:

> The Union of the States never was a purely artificial and arbitrary relation . . . It received definite form and character and sanction by the Articles of Confederation. By these the Union was solemnly declared to be "perpetual." And when these articles were found to be inadequate to the exigencies of the country, the Constitution was ordained "to form a more perfect Union." It is difficult to convey the idea of indissoluble unity more clearly than by these

words. What can be indissoluble if a perpetual union, made more perfect, is not? But the perpetuity and indissolubility of the Union by no means implies the loss of distinct and individual existence, or of the right of self-government by the States....It may be not unreasonably said that the preservation of the States and the maintenance of their governments are as much within the design and care of the Constitution as the preservation of the Union and the maintenance of the national government. The Constitution, in all its provisions, looks to an indestructible Union composed of indestructible States.

The pre-war court had developed, for use in the legal analysis of the American federal system, a concept of state and federal powers lacking the characteristic of unlimited, absolute absoluteness that was central in the reigning jurisprudence. The Civil War validated this enterprise. *Everyone* within the legal elite seemed to conceive the absoluteness of the state and federal governments *within* their spheres as consistent with a condition of peace, of legitimate harmony, rather than as the provisional and contingent outcome of the struggle to establish the states or the Union as the "real" sovereign. The formulas of Marshall's and Taney's commerce clause cases passed from the status of uneasy compromises, always open to attack as disingenuous and politically self-serving, to the status of revered monuments, unquestionably right, and, just as important, unquestionably *legal*. Henceforth the fundamental *legal* conception in America was not the sovereign of positivism but a form of governmental power that was (a) inherently limited rather than inherently expansive, and (b) not intrinsically linked to the notion of plenary jurisdiction over a territory, but rather sufficiently abstract so that it could exist over a "subject matter" (e.g. commerce, internal police) or a type of "question" (judicial question; legislative question) within a territory. Bryce, writing in 1889, puts this clearly:

A State is, within its proper sphere, just as legally supreme, just as well entitled to give effect to its own will, as is the National government within its sphere; and for the same reason. All authority flows from the people. The people have given part of their supreme authority to the Central, part to the State governments. Both hold by the same title, and therefore the National government, although superior wherever there is a concurrence of powers, has no more right to trespass upon the domain of a State than a State has upon the domain of Federal action...

... The inextricable knots which American lawyers and publicists went on tying down till 1861, were cut by the sword of the North in the Civil War, and need concern us no longer. It is now admitted that the Union is not a mere compact between commonwealths, dissoluble at pleasure, but an instrument of perpetual efficacy, emanating from the whole people, and alterable by them only in the manner which its own terms prescribe. It is "an indestructible Union of indestructible States."

He also saw the peculiarity, from a European point of view, of non-territorial sovereignty:

The French or English reader may ask how it is possible to work a system so extremely complex, under which every yard of ground in the Union is covered by two jurisdictions, with two sets of judges and two sets of officers, responsible to different superiors, their spheres of action divided only by an ideal line, and their action liable in practice to clash. The answer is that the system does work, and now, after a hundred years of experience, works smoothly.

In The Unwritten Constitution, a brilliant conservative tract of 1890, now forgotten, Christopher G. Tiedeman argued the special significance of this development in a passage that deserves full exhumation:

... It was reserved for an American to create an absolutely new political idea of the most transcendent importance, and which has ultimately solved the problem of combining a strong central government with an independent local government.

In February, 1783, Pelatial Webster published "A Dissertation on the Political Union and Constitution of the Thirteen United States of North America," which was a year later followed by

38   another of the same tenor, by Noah Webster, in both of which was proposed "a new system of government which should act, not on the States, but on individuals, and vest in Congress full power to carry its laws into effect." When we consider for a moment the wonderfulness of two separate and in many respects independent governmental agencies exerting their powers over the same territory, and each within its own sphere commanding the obedience of the same people, there is no occasion for surprise that it required a century of experience under the new government to fully appreciate its significance and effect. The successful maintenance of the separate autonomy of the Federal and State governments for a century, through all the vicissitudes of political fortune which fell to the lot of the people of the United States, furnished an enigmatical contradiction of the prevalent notions of an indivisible sovereignty.

If there be such a thing in politics as sovereignty, it is necessarily indivisible, and hence it is impossible to subject a territory and people to two separate and independent governments without one of them becoming subordinate toward the instrument of the other. And I am satisfied that the political leaders of the day, such as Hamilton, Madison, and Randolph, who made such strenuous efforts to establish a strong federal government, put no faith in the feasibility of a dual government of this sort. For, upon the assembling of the constitutional convention, these statesmen advocated the establishment of a supreme federal government, which would reduce the States to subordinate provinces; and they did not yield to the demands of the advocates of State rights until it was demonstrated that the convention would not adopt a centralized government. They feared, and the struggles of seventy five years justified their fears, that the two governmental agencies could not maintain their independent autonomy. But against their will and in spite of their fears this became the fundamental principle of the American governmental agencies, about which the political force, played with more or less vehemence for three quarters of a century, until, as a declaration of the results of the mighty crisis, the Supreme Court of the United States pronounced this country to be "an indestructible Union composed of indestructible States."

Within the system of co-equal powers, the role of the federal judiciary was that of umpire and line drawer. Given the premises of the system, there could be no presumption in favor of any participant's status at the expense of the other's. The problem of burden of proof was ingeniously solved through Marshall's formula that the federal government being of enumerated powers, bore the burden of establishing the existence of authority over a subject matter, but that authority once established included all reasonable subsidiary implications and superseded all conflicting state interests. The point was that the federal judiciary was in theory impartial among the contenders.

Nonetheless, before the Civil War, the Court did not once, except in the Dred Scott case, strike down a federal statute as invasive of state powers, although it frequently struck down state laws on the inverse ground that they invaded the sphere of Congress (which had, often, not legislated or otherwise expressed itself on the subject matter). In 1869, however, Chief Justice Chase applied the symmetrical conceptual scheme of Marshall and Taney to a federal law banning the sale of a dangerous illuminating gas:

> That Congress has power to regulate commerce with foreign nations and among the several States, and with the Indian tribes, the Constitution expressly declares. But this express grant of power to regulate commerce among the States has always been understood as limited by its terms; and as a virtual denial of any power to interfere with the internal trade and business of the separate States; except, indeed, as a necessary and proper means for carrying into execution some other power expressly granted or vested.

Chase then rejected the government's contentions that the act was in aid of federal taxes on other items. "Standing by itself, it is plainly a regulation of police. . . ." The decision in the case followed as a matter of deduction from major and minor premises:

> As a police regulation, relating exclusively to the internal trade of the States, it can only have effect where the legislative authority of Congress excludes, territorially, all State legislation, as for example, in the District of Columbia. Within State limits, it can have no

40   constitutional operation. This has been so frequently declared by this court, results so obviously from the terms of the Constitution, and has been so fully explained and supported on former occasions, that we think it unnecessary to enter again upon the discussion.

As a federal institution, the Court was not, and could not well have been truly neutral in the pre-War struggle over the nature of the Constitution. The *De Witt* case marked the beginning of a new attitude, one that led the Court to attempt to strike in practice a balance that had previously been theoretical and rhetorical rather than actual. As Bryce put it twenty years later, though it might be "in the last resort a federal court," yet it was not supposed to be "biased in favor of the Federal government," but rather to avoid "unfairness" as between the powers. [See *The Collector v. Day*, 11 Wall. 113 (1870) for another example.]

∾ 3 ∽

The other system that eventually emerged within legal consciousness, that of individual rights, had exactly this same structure: substantive authority was divided, along both territorial and "ideal" or "subject matter" lines, between public and private powers absolute but limited within their spheres. The parallel is easy to grasp today; in fact, it is almost second-nature to us, along with the various critical routines by which the analogies can be redissolved into their constituent parts. In the making, however, the possibility of constructing two parallel systems was by no means obvious, and the tortuosity of the path of emergence suggests something factitious in our most familiar habits of thought.

I believe that the post-war conception of the state-state-federal relationship served as a model or exemplar or paradigm in the construction of the citizen-citizen-state relation in Classical legal thought. For purposes of analogical borrowing, the important things about the federal system were (a) that sovereignty within the system, whether state or federal, was an inherently limited concept, (b) that state sovereignty was a unified or "multi-dimensional" legal concept: the State of Massachusetts was legally the same entity in relation to Rhode Island that it was in relation to the federal government, although in the latter case its boundary was, as Bryce put it, "ideal" rather than physical; (c) that state and federal governments were "absolute within their spheres" while (d) the federal judiciary was the equally absolute master of the operation of drawing the boundary lines between spheres, using a technique of construction of the Constitution that was legal rather than prudential or political.

By 1898, there existed a federal jurisprudence of the citizen-citizen-state relation which was identical, in each of the respects just mentioned, to the federal system. (a) The concepts of state power and individual right were equated as instances of legally effective will limited by the Constitution. (b) The individual rights of property and contract were unified or "multi-dimensional" legal entities, equally applicable to private disputes and to conflicts between state and citizen. The freedom of contract protected by the 14th Amendment against legislative interference was the same entity as the freedom of contract enforced by the common law in litigation between businessmen. (c) Private right and state power were each "absolute within their spheres," while (d) the federal judiciary had the exclusive power to draw the boundaries of the spheres, using a technique of construction that was legal rather than prudential or political.

This very broadly integrated system of thought was unique in American history. Such a system of thought could not easily come into existence at the state level since the federal analogy was not available there as a constant source of guidance in the evolution of the theories of private and public law rights. And it could not exist at the federal level before the Civil War: there was no general acceptance of the legal character and legitimacy of the Marshallian federal formulas, and there was no general federal jurisdiction over private rights against the state. Finally, until the 1870's and 1880's there were no theories of public and private law of a type capable of sustaining the analogy to the theory of federalism.

In Classical legal thought, rights against the state occupied a central position: they were part of public, of constitutional law,

42   and were therefore thought of as in the same general universe as the law of federalism. On the other hand, they were "rights" of private parties, and so bore a close relationship to the "rights" of private parties the courts protect through the common law of property or contracts or torts. The law of federalism and private law were much more clearly autonomous from one another than rights against the state from either.

In *pre*-Classical legal thought, rights against the state were much more closely linked to federalism, within the rubric of public or constitutional law, than to private law. The creation of an individual-individual-state parallel to the state-state-federal system was a slow process. The individual-state relation was analogized to that of state and federal power before there was a clear identification of the private law rights and property and contract with those federally guaranteed against the state as the "life, liberty of property" of the 14th Amendment. For this reason, it seems best in expounding the pre-Classical system to present rights against the state in juxtaposition with the law of federalism, and to save for later the back and forth interaction between public law and private law rights.

It is important to keep in mind that the emergence of rights against the state within Classical legal thought involved, in fact, a *double* relationship to the law of federalism. First, the power of the federalism model derived from more than intrinsic aptness. The federal courts were trying to develop a brand new federal law of individual rights against the state. They had to go somewhere for models of legal relationship. The federal model was both intimately familiar and recently vindicated as legally legitimate.

The second kind of interrelationship is more complex. The theories of public and private rights within Classicism were what they were partly because they were theories of what the *federal* courts could and should do about rights. When federal courts dealt with public and private law rights, they did so *always* in a context of jurisdictional uncertainty. In principle, according to the original understanding, the main job of protecting rights in general belonged to the states. The federal rules were a system grafted onto or imposed upon a state system which everyone, at least as late at 1885, took to be the "real" system.

The substantive theories of public law rights that emerged within Classicism were shaped by the necessity the federal judges felt of creating doctrines that would be compatible with the peculiar federal role. Unlike state court judges, federal court judges had to defend themselves against attacks on the very existence of a rights jurisdiction. Their choice among theories of rights was therefore responsive to a whole range of tactical pressures absent at the state level. For example, the first federal personal rights against the states (aside from those explicitly guaranteed by, e.g., the Contracts Clause) were, according to the judges, logical derivations from the existence and peculiar characteristics of a federal system. Such were the right to travel from state to state and the right to engage in interstate commerce. Only with time and abstraction did these develop into fundamental rights unrelated to the peculiarities of federalism, such as the freedom of contract.

There is a striking analogy between the emergence of Classicism and the emergence of the common law of the national courts of England after 1066. In both cases, the necessity of establishing the jurisdiction of the central authority against a background of autonomous local legal systems profoundly influenced the substantive doctrines that courts could adopt. Maitland and Milsom seem to agree that the law of torts and contracts was secreted "in the interstices of the rules of procedure" not because of some inherent primitivism of the medieval legal mind, but because the procedures were the only way to get a case out of the control of local authority. The federal law of individual rights against the state was secreted in the interstices of the rules governing the relations of state and federal powers. This origin made the federal law of rights as different from state law based on state constitutions as the manorial law of contracts was from that administered in the Court of King's Bench.

~ 4 ~

In most important respects, the legal concept of a constitutional right—a right the courts are legally bound to vindicate against the

44   legislature—is the same today as it was in 1900. The Classical conception that emerged in the interpretation of the Fourteenth Amendment was that individual rights and governmental powers are opposed entities. The claims of right of the individual conflict with and encroach on legislative claims of power. The courts find themselves in the middle, without any other help than the Constitution. The Constitution, in turn, recognizes if it does not positively create the dilemma. When the judge refers to it, he finds both rights and powers given extensive treatment as indisputably real legal entities with which he must reason legally, but precious little concrete information about how he is to resolve conflicts between them.

We have shifted the emphasis from property rights to personal rights. But the great difference between our view and that of 1900, is that we no longer believe in the existence of an objective or scientific method of reasoning the judge can apply to the resolution of the dilemma of opposing entities. The court speaks of "fundamental" individual rights vs. "compelling" state interests, but just about everyone seems to agree that these are simply ways of structuring a process of "balance" which is essentially prudential, or political or subjective in character. It is simply a premise that legislative power and individual rights are, as Corwin put it in 1929, "balanced and antithetical concepts" whose "essential contradiction" is "manifest." [42 HLR 149] The basic anti-interventionist argument follows directly.

It is that the judge should defer to the legislature in cases of any doubt at all: the legislature's balance of preference has the warrant of democracy, if not of Reason. In 1900, it seems the judges had much greater confidence in their tools for performing the job the Constitution thrust upon them. They perceived rights and powers as in conflict, but not as contradictory. The essence of judicial method was the correct resolution of conflict. There was correspondingly less need to defer to popular bodies when the meaning of the document was in doubt.

1870 was a different matter altogether. In this section, I will attempt a conceptual map of what, by analogy with early English law, we might call the "manorial" doctrine of rights that existed before the conflict of state and federal jurisdictions forced conceptual innovation. The concepts are those of "general constitutional law" (i.e. state as opposed to federal). My purpose is to explain how it was that pre-Classical thinkers dealt with the rights-powers problem without resort either to the notion of a pseudo-scientific legal method for resolving a conflict, or to the various counsels of despair we adopt in dealing with our contradiction.

The first striking difference between the pre-Classical and the Classical (and modern) approaches is that earlier thinkers split the problem up. In the Classical and post-Classical models, the relation of rights to powers is diadic: there are two and only two concepts which are in conflict in a rather fundamental fashion. The choice of the judge is typically to support one at the expense of the other. In pre-Classical legal consciousness there were at least four different conceptual contexts within which the right-power problem might arise:

(1) A claim that legislative action violated the natural rights of the individual. Judges were sometimes asked to disregard or set aside legislative action, even in the absence of an explicit constitutional provision, a legally vested right, or an implied limitation, because it violated principles of justice that were *intrinsically* binding on everyone, whether or not institutionally recognized. The usual example was a legislative decree forcibly transferring the property of A to B, or declaring X to be the wife of Y rather than of Z.

(2) A claim that the legislature had violated some particular, defined, "legally vested right" of the plaintiff protected under one or another of the general clauses of the constitution in question, or as part of a practice of judicial review to secure natural rights. It would violate a vested right if the legislature were to revoke arbitrarily privileges that had been granted a corporation in order to induce it to invest large sums in some development project.

46   (3) A claim that the legislature had violated an explicit limitation on its power, a limitation created to protect the
plaintiff (for example a Just Compensation Clause, or the
Contracts Clause of the federal constitution).

(4) A claim that the legislative action exceeded one of the
"implied limitations" imposed by the constitutional separation of powers. For example the legislature might be
"usurping the judicial function" or acting in a way that
was simply "not within the definition of legislative powers" if it were to take it upon itself to determine the
amount of compensation to be paid in an eminent
domain proceeding.

Within each of these categories there could be endless dispute
not just about particular cases, but also about the definition and
use of concepts. But the dispute was *within* the concepts, not about
their meaningfulness. For example, it was a difficult question
whether the contracts clause of the federal constitution applied to
a corporate charter. But no one disputed that the Contracts Clause
had *some* meaning and was judicially enforceable against the
states.

Likewise with the vested rights doctrine. Today, we find the
notion that there is an objectively determinable moment when a
legal advantage vests, and becomes a constitutionally protected
right, absurd. For a writer like Thomas M. Cooley, whose treatise
on constitutional law sums up the pre-Classical wisdom, there
might be a difficulty in fixing the moment of vesting. It might be
necessary to resort to case by case analysis to cover the diverse
judicial solutions in different situations. But there was no question
of the reality of the distinction the judge struggled to apply correctly. A phrase of Justice Bradley, dissenting in a case decided in
1885, gives a sense of the striking difference between our conceptions and theirs:

> The suggestion that the words "vested rights" are not to be found
> in the Constitution does not prove that there are no such rights.
> The name of the Supreme Being does not occur in the

Constitution; yet our national being is founded on a tacit recognition of His justice and goodness, and the eternal obligation of His
laws.[115 U.S. 620, 632]

A more difficult example: there was a perennial argument
about whether a judge could legitimately strike down or disregard
a law for no other reason than that it violated natural right. But
everyone seems to have agreed that the natural rights concept was
meaningful. Those most opposed to making it a basis of jurisdiction did not hesitate for a moment to appeal to the concept in
deciding how to interpret an ambiguous constitutional clause.
Moreover, it seemed to be accepted as a matter of course that a
judge could legitimately choose between two plausible interpretations of a statute on the ground that one of them was less in conflict with natural justice than the other.

For example, in *Pumpelly v. Green Bay Company* (1872), Justice
Miller had to construe the clause of a state constitution forbidding
the taking of property without just compensation. The agents of
the state had, without instituting condemnation proceedings or
paying compensation, rendered the plaintiff's land useless by
flooding it. The defendant's argued that there had been no "taking" of property.

It would be a very curious and unsatisfactory result, if in con-
struing a provision of constitutional law, always understood to
have been adopted for protection and security to the rights of the
individual as against the government, and which has received the
commendation of jurists, statesmen, and commentators as placing
the just principles of the common law on that subject beyond the
power of ordinary legislation to change or control them, it shall
be held that if the government refrains from the absolute conversion of real property to the uses of the public it can destroy its
value entirely, can inflict irreparable and permanent injury to any
extent, can, in effect, subject it to total destruction without making
any compensation, because in the narrowest sense of that word, it
is not taken for the public use. . . .

In the case of Gardner v. Newburgh, Chancellor Kent granted

an injunction to prevent the trustees of Newburg from diverting the water of a certain stream flowing over plaintiff's land from its usual course, because the act of the legislature which authorized it had made no provision for compensating the plaintiff for the injury thus done to his land. And he did this though there was no provision in the Constitution of New York such as we have mentioned, and though he recognized that the water was taken for a public use. After citing several continental jurists on this right of eminent domain, he says that while they admit that private property may be taken for public uses when public necessity or utility requires, they all lay it down as a clear principle of natural equity that the individual whose property is thus sacrificed must be indemnified. . . .

If these be correct statements of the limitations upon the exercise of the right of eminent domain, as the doctrine was understood before it had the benefit of constitutional sanction, by the construction now sought to be placed upon the Constitution it would become an instrument of oppression rather than protection to individual rights.

What today is an argument about the meaningful existence of natural rights was then an argument about their justiciability.

As they existed in pre-Classical legal consciousness, the concepts of natural and vested rights and express and implied limitations overlapped, but were largely autonomous from each other. *Legally* speaking, they were not just four instances of a general conflict between individual right and legislative power. The legal operations the judge performed in each situation were *sui generis*, rather than instances of the application of a single scientific method, or occasions for performing the essential judicial task of balancing interests. The tendency to reduce all situations involving either a right or power of any kind to a single situation of right-power confrontation did not exist even in the most sophisticated constitutional writing.

Moreover, in *none* of the four situations did the judges use concepts like those modern legal writers apply to all questions of the opposition of rights and powers. Some typical Classical legal rights are freedom of contract secured by the Due Process Clause of the Fourteenth Amendment; the right to Just Compensation secured in the same way; and the right to Equal Protection typified by a case like *Yick Wo v. Hopkins* (differential enforcement of a local ordinance so as to discriminate against Chinese laundries). The modern equivalents are rights like Free Speech, inferred from the First Amendment's prohibition on federal laws abridging freedom of speech; privacy, inferred from a variety of amendments; and the 'new' equal protection the Court has developed in cases like *Brown v. Bd. of Education* and the *Reapportionment Cases*.

The characteristics of Classical and post-Classical rights are: abstraction (the right as formulated applies over a broad, initially indeterminate range of very disparate situations); firm formal grounding in explicit constitutional language, rather than in extralegal concepts like natural justice; appeal to concepts of individual autonomy and legal equality; and hence inconsistency with unlimited exercise of legislative powers that are equally if not more firmly grounded in the Constitution.

The modern liberal enemies of the right-wing Classical Court have looked for the origins of the Classical and modern sort of rights in natural rights, vested rights and implied limitations. Classical thinkers, by contrast, claimed that Fourteenth Amendment rights were an instance of the fourth category of concrete and explicit constitutional limitation. For our purposes, what is important is that the very heterogeneous structure of the pre-Classical concepts probably reduced the perception of conflict and masked the flat contradictions that emerged with a more abstract and coherent treatment.

In other words, I am asserting that a purely formal characteristic of the pre-Classical doctrines, their heterogeneity, made it easier to believe that taken together they represented an adequate treatment of the problem. We will encounter similar structural traits in the discussion of private law. But, at least for rights, there were also substantive aspects to the pre-Classical concepts that allowed legal thinkers to fit them together with a degree of harmony long since passed beyond our powers.

℘ 5 ℘

In pre-Classical thought, natural rights animate all of public law. Vested rights, and express and implied limitations, as well as sovereignty itself, were comprehensible only by reference to the long tradition of thinking about a transcendent ordering of the social universe, an ordering that actual government could mirror but whose principles were beyond change by human agency. Within this tradition, it was possible to order the concepts of right and power in such a way as to sharply reduce what we regard as inherent incompatibilities.

Pre-Classical natural rights have abstraction in common with the Classical (and modern) variety, and they were even then strongly associated with the idea of autonomy. But they were not fully legal. We tend to see the rights-powers relation in terms of two diadic opposition representing a single structure on two levels:

| Natural Rights | Sovereignty |
| Legal Rights | Legal Powers |

In pre-Classical legal consciousness, the relationship was hierarchical:

Natural Rights
Sovereignty
Legal Powers
Legal Rights

Within this arrangement, natural rights and sovereignty were defined, in utterly incompatible terms, as unlimited, absolutely absolute, unconstrainable concepts. Natural rights were entitled to vindication no matter what. As Justice Bradley put it in the *Slaughterhouse Cases:*

> In this free country the people of which inherited certain traditionary rights and privileges from their ancestors, citizenship means something. It has certain privileges and immunities attached to it which the government whether restricted by express or implied limitations, cannot take away or impair. It may do so temporarily by force, but it cannot do so by right. [16 Wall.114]

Likewise, sovereignty was absolute dominion and knew no restraints of any kind, including constraints of right. But this situation of logical incompatibility of concepts posed (almost) no problem at all for the judge. The absoluteness of natural rights was a *political* datum. The kind of rights he dealt with as a lawyer were *legal* rights, and these were not only not absolute, they were wholly the creatures of legal powers derived from sovereignty. In pre-Classical legal consciousness, law of the positive kind, the law of the actual legal system in force in the United States, the law of treatises and judicial opinions and advice to clients, was the law of legal powers. Rights, within the system of legal reasoning, were the reflex of powers, what one secured by the manipution of powers.

Right into the Classical period, judges who wanted to deny individual claims to rights against the state used language suggesting that, not only in private, but also in public law, legal power was anterior to legal right. As Justice Harlan put it in an 1887 opinion:

> Nor can it be said that government interferes with or impairs any one's constitutional rights of liberty or of property, when it determines that the manufacture and sale of intoxicating drinks, for general or individual use, as a beverage, are, or may become, hurtful to society, and constitute, therefore, a business in which no one may lawfully engage. Those rights are best secured, in our government, by the observance, upon the part of all, of such regulations as are established by competent authority to promote the common good. No one may rightfully do that which the law-making power, upon reasonable grounds, declares to be prejudicial to the general welfare.

But even judges famous for their uncompromising endorsement of judicial review based on natural rights adopted the same perspective. For example, in *Calder v. Bull* (1798), Justice Chase, often treated as the original natural law advocate, spoke of rights as follows:

> It seems to me, that the right of property, in its origin, could only arise from compact express, or implied, and I think it the better opinion, that the right, as well as the mode, or manner, of acquiring

52

property, and of alienating or transferring, inheriting, or transmit-
ting it, is conferred by society; is regulated by civil institution, and is
always subject to the rules prescribed by positive law. [3 Dall. 394]

The pre-Classical notion was that men created the sovereign,
namely the People gathered in their constitution-making capacity,
in order to secure their natural rights against lawless neighbors.
This the sovereign did by creating legal powers, legislative and
judicial, which in turn operated to protect the citizen against his
neighbors' encroachments. The judicial power was that of applying to particular fact situations the general rules set by the legislative power to this purpose. The result was the *indirect* protection
of natural rights through the medium of positive law. A hierarchical arrangement of institutions (the People; the legislature; the
courts; individual citizens) mirrored that of concepts.

In their constitutions, the sovereign people limited the legal
powers they created so as to prevent the legislatures in particular
from becoming subverters of the natural rights they were meant
to protect. The courts enforced these limitations imposed by sovereign power on legislative power, just as they enforced the limits
legislative power laid on private autonomy. In each case, the court
carried out a purely legal task — the interpretation and execution
of a power — in order to *indirectly* secure natural right. The operation of enforcing at least the explicit limitations in the texts was
thus sheltered from the problem of the logical incompatibility of
sovereignty and natural right.

It followed, within this conception of the legal universe, that an
appeal beyond the structure of powers to the natural rights motivat-
ing its creation could not claim to be judicial in the conventional sense.
There was an argument that the judge who heeded the appeal was
scrambling the hierarchical arrangement of concepts and institutions
that suppressed the contradiction of natural right and sovereignty. As
Justice Clifford put it, dissenting in *Loan Assoc. v. Topeka* (1874):

Courts cannot nullify an act of the State legislature on the vague
ground that they think it opposed to a general latent spirit supposed to pervade or underlie the constitution, where neither the
terms nor the implications of the instrument disclose any such
restriction. Such a power is denied to the courts, because to con-

cede it would be to make the courts sovereign over both the constitution and the people, and convert the government into a judicial depotism. [12 Wall. 669]

On the other hand, the system of powers was designed to secure particular objectives, the protection of certain real, God-given transcendentally rational human entitlements. When the judge saw that the set of indirect checks and balances were not working to their proper end, he might feel himself bound in conscience to use his power to intervene to prevent a subversion of the original scheme. Natural right was far from the inherently subjective concept we know today. The judge enforcing it might feel he was taking an advanced or controversial or statesmanlike position on a difficult question of legal philosophy; he need not concede that he was engaged in an act of usurpation. As Justice Miller pointed out in the *Loan Association* case just cited, when the argument is about natural rights the charge of despotism can go in either direction:

. . . A government which recognized no such rights, which held the lives, the liberty, and the property of its citizens subject at all times to the absolute disposition and unlimited control of even the most democratic depository of power, is after all but a despotism. It is true it is a despotism of the many, of the majority, if you choose to call it so, but it is none the less a despotism . . .

The theory of our governments, State and National, is opposed to the deposit of unlimited power anywhere. The executive, the legislative, and the judicial branches of these governments are all of limited and defined powers.

There are limitations on such power which grow out of the essential nature of all free governments. Implied reservations of individual rights, without which the social compact could not exist, and which are respected by all governments entitled to the name. No court, for instance, would hesitate to declare void a statute which enacted that A. and B. who were husband and wife to each other should be so no longer, but that A. should thereafter be the husband of C., and B. the wife of D. Or which should enact that the homestead now owned by A. should no longer be his, but should henceforth be the property of B. [20 Wall. 662-3]

54   The modern reader, reacting to these declarations of Justices Miller and Clifford, may have in the back of his or her mind that there was an association between solicitude for big business, for the rich, for entrepreneurs and the middle class, latent in the appeal to natural rights against a "despotism of the many." Conversely, Clifford's appeal to the sovereignty of the people and the Constitution over the judges suggests the populist, progressive, liberal rhetoric of the period 1890-1940. This set of associations cannot be extrapolated back to 1874, as the facts of *Loan Association* show clearly enough.

Topeka had issued bonds, promising to pay the interest from taxes, and handed over the capital raised to local manufacturers as an inducement to set up business in the city. Miller's opinion, applying the general constitutional law of the state in the context of diversity jurisdiction, held that the bonds were worthless because the city could not tax for the "private purpose" of subsidizing manufactures. The political context in which *he* saw the question is clear enough:

> If it be said that a benefit results to the local public of a town by establishing manufactures, the same may be said of any other business or pursuit which employs capital or labor. The merchant, the mechanic, the innkeeper, the banker, the builder, the steamboat owner are equally promoters of the public good, and equally deserving of the aid of the citizens by forced contributions. No line can be drawn in favor of the manufacturer which would not open the coffers of the public treasury to the importunities of two-thirds of the business men of the city or town.

By contrast, Justice Clifford saw the issue in terms of that holy of holies of the propertied classes, the public credit:

> In my judgement there is much more to be dreaded from judicial decisions which may have the effect to sanction the fraudulent repudiation of honest debts, than from any statutes passed by the State to enable municipal corporations to meet and discharge their just pecuniary obligations.

Because he was anxious to defend him against the clearly spurious charge of being an early Classical reactionary, Charles Fairman was led to try to state precisely how Miller's assumptions in *Loan Association* differed from those of *Lochner*:

> It would wrench Miller's words out of historical context to imagine him to have been a forerunner of the defenders of economic laissez faire, on the Court and in the country, in the latter part of the nineteenth century and for nearly four decades of the twentieth. He was affirming that no man should be taxed - not even by vote of the majority - to make a lure for private businesses. He maintained, as he had said in a dissent (Chase, C.J., and Field, J., concurring) -
>
> "We do not believe that any legislative body, sitting under a State constitution of the usual character, has a right to sell, to give, or to bargain away forever the taxing power of the State . . .
>
> "The result of such a principle, under the growing tendency to special and partial legislation, would be, to exempt the rich from taxation, and cast all the burden of the support of government, and the payment of its debts, on those who are too poor or too honest to purchase such immunity."

He argued that for Miller the existence of rights reserved to the people was "axiomatic." These rights and the express limitations of the constitutions "belonged to one universe of discourse," which was that of the late 18th, early 19th century rhetoric of the Rights of Man.

What was important about pre-Classical natural rights was not that they were inherently biassed in favor of one class of the community or another. It was that they existed right at the borderline of operativeness within legal consciousness. They defined the context and limits of judicial daring within public law, drawing the judge onward to intervene, but also into the danger that a strong dissent would make the label of usurper stick.

Unlike his successors, the pre-Classical judge made up his mind about this problem as one of choice between two compelling ideals: the defense of the unquestionably real, cognizable, politically fundamental concept of rights, or deference to the pos-

56   itivist institutional scheme that allocated the political role to the
legislature. He did not confront the modern dilemma: there was
no contradiction of equally legitimate 'balanced' concepts, and
no gnawing worry about the very possibility of deciding in a
rational, objective fashion whether or not a legal wrong had been
committed.

∾ 6 ∽

The hierarchical structure of natural rights, sovereignty, legal
power and legal right was one characteristic of the pre-Classical
concepts that mediated the contradiction of rights and powers. A
second characteristic was the availability of the notion of an
implied limitation on legislative power. Implied limitations were a
half-way house between unabashed appeal to natural rights and
the relatively legal and respectable notion of judicial review of
express limitations.

Implied limitations were those that assertedly arose from the
fact that the constitutions expressly delegated to the legislature
only "the legislative power." It followed, according to the argument, that if the legislature performed acts that were not legislative, they violated the constitution by usurping a part of sovereign
power not granted them by the sovereign people. It was then up to
the judges to enforce the document by denying recognition to the
pseudo-legislative act.

If a "legislative act" was simply "whatever the legislature
does," then the doctrine of implied limitations would have been
without importance. But pre-Classical commentators argued that
the term had an ascertainable meaning, and that actual practice
was no more than strong evidence of legality. For example, trying
and rendering judgment in private law disputes between individuals was part of the judicial, not the legislative function. The legislature would therefore act illegally, and the judge should ignore it
or countermand it, if it attempted to do such a thing.

It was apparently possible to believe that the implied limitations argument involved only a minor extension of that of express
limitations. It was also possible to argue sincerely that the legisla-

tive power was not an undifferentiated mass split off from the people's sovereignty, but rather structured. It consisted of the police, eminent domain, and taxing powers. Each of these had its own definition. A legislative act that could be assimilated to none of the three sub-powers was necessarily *ultra vires*. Under this interpretation, the doctrine of implied limitations acquired both generality and bite so that it might serve as a vehicle for wide ranging judicial review of legislation. But it lost, at the same time, some of its claim to being merely an instance of judicial execution of the sovereign will.

Express limitations were hard to interpret at all if they were not binding conditions placed on the grant of legislative power, intended to prevent specific abuses by the people's representatives. Implied limitations lacked this quality. It was not obvious that the separation of powers had as an implication that a vast range of actions not explicitly forbidden the legislature could be struck down by the courts. It was at least plausible that the meaning of the separation of powers was the creation of mutually checking institutions by the parceling out of aspects of sovereignty. The legislature would then have full, uncontrollable, absolutely absolute law making authority except in those cases where the higher sovereign had plainly and explicitly withheld it.

In this situation of theoretical conflict, there was a tendency on both sides to merge the implied limitations argument into that about the justiciability of natural rights. In *Calder v. Bull* (1798), for example, the famous dictum of Justice Chase seems intended to obliterate the distinction:

> I cannot subscribe to the omnipotence of a State Legislature, or that it is absolute and without control; although its authority should not be expressly restrained by the Constitution, or fundamental law, of the State. The people of the United States erected their Constitutions, or forms of government, to establish justice, to promote the general welfare, to secure the blessings of liberty; and, to protect their persons and property from violence. The purposes for which men enter into society will determine the

nature and terms of the social compact; and as they are the foundation of the legislative power, they will decide what are the proper objects of it: The nature, and ends of legislative power will limit the exercise of it. This fundamental principle flows from the very nature of our free Republican governments, that no man should be compelled to do what the laws do not require; nor to refrain from acts which the laws permit. There are acts which the Federal, or State Legislature cannot do, without exceeding their authority. There are certain vital principles in our free Republican governments, which will determine and overrule an apparent and flagrant abuse of legislative power; as to authorize manifest injustice by positive law; or to take away that security for personal liberty, or private property, for the protection of which the government was established. An act of the Legislature (for I cannot call it a law) contrary to the great first principles of the social compact, cannot be considered a rightful exercise of legislative authority. The obligation of a law in governments estab-lished on express compact, and on republican principles, must be determined by the nature of the power, on which it is founded. A few instances will suffice to explain what I mean. A law that punished a citizen for an innocent action, or in other words, for an act, which, when done was in violation of no existing law; a law that destroys, or impairs, the lawful private contracts of citizens; a law that makes a man a Judge in his own cause; or a law that takes property from A and gives it to B: It is against all reason and justice, for a people to entrust a Legislature with such powers; and, therefore, it cannot be presumed that they have done it. The genius, the nature, and the spirit, of our State Governments, amount to a prohibition of such acts of legislation; and the general principles of law and reason forbid them [3 Dall. 387-88]

Eighty years later, the same elision occurs in Justice Miller's *Loan Association* (1874) opinion:

We have referred to this history of the contest over aid to railroads by taxation, to show that the strongest advocates for the validity of these laws never placed it on the ground of the unlim-

59

ited power in the State legislature to tax the people, but conceded that where the purpose for which the tax was to be issued could no longer be justly claimed to have this public character, but was purely in aid of private or personal objects, the law authorizing it was beyond the legislative power, and was an unauthorized invasion of private right.

It must be conceded that there are such rights in every free government beyond the control of the State. . . . To lay with one hand the power of the government on the property of the citizen, and with the other to bestow it upon favored individuals to aid private enterprises and build up private fortunes, is none the less a robbery because it is done under the forms of law and is called taxation. This is no legislation. It is a decree under legislative forms.

Nor is it taxation. A "tax," says Webster's Dictionary, "is a rate or sum of money assessed on the person or property of a citizen by government for the use of the nation or state." "Taxes are burdens or charges imposed by the legislature upon persons or property to raise money for public purposes."

Coulter, J., in Northern Liberties v. St. John's Church, says, very forcibly, "I think the common mind has everywhere taken in the understanding that taxes are a public imposition, levied by authority of the government for the purpose of carrying on the government in all its machinery and operations—that they are imposed for a public purpose."

We have established, we think, beyond cavil that there can be no lawful tax which is not laid for a public purpose. [20 Wall. 662-64]

In both cases, the opinions taking the opposite view of legislative power simply ignore the implied limitations gambit. Iredell, in *Calder v. Bull*, is clear that in the absence of express limitations "whatever the legislative power chose to enact, would be lawfully enacted," but he proceeds to refute only the position of "some speculative jurists" that "a legislative act against natural justice, must, in itself, be void." The refutation is not inconsistent with the existence of implied limitations:

60   If, . . . the Legislature of the Union, or the Legislature of any
         member of the Union, shall pass a law, within the general scope of
         their constitutional power, the Court cannot pronounce it to be
         void, merely because it is, in their judgments, contrary to the prin-
         ciples of natural justice. The ideas of natural justice are regulated
         by no fixed standard: the ablest and the purest men have differed
         upon the subject; and all that the Court could properly say, in such
         an event, would be, that the Legislature (possessed of an equal
         right of opinion) had passed an act which, in the opinion of the
         judges, was inconsistent with the abstract principles of natural jus-
         tice. There are but two lights, in which the subject can be viewed:
         1st. If the Legislature pursue the authority delegated to them,
         their acts are valid. 2d. If they transgress the boundaries of that
         authority, their acts are invalid. In the former case, they exercise
         the discretion vested in them by the people, to whom alone they
         are responsible for the faithful discharge of their trust: but in the
         latter case, they violate a fundamental law, which must be our
         guide, whenever we are called upon as judges to determine the
         validity of a legislative act. [3 Dall. 398-99]

Clifford, dissenting in *Loan Association*, conceded that the courts
enforce constitutional prohibitions, "express or implied," against
the legislature. [20 Wall. 668] He then proceeded to argue against
a "natural justice" jurisdiction as though that were the only argument Miller had made.

I think it a fair inference that the implied limitations concept
had a good deal of force in legal argument, bridging the gap
between natural rights and express limitations. Edward Corwin
writing in 1914, treated the attempt to distinguish implied limitations from natural rights as pure obscurantism but conceded that,
before the Civil War, the former doctrine had been "of most varied and widest serviceability" to the latter. Implied limitations had
brought natural rights "within reach of the haven of the written
constitution." He even argued that the use of the separation of
powers as a basis of implied limitations had had an impact on
results:

    Courts which continued to appeal to natural rights were com-
    pelled by their own logic to consider constitutional questions not

simply in their legal aspects but in their moral aspects as well. . . . Those courts, on the other hand, which sought to effect an absolute separation of legislative and judicial powers regarded any enactment disturbing vested rights, whatever the justification of it, as representing an attempt by the legislature to exercise powers not belonging to it and ipso facto void. [14 Mich. L. Rev. 259-261]

While natural rights existed as available concepts at the outer limits of the operative core of legal consciousness, they were almost always fused in argument with implied limitations. My point in this section has been that this fusion helped soften what was to be the conflict and then the contradiction of rights and powers.

∞ 7 ∞

The last structural characteristic of pre-Classical thought that helped to reduce the sense of contradiction within it was the existence of vested rights as a mediator between natural rights and legal rights. The concept of a vested right is by a good deal the most exotic in the pre-Classical repertoire. "When I say that a *right* is vested in a citizen," said Chase in *Calder v. Bull* (1798), I mean, that he has the *power* to do certain actions; or to possess *certain things, according to the law of the land*." [3 Dall. 394] Here is Corwin's definition of 110 years later:

a right which a particular individual has equitably acquired under the standing laws to do certain acts or to possess and use certain things, [and] the doctrine of vested rights regards any legislative enactment infringing such a right, whether by direct intent or incidentally, without making compensation to the individual affected, as inflicting a penalty *ex post facto*. [24 HLR 375]

It seems to have been more or less universally believed that to disturb a vested right was to violate a natural right. In other words, once the property or whatever (a crucial whatever) had vested "equitably," "under the standing laws," "according to the law of the land," it was an outrage against natural justice for the state to

62   interfere with it. There were, as well, two senses in which a vested right was "legal." First, its existence, as the definitions show, could be ascertained only by the careful examination of the body of positive law under whose auspices the owner had allegedly acquired it. Second, given that it existed, and that the state had interfered with it, and that this constituted a violation of the owner's natural right to retain it, there might or might not be a constitutional text authorizing a judge to give it legal protection through judicial review.

During most of the pre-Classical period, there seems to have been a degree of consensus that judges could protect vested rights against the legislature either through the direct appeal to natural justice, through the implied limitations-separation of powers notion, or through express prohibitions such as the Contracts and Just Compensation Clauses. The question for us is: What did they think they were protecting? The core notion seems to have been based on an imagined fact situation: a person acquires title to real property by legal means (say, purchase), such that any court would enforce his property rights; the legislature then arbitrarily and for base motives passes a law purporting to transfer the title to another; a court refuses to enforce the legislative "sentence."

Now this same dramatic scenario also played a prominent role in Classical legal thought. For example, in the case of *Reagan v. Farmer's Loan and Trust* (1894), Justice Brewer used it in arguing for a judicial power to determine the reasonableness of railroad rate fixing by the states:

> This, as has been often observed, is a government of law, and not a government of men, and it must never be forgotten that under such a government, with its constitutional limitations and guarantees, the forms of law and the machinery of government, with all their reach and power, must in their actual workings stop on the hither side of the unnecessary and uncompensated taking or destruction of any private property, legally acquired and legally held. It was, therefore, within the competency of the Circuit Court of the United States for the Western District of Texas, at the instance of the plaintiff, a citizen of another State, to enter

upon an inquiry as to the reasonableness and justice of the rates
prescribed by the railroad commission.

In both Classical and pre-Classical thought, the importance of the
scenario was as the starting point in an argument: So you accept
that it is abhorrent for the legislature to take A's goods and give
them to B? Then you must also accept that it is abhorrent for the
legislature to.. . . But the nature of the argument that followed, the
list of asserted implications of the premise, changed greatly
between one period and the other.

In Classical legal thought, the point of the scenario was that the
legislature had arbitrarily assaulted the autonomy of the individual, his freedom or liberty to go about the activity of acquiring
and enjoying. The implications of our abhorrence of this interference had to do with other ways in which the legislature might
arbitrarily assault individual autonomy. The form of the argument was that "in reason" our legal liberty to do *anything* is a kind
of property, because it is an area of autonomy. Classical thinkers
reasoned from the case of legislative confiscation toward the
establishment of the system of Classical rights of property and
contract. As I said above, these were highly abstract yet legal in
character, and their relationship to powers was one of "balanced
antithesis."

At the end of the road of Classical reasoning, our abhorrence
at confiscation led to the fusion of the concepts of property and
liberty. Justice Harlan's opinion for the court in *Adair v. U.S.*
(1908) makes this clear. The case raised the question of the con-
stitutionality of a federal statute making it a crime for an employer to fire an employee for union membership:

> [A]s agent of the railroad company and as such responsible for the
> conduct of business of one of its departments, it was the defen-
> dant Adair's right—and that right inhered in his personal liberty,
> and was also a right of property—to serve his employer as best he
> could, so long as he did nothing that was reasonably forbidden by
> law as injurious to the public interests. It was the right of the
> defendant to prescribe the terms upon which the services of
> Coppage would be accepted, and it was the right of Coppage to

become or not, as he chose, an employee of the railroad company upon the terms offered to him.

Pre-Classical legal thinkers were aware of the argument by which
the concept of property could be abstracted to cover most human
activity. Locke in the *Second Treatise* referred to men's "Lives,
Liberties and Estates, which I call by the general Name, *Property*."
[123, Laslett] Hamilton speaks of a "property in rights." But within the *legal* consciousness of the period, the operative legal concepts derived from abhorence of legislative spoliation were those
of the vested rights doctrine, and, according to Corwin,

> the doctrine of vested rights was interposed to shield only the
> property right, in the strict sense of the term, from legislative
> attack. When that broader range of rights which is today connot-
> ed by the terms "liberty" and "property" of the Fourteenth
> Amendment were in discussion other phraseology was employed,
> as for example the term "privileges and immunities" of Art. IV,
> S.2, of the Constitution. In his famous decision in Corfield v.
> Coryell, rendered in 1823, Justice Washington defined this phrase
> to signify, as to "citizens in the several states," "those privileges
> and immunities which are in their nature, fundamental, which
> belong of right to the citizens of all free governments; and which
> have, at all times, been enjoyed by the citizens of the several states
> which compose this union." "What these fundamental principles
> are," he continued, "it would perhaps be more tedious than diffi-
> cult to enumerate. They may, however, be all comprehended
> under the following heads; protection by the government of the
> enjoyment of life and liberty, with the right to acquire and possess
> property of every kind, and to pursue and obtain happiness and
> safety; subject nevertheless to such restraints as the government
> may justly prescribe for the good of the whole."
>
> But now of all the rights included in this comprehensive sched-
> ule, one only, and that in but a limited sense, was protected by the
> doctrine of vested rights, the right namely of one who had already
> acquired some title of control over some particular piece of prop-
> erty, in the physical sense, to continue in that control. All other
> rights, however fundamental, were subject to limitation by the

legislature, whose discretion as that of a representative body in a   65
democratic country, was little likely to transgress the few, rather
specific, provisions of the written constitution. [12 Mich. L. Rev.
275]

Insomuch as Corwin here tried to distinguish the Classical (and
modern) from the pre-Classical variety of legal rights by emphasizing "property, in the physical sense," he was misleading. Most
of the pre-Civil War federal cases involving vested rights arose
under the Contracts Clause, which, after the *Dartmouth College
Case* (1819), applied to corporate charters. The corporations
involved were virtually *never* defending "some title of control
over some piece of property." They wanted to retain particular
legal advantages of a non-physical kind, such as monopolies and
exemptions from taxation. Cooley's definition makes this clear
enough:

> And it would seem that a right cannot be regarded as a vested
> right, unless it is something more than such a mere expectation as
> may be based upon an anticipated continuance of the present gen-
> eral laws: it must have become a title, legal or equitable, to the
> present or future enjoyment of property, or to the present or
> future enforcement of a demand, or a legal exemption from a
> demand made by another. [391]

The true distinction between vested rights and Classical (and
modern) property rights is that the older variety was concerned
with the effects on expectations formed under existing legal rules
of legislative changes in those rules. The vesting of a right created an entitlement, as against the legislature, to the maintenance of
some advantage created by reliance. The great theoretical problem with the concept was to decide, in some at least apparently
judicial (as opposed to legislative) fashion when particular established expectations about the continuance in force of legal rules
were legitimate and when not. The practical problem was to do so
in such a way as to avoid both the freezing of the legal system
around a static distribution of advantages, and a state of insecurity such that men would not take the risks involved in creating
wealth.

The vested rights involved in actual litigated cases were highly particularized advantageous positions, often in the form of corporate charters. Likewise the alleged infringements took the form of highly particularized assaults on agglomerations of private economic power, as by the repeal or circumvention of corporate privileges in favor of competitors or the community at large, the repudiation by municipalities of bonds issued to finance private railroads, or the depreciation of debts by changing the medium of payment or the remedies available to creditors.

The difference between the right to be free of this kind of legislative interference and the right of free speech or of contract is obviously important, but difficult to formulate clearly. The vested right is fully consistent with the notion that legal rights are merely the reflection of legal powers. The right is to the continued existence of a legislatively created arrangement. The right of speech, on the other hand, inheres in the individual regardless of the legislative schemes that regulate it. It exists *in opposition* to them rather than as a position of security in their interstices.

The vested rights doctrine applies in principle to every kind of right. It is not restricted to a particular part of social life or a particular type of activity. In this sense, it is much more general, more abstract than the First Amendment, which applies only to speech, press and religion, or the Fourth, which concerns very specific kinds of official behavior such as warrantless searches. The vested rights doctrine is more like our notion of procedural due process, which applies to every kind of governmental activity.

But the abstraction of vested rights did not mean that they were more restrictive of the state than our particular substantive rights. The doctrine protected only the results of *reliance* on a previously existing legal regime, for example, the acquisition of a mortgage in the expectation that judicial process would be available to foreclose it if necessary. The doctrine created no substantive limitation on legislative power, no limitation at all on the rules that the state could impose on those who had not yet relied. The trustees of Dartmouth College could not be deprived of the privilege of running it, given the terms of their charter. But the court in so holding imposed no general restriction on legislative power over educational corporations. It remained free to insert in every future charter a clause reserving its power to replace the trustees at will.

By contrast, incidents of protection of First Amendment rights do delimit legislative power for the future. Indeed, they commit the court to a program of limitation involving efforts to prevent the legislature from doing indirectly what it cannot do openly. Again, the modern analogy, though imperfect, is procedural due process, which tells the legislature how but not what. The vested rights doctrine was a sort of constitutional grandfather clause, likewise in theory concerned with means rather than ends.

The common law analogue was the equitable doctrine of estoppel, which prevents a party from taking advantage of an acknowledged legal right or power because his prior actions and another's reliance would make his doing so unjust in the particular circumstances. Like the party estopped, the legislature had an acknowledged power to change the law, and by derivation to change private rights, at will. But in some specific circumstances, the judges refused to permit this. No one questioned the general validity of power. There was no subject matter and no particular action distinguished by the judges as an exception to power. No counterrules protecting an area of individual autonomy from state interference came into existence. Equity intervened to prevent an abuse of a system whose fundamental legitimacy was not in doubt for an instant. As Cooley put it:

> In its application as a shield of protection, the term "vested rights" is not used in any narrow or technical sense, or as importing a power of legal control merely, but rather as implying a vested interest which it is right and equitable that the government should recognize and protect, and of which the individual could not be deprived arbitrarily without injustice. The right to private property is a sacred right; not, as has been justly said, "introduced as the result of princes' edicts, concessions and charters, but it was the old fundamental law, springing from the original frame and constitution of the realm."

But as it is a right which rests upon equities, it has its reasonable limits and restrictions; it must have some regard to the general welfare and public policy; it cannot be a right which is to be examined, settled, and defended on a distinct and separate consideration of the individual case, but rather on broad and general grounds, which embrace the welfare of the whole community, and which seek the equal and impartial protection of the interests of all. [358]

It is of the utmost importance to distinguish between the theory of vested rights and their actual significance in pre-Civil War America. I have been emphasizing how different they were in theory from the Classical rights which were supposed to guard the autonomy of private economic actors against attempts at regulation of business practices and the redistribution of business profits. In practice, the system of corporate charters, combined with sporadic business control of legislatures, could operate under the vested rights doctrine to withdraw a large part of the economy from public control. Eventually exemptions from taxation ran out and new businesses and new economic activities grew up without the benefit of charter protection. In the long run, the vested rights doctrine could not eliminate the threat of legislative control. But "in the long run" meant after the initial advantages had been seized: time was worth something, even though external, substantive, direct protection of the same advantages *might* have been even better.

I am not concerned, as a general matter, with the quantum of power that business, or for that matter other groups such as racial or religious minorities, were able to exercise under one regime of rights rather than another. With respect to all such questions, I am content to suspect the worst without being able to prove it. My point has been that the pre-Classical concept of vested rights was an intermediary or mediator between natural rights whose legality was doubtful and legal rights that existed only as the reflex of legislative powers. They focused courts and commentators on questions like: Does a shortening of the period of the statute of limitations, which bars a cause of action that would otherwise have been valid, interfere with a vested right of the "owner" of that cause of action? Given such a focus, the problem of the direct confrontation, of individual legal rights to autonomy, with public legal powers to regulate individual action, could remain peripheral.

I do not mean, in anything I have said, to suggest that our conception of a contradiction of rights and powers is in any sense an obvious, natural, inevitable, or intrinsically correct one. Quite the contrary. The investigation of pre-Classical thought shows, I think, the contingent character of the conceptual schemes that make the legal universe intelligible at any given moment. It is as true of our notions as of theirs that we must understand them historically if we are to understand them at all.

[The reader interested in pursuing the subjects of natural and vested rights, implied limitations and vested rights should begin with Cooley's discussion in his *Constitutional Limitations*, Chapters VII and XI. My treatment is based primarily on the cases cited by Cooley in the notes on pages *174-*176 and *353-*358.]

∾ 8 ∾

The transformation of rights against the state in the years after 1870 involved the slow breakdown of the hierarchical manner of suppressing the contradiction of rights and powers, and the fading of both implied limitations and vested rights. By 1900, their presence in a federal judicial opinion was exceptional and faintly embarrassing rather than the norm. In Classical (and modern) legal thought, the judge deals with legal rights he must protect up to their boundary with equally legal powers, or must balance the two entities one against the other. The irony is that the rise of the younger generation of legal rights has corresponded to the agonized demise of the older generation of natural rights. They lived to see their offspring admitted to the center of the legal universe, and then deprived the event of what should have been its meaning by disappearing from the scene.

Over a period of 100 years, there was a progressive legalization first of the express limitations in constitutional texts, second of

70   the ground rules of federalism, and third of the general right of freedom from legislative regulation. In the process, the model of a political equilibrium stable *only* because of the skillful distribution of political power among mutually checking institutions was abandoned. The contrary model of an equilibrium stabilized by the neutral enforcement of ground rules—the vision of Hamilton—won the day. One way to understand this process is in terms of the contrast between the core of legal consciousness and the periphery of inoperative or weakly operative concepts.

I have already mentioned those general legal categories we use routinely to group rules, without any sense that they influence those rules. Contract law and corporations are examples.

There are also, in legal consciousness at any moment, concepts that legal thinkers find in the legal literature of a preceding age, and perhaps themselves mouth ritualistically, without any confidence that they have a meaning. This is an inoperativeness of a much more decisive kind than that of the taxonomic doctrinal categories. Such is the concept of natural rights today and of legal fictions in their decadence. Illusory concepts of this kind do not add to an argument (except perhaps sometimes esthetically). They are not useful in the task of convincing an interlocutor because no one believes in them *at all* any more.

Natural rights belonged in 1870 to yet a third variety of legally inoperative concepts: that of entities of acknowledged reality, meaning, and relevance to legal thought, but of doubtful legitimacy in legal argument because falling within the province of the legislature. All legal powers and their derivative rights might spring from the enterprise of protecting natural rights. The legal universe might therefore be unintelligible without reference to the concept. Yet the judge could not refer to them directly as the sole basis of decision without opening himself to criticism. "Social policy" plays a similarly ambivalent role in modern legal consciousness.

Finally, within the consciousness of an historical period, there will be principles, concepts, operations, that everyone accepts as typically, unquestionably, both operative and legal. Judges use them to explain and justify decisions, without doubts or even con-

sciousness of a problem of correct legal method or of definition
of the judge's institutional role. To challenge these operations
seems pointless: if there is anything the judge can undertake without qualms, they are it. A modern legal thinker occasionally feels
impelled to articulate what he thinks is in this core. Here is an
example:

> But am I not too much obfuscating what is basically clear? The
> function of the judiciary is simply, is it not, to administer justice?
> It is, indeed, and there is a sense in which this is the unique and the
> most important task of the judiciary. A man is put on trial for, we
> will say, murder; his liberty, perhaps his life, is at stake. Under the
> systems prevailing in modern Europe and America, the facts must
> be proven by relevant, only by relevant, evidence produced at a
> trial—the adequacy of the evidence must be measured in terms of
> the law, the law as it is authoritatively understood. The judges and
> the jury must be impervious to considerations of state or to howls
> for blood. The accused may be politically noxious; the victim may
> have been a popular figure. No matter. Every person, however
> high or low, where life or liberty is concerned, is to be judged by
> the known law, pursuant to the due observance of the established
> rules for the law's enforcement. And in the private law—the law
> of meum and tuum—the objectives are the same. No person, pub-
> lic or private, if he unlawfully injures my person, or fails to fulfill
> his obligations, or takes my property, shall escape the disinterest-
> ed judgment of the law.
>
> . . .In this sense, then, of the unqualified application of the
> known law to facts fairly found, we have a definition of the cen-
> tral core of the administration of justice as that term is under-
> stood, a definition for which we can claim near universality in
> modern societies. But once this much is agreed upon, the next step
> in the argument is confounded by doubt. [Jaffe]

For any given moment, all the concepts, doctrines and operations
in legal consciousness might be distributed among or on the bor-
derlines of the categories I have just described. Yet if we look at
consciousness as it evolves through time, it is clear that a static
map would be misleading. First, concepts can move from one class

72   to another, as natural right has done. Second, there are differences among the elements within a given category. When a new doctrine or concept or problem appears, or when the operativeness of an existing concept is for some reason brought into question, legal thinkers have to find analogies. They do so by comparing the new matter to the core of each category. If it resembles core illusory, or core alegal, or core legal elements, then it will be so classified. Its relation to other, peripheral members of these categories is much less important.

Throughout the period with which we are concerned, the core legal concepts and operations, the models to which other elements were compared, were the execution of legal powers (doing of the will of the sovereign) by statutory interpretation, and the common law (not equitable) adjudication of private rights. A good deal that is confusing to us in pre-Classical legal thought becomes clearer if we keep in mind that until the Classical synthesis of the '80s and '90s, these two powerful models seemed to exist in different universes from one another. There were few cross-references. Much that was most characteristic in each was flatly contradicted or rejected out of hand in the other. No one seemed to mind.

If we look at the matter statically, the feeling of conflict and disorder that would have existed had legal thinkers attempted to integrate public and private law was avoided simply by thinking in pigeon-holes. Looked at dynamically, a process of change and convergence had been going on imperceptibly for decades. But the impulse of self-conscious integration still had ample scope *within* the pigeonholes, in the tasks of rationalizing the apparent chaos of the common law, and of first preserving then rebuilding the fragile structure of American federalism.

Both the exemplar of statutory interpretation and that of common law adjudication exercised an enormously powerful modeling influence on peripheral bodies of doctrine whose full legality was less clear, on doctrinal solutions for new problems, and on arguments about how judges should respond to legal challenges from other institutions. The basic mode of influence of the core on the peripheral elements arose from the fact that there was often *advantage* to be gained from making a given doctrine look very legal, or very non-legal, or illusory.

If a particular judicial operation could be made to look like common law or statutory interpretation, then the judge's action was legitimized at least in the large. He might be open to challenge on the merits, but not for the bare act of assuming jurisdiction to determine them. The eagerness of lawyers to exploit this sort of advantage in the interests of their clients was a source of energy, like the reproductive urge in biological evolution or the profit motive in the theory of economic competition. A large number of legal actors constantly strained their ingenuity to recast legal doctrines just enough to win a case, so that judges were constantly offered the chance to engage in the incremental modification of the system of concepts.

The first great public enterprise of this kind was the legitimation of judicial review of legislation by application of express constitutional limitations. Express limitations were most obviously compatible with the model of law as will of the sovereign people. In form, they were legal limitations on the grant of the legal power of legislation. If law was the will of the sovereign, and the people were the sovereign, then the will of the people constitutionally expressed was law. If it was law, it was the duty of the judges, trustees of the judicial power, to enforce it.

Commentators have been insisting off and on for 200 years that there is nothing either logically or historically necessary about this argument. It may be true that the judges are bound to obey the will of the sovereign as the only source of law. Does it follow, then or now, that the judges have the final power to decide whether the legislature's action is in accord with the Constitution? But there is no question that there is a strong legal argument, based precisely on the premise of positivism, that the judge should not enforce a congressional statute that to his mind plainly and deliberately "abridges the freedom of religion" by, say, prohibiting the observance of the rites of the Catholic Church. That this will involve him in difficulties when a case arises involving a religious group using dangerous and illegal drugs in its service is obvious. But it weakens the underlying argument only a little, if at all.

74   Express limitations were compatible with the idea that sovereignty is the primary legal conception, but this alone did not establish their legitimacy as legal doctrines. Insomuch as they were successful they drew on the common law analogy as well. The argument was that the people were a legal principal or a cestui qui trust, who had created an agency or trust and an agent or trustee. No one could doubt the fully legal character of what a common law judge did in enforcing the limits on the scope of an agency or the terms of a trust.

      The use of the common law analogy gave both structure and legitimacy to the judicial role. Since the constitutions generally said nothing at all about the theory and practice of review, it was necessary to go somewhere else for suggestions about the basic organization of the process. Take the question of whether the court should enjoin the enforcement of an unconstitutional statute the day it is enacted into law. The analogy to the common law suggested that the role of the courts was the passive one of responding to concrete complaints by particular parties aggrieved. Against this analogical background, the rather involved consequences that are said to be the will of the sovereign people expressed in the limit of federal jurisdiction to "cases or controversies" become more plausible.

      But the common law agency or trust analogy served also to legitimate review by affirming its wholly legal, apolitical, everyday character. It was not plausible that the Founding Fathers intended to create a radically innovative legal institution without precedent anywhere in the world, yet failed to mention it explicitly. It was much more plausible that as skilled lawyers they adapted an utterly familiar common law technique, from agency or the law of trusts, to the problem of the sovereign's control of the legislature. This kind of activity might be carried on without the need of fanfare: the legal meaning of the language used would be clear within the community of the initiated.

      Through the alternate appeal to the Constitution as "law like any other law" and to the common law of agency and trusts, judicial review achieved full legality, at the price of renouncing any reference at all to the concept of rights. The argument was fully consistent with, indeed it was an aspect of the idea that natural rights were political while legal rights were simply the outcome of the exercise of legal powers. The judge carried on the task of policing the legislature *as though* there were no other entities involved than the Constitution and the Statute to be reviewed. Of course, his every move was guided by the "nonlegal" knowledge that powers were both created *and* limited to secure rights. It was simply that rights could speak neither for themselves nor through legal intermediaries like the modern equal protection clause. They were shielded but never expressed.

At this point, we confront a second phenomenon complementary to that just described: the influence exercised on the core concepts by the elements assimilated to them. In other words, the core organizing concepts transform, but are at the same time transformed. The point about the core elements is that their *location* in the set of categories is unquestioned, so obvious as not to merit discussion. By contrast, their *nature* is open to dispute, and changes according to the composition of legal consciousness as a whole. In fact, we change the concept of statutory interpretation by extending it to cover judicial review of legislative acts. We change the notion of enforcing the scope of an agency by treating constitutional limitations on legislative power as an instance of that general category.

The conflict over federalism already described illustrates the process. The initial effort of the Court and the nationalist opinion was to present the task of drawing the lines between state and federal power as one identical with, or at least analogous to, the interpretation of the statutory will of a legislative sovereign. A second string to the bow was that the court merely interpreted the scope of the agencies entrusted by the sovereign people to state and federal governments respectively. This argument was highly controversial: many countered that the court's action was not the carrying out of sovereign will or the enforcement of an agency, but the usurpation of an autonomous judicial power in derogation of the "real" sovereignty of the states or of Congress. My argument is that after the Civil War, the Marshallian vision was accepted as fully legal, and transformed the legal core to which he had struggled to assimilate it.

The post-Civil War notion was that the judicial interpretation

76   of the Constitution on the basis of the limited, bounded absolute-
         ness of state and federal governments, was the very essence of the
         federal judicial role. But the success of the analogy of judicial
         review to statutory interpretation of the scope of agencies had a
         significant implication. It meant acceptance of the legal character
         of the basic Marshallian conceptual tool: the notion of state and
         federal powers as neither beyond the control of the court—i.e.
         sovereign—nor subject to detailed review by an omnipresent
         superior acting through the court. The judges could review the
         action of a power holder without annihilating the power, because
         the power was, in theory, just as absolute within its sphere as it was
         void outside of it.

         This new core of fully legal activity served, in turn, as a model
         and incentive for the transformation of the concept of rights
         against the state. The dilemma of the logical incompatibility of
         natural rights and sovereignty was identical in structure to that of
         state and federal sovereignties. The pre-Classical solution to the
         rights-powers dilemma was the relegating of rights against the
         state to the domain of the political. The success of the pre-
         Classical solution for federalism suggested that banishment might
         be outmoded. If sovereignties could co-exist, with the court in the
         role of setting, by legal action, their legal limits, then the same
         might be true of rights and sovereignty. Once it was possible to
         imagine a system of sovereignties that were fully legal, absolute
         only within their spheres, subject to judicial control as well as to
         judicial obeisance, then the same might be imagined of rights.
         They could cease to be natural and political, and become legal and
         judicially enforceable.

         Classical legal thinkers took up the challenge and attempted to
         reconcile sovereign power and legal right without subordinating
         one to the other. The judiciary assumed the role of carrying out
         the terms of reconciliation, without bias in favor of either side.
         The direct appeal to natural right no longer figured as a sporadi-
         cally operating balance wheel to legislative power. But natural
         rights found permanent representatives within legal consciousness
         in the form of the highly abstract rights of person and property
         secured by the 14th Amendment.

A hallmark of Classical legal thought was thus the denial of the
logical incompatibility of important legal concepts. Classical legal
thinkers asserted that the Constitution provided a charter for the
direct, scientific, judicial resolution of the perennial but non-
essential conflict of rights and powers, state and federal authority.
They rejected the notion of a balance of power among mutually
checking institutions in favor of that of a rational division of
functions in accordance with an overarching legal settlement
entrusted by the people to judicial enforcement.

~ 9 ~

The *Slaughterhouse Cases* (1872) illustrate various aspects of the
pre-Classical consciousness I have been describing in this chapter.
They represent, besides, the first in the line of great cases that
were to be the vehicle of the development of Classical legal
thought. The cases were great because they involved politically
volatile issues that combined difficult questions of federalism with
equally difficult questions of individual rights against the state,
before a Court with four or five members blessed with breadth of
understanding and technical legal skill. Even occurring in isolation, such circumstances were likely to produce conceptual innovation. But once the *line* of cases had come into existence, this tendency was multiplied many times over. The judges knew, in the
later cases, that they were participating in the tradition of powerful thinking, and they studied to fit themselves within it, seeing
their chance at what passes for immortality in law.

But the *Slaughterhouse Cases* are more than the first in the line.
Because they were first, they are the only ones that can also serve
as a full embodiment of an earlier legal universe. They represent
the very brief transitional moment during which all of the past
was in the presence of much of what was to come. For our purposes, the cases provide a test of the conceptual map of pre-
Classical legal consciousness. I believe that a great deal that is otherwise simply unintelligible to the modern reader springs into life
and significance once we understand it within their lost conceptual scheme.

78   The factual background of the case was as follows: the Carpetbag legislature of Louisiana had passed a set of sanitary regulations governing the slaughtering of livestock in and around New Orleans, and included in the new regime a requirement that the trade be carried on in a single slaughterhouse. This establishment was to be run by a private corporation whose charter required it to provide space to all comers at legislatively fixed prices. It was clear that the future monopolists had bribed everyone in sight several times in order to secure their exclusive privilege. On the other hand, the scheme itself was of a general type to be adopted successfully, for purely sanitary reasons, in many other states. (Sometimes the single slaughterhouse was State owned, but often it was a private corporation, exactly as in New Orleans.)

When the cases came to the U.S. Supreme Court, the issue was whether butchers who had previously slaughtered on their own premises were denied rights under the brand new Fourteenth Amendment by the requirement that they move to the new facility and pay a fee there. The language in the Amendment that seemed most relevant went as follows:

> All persons born or naturalized in the United States . . . are citizens of the United States and of the State wherein they reside. No State shall make or enforce any law which shall abridge the privileges or immunities of citizens of the United States, nor shall any State deprive any person of life, liberty or property without due process of law, nor deny to any person within its jurisdiction the equal protection of the laws. Congress shall have power to enforce this article by appropriate legislation.

Although the basis of federal jurisdiction was the claim that the statute violated this Amendment, Justice Miller's opinion for a majority of five sustaining the statute began with a discussion of its validity under the general constitutional law of the American states. Miller was part of that pre-Classical camp that believed in the justiciability in state courts of individual claims based on an amalgam of natural rights and implied limitations. (See his statements in *Loan Association* and *Pumpelly v. Green Bay*, quoted above.) The Court had no jurisdiction to hear such a claim in this non-diversity case, but as always in pre-Classical thought, the natural rights perspective on the situation was important in deciding how to interpret whatever federal constitutional provisions did apply.

The discussion began as follows:

> It is true that [the statute] grants, for a period of twenty-five years, exclusive privileges. And whether those privileges are at the expense of the community in the sense of a curtailment of any of their fundamental rights, or even in the sense of doing them an injury, is a question open to considerations to be hereafter stated. But it is not true that it deprives the butchers of the right to exercise their trade, or imposes upon them any restriction incompatible with its successful pursuit, of furnishing the people of the city with the necessary daily supply of animal food. [16 Wall. 60]

Miller thus distinguished two questions: the rights of the butchers to carry on their trade — a typical "natural" but not "vested" right — and the "fundamental rights" of the "community." The second head is that of implied limitations: the whole community, as opposed to just the plaintiff butchers, had a right that the legislative branch should not violate its grant of powers.

The answer to the argument based on the butcher's natural rights is as follows:

> The statute under consideration defines these localities and forbids slaughtering in any other. It does not, as has been asserted, prevent the butcher from doing his own slaughtering. On the contrary, the Slaughter-House Company is required, under a heavy penalty, to permit any person who wishes to do so, to slaughter in their houses; and they are bound to make ample provision for the convenience of all the slaughtering for the entire city. The butcher then is still permitted to slaughter, to prepare, and to sell his own meats; but he is required to slaughter at a specified place and to pay a reasonable compensation for the use of the accommodations furnished him at that place.

The wisdom of the monopoly granted by the legislature may be opened to question, but it is difficult to see a justification for the assertion that the butchers are deprived of the right to labor in their occupation, or the people of their daily service in preparing food, or how this statute, with the duties and guards imposed upon the company, can be said to destroy the business of the butcher, or seriously interfere with its pursuit. [16 Wall.61-62]

I will argue a little further on that Miller's approach to the "right to labor in [an] occupation" was strongly conditioned by the fact that he saw this as a natural right whose *legal* definition was wholly a legislative matter. In other words, his jurisdiction under general constitutional law had nothing to do with making out its precise contours. Since in that jurisdiction he must appeal to a quasi-legal entity, the question was simply one of preventing abuses so gross as to subvert the purposes for which the people had created the sovereign. He was quite aware that the butchers lost something when they had to move and pay rent. But the quasi-legal natural rights concept was consistent not only with legislative power to define legal rights, but with much arbitrariness therein, before it rose to a level justifying a kind of judicial civil disobedience.

The implied limitations argument was a good deal more legal, and Miller considered it much more seriously. The statute was, at least in form, a police regulation, so that the question was whether it was "really" an exercise of the police power. Recall the discussion of the taxing power in *Loan Association.*

Miller began by quoting various definitions of the police power, some of them explicitly referring to butchering as a proper subject of regulation. He then considered the rationale and operation of the statute in detail, arguing that it fitted within the definition of power. A crucial point was that "the interested vigilance of the corporation will be more efficient in enforcing the limitation prescribed for the . . . slaughtering business . . . than the ordinary efforts of the officers of the law." But Miller also pointed out how little the rules interferred with the trade of butchering, and that the prices to be charged for space were limited by statute, and "we are not advised that they are on the whole exorbitant or unjust." He then considered and rejected the idea of a flat per se rule against exclusive privileges, on the ground that the legislative police power had never been understood to be subject to any such restriction. [16 Wall. 65-6].

It was implicit in the discussion that one way of deciding whether a statute was a police regulation, and so within the implied limitations on legislative power, was to ask whether it was reasonably adapted to achieve a community purpose, here sanitation, without doing any more harm than necessary to the butchers. Be it noted that this was a relatively activist approach that many judges, like Iredell and Clifford in *Calder v. Bull* and *Loan Association*, would have rejected. But the important thing was that he confirmed state power. In other words, in his preliminary discussion he reached the conclusion that as a state supreme court judge he would have upheld the statute, so far as "general constitutional law" was concerned.

Any applicable express limitations in the Louisiana constitution had been finally passed on by the State Supreme Court. It followed that the only remaining basis of attack was the Fourteenth Amendment, and in particular the clause forbidding states to abridge the privileges and immunities of U.S. citizens.

The important point about the *Slaughterhouse Cases* is that both for Miller and for the dissenters, to admit that the butchers' "right to labor in their profession" was protected as a privilege or immunity of U.S. citizenship *would change its nature from a natural right to a legal right.* The state constitutions contained no express prohibitions against a state "abridging the privileges and immunities of the citizens." All those natural rights to autonomy in the business of life that the Court had defined as privileges and immunities in *Corfield v. Coryell* [see quote on page 64 supra] were open to full legislative definition and control, subject only to the kinds of review based on implied limitations, vested rights or natural rights that I have already described. Miller's first point had been that none of these bases of review would avail the plaintiffs.

But if these privileges and immunities were those of citizens of the U.S., then there was now an express federal constitutional prohibition against abridging them. They became, *ipso facto*, legal rights the federal courts must protect through judicial review of the most conventionally legal kind. As was to be the case over and over again, the struggle to *federalize* rights was also a struggle to *legalize* them.

There was considerable irony in the outcome. Miller refused to federalize rights, on the basis of arguments that legitimized the Marshallian conception of federalism. As a result, that conception was available, as it would not have been had the dissenters prevailed, as a model for rights when they finally were both federalized and legalized under the due process clause. Miller prevented a premature legalization but strengthened, unwittingly, the structures within legal thought that would eventually make legalization seem easy. The dissenters developed the concept of rights, and thereby contributed mightily to the evolution that was to come. But they did so in the context of arguments about federalism inconsistent with the notion of due process that was ultimately to win acceptance.

Miller's federalism argument began with a quotation from Marshall's opinion in *Gibbons v. Ogden* (1824):

> In Gibbons v. Ogden, Chief Justice Marshall, speaking of inspection laws passed by the States, says: "They form a portion of that immense mass of legislation which controls everything within the territory of a State not surrendered to the General Government - all which can be most advantageously administered by the States themselves. . . . No direct general power over these objects is granted to Congress; and consequently they remain subject to State legislation." [16 Wall. 63]

He then referred to the illuminating gas case (*U.S. v. DeWitt*) already described. A few pages later, he pointed out that the various rights traditionally classed as privileges and immunities also fell within the domain of State law. The phrase privileges and immunities, he said,

> embraces nearly every civil right for the establishment and protection of which organized government is instituted. They are, in

the language of Judge Washington [in Ward v. Maryland], those
rights which are fundamental. Throughout his opinion they are
spoken of as rights belonging to the individual as a citizen of a
State . . . . And they have always been held to be the class of rights
which the State governments were created to secure. [16 Wall. 76]

Miller's repeated reference to the establishment of State government to protect rights meant *both* that they had been understood
to be outside federal jurisdiction *and* that rights of the kind
involved here were, in the main, the reflex of legal powers. The
rights did not exist, legally, separated from the sovereign who
defined and enforced them. For this reason, a holding that the 14th
Amendment put all "those rights which are fundamental" under
Federal protection would overthrow the Marshallian scheme:

But with the exception of those and a few other restrictions, the
entire domain of the privileges and immunities of citizens of the
States, as above defined, lay within the constitutional and legislative power of the States, and without that of the Federal government. Was it the purpose of the fourteenth amendment, by the
simple declaration that no State should make or enforce any law
which shall abridge the privileges and immunities of citizens of
the United States, to transfer the security and protection of all the
civil rights which we have mentioned, from the States to the
Federal government? And where it is declared that Congress shall
have the power to enforce that article, was it intended to bring
within the power of Congress the entire domain of civil rights
heretofore belonging exclusively to the States?

All this and more must follow, if the proposition of the plaintiffs in error be sound. For not only are these rights subject to the
control of Congress whenever in its discretion any of them are
supposed to be abridged by State legislation, but that body may
also pass laws in advance, limiting and restricting the exercise of
legislative power by the States, in their most ordinary and usual
functions, as in its judgment it may think proper on all such subjects. And still further, such a construction followed by the reversal of the judgments of the Supreme Court of Louisiana in these
cases, would constitute this court a perpetual censor upon all leg-

islation of the States, on the civil rights of their own citizens, with
authority to nullify such as it did not approve as consistent with
those rights, as they existed at the time of the adoption of this
amendment. The argument we admit is not always the most conclusive which is drawn from the consequences urged against the
adoption of a particular construction of an instrument. But when,
as in the case before us, these consequences are so serious, so far-
reaching and pervading, so great a departure from the structure
and spirit of our institutions; when the effect is to fetter and
degrade the State governments by subjecting them to the control
of Congress, in the exercise of powers heretofore universally conceded to them of the most ordinary and fundamental character;
when in fact it radically changes the whole theory of the relations
of the State and Federal governments to each other and of both
these governments to the people; the argument has a force that is
irresistible, in the absence of language which expresses such a purpose too clearly to admit of doubt [16 Wall. 77-78]

As Miller saw it, the interdependence of legal powers and legal
rights meant that the premise of "powers absolute within their
spheres" would fall if rights were federalized. The other consequence, that "fundamental" rights would become legal entities the
Federal courts were responsible for defining and protecting, was
also present to his mind. There is his famous phrase about the
Court as "censor upon all legislation of the States, on the civil
rights of their own citizens, with authority to nullify such as it did
not approve as consistent with those rights as they existed at the
time of the adoption of this Amendment." I do not think he was
talking about the kind of review under "general constitutional
law" that he himself had gratuitously performed on this statute
earlier in the opinion. He anticipated, if he read the dissents, that
the creation of an independent federal jurisdiction would mean
the recognition of privileges and immunities as legal entities of an
altogether novel kind.

～ 10 ～

I think it plausible that if the dissenters could have broken out of
the conceptual impasse of contradictory theories of rights and

federalism, they might have carried the day. They did not. Both
Field and Bradley conceded that the recognition of a broad range
of rights as privileges and immunities of U.S. citizenship would
profoundly change the nature of the union. According to Bradley,
the Fourteenth Amendment meant that "citizenship of the United
States is the primary citizenship in this country; and that state citizenship is secondary and derivative. . . ." [112] Field's statement
was even stronger:

> A citizen of a state is now only a citizen of the United States resid-
> ing in that state. The fundamental rights, privileges, and immuni-
> ties which belong to him as a free man and a free citizen, now
> belong to him as a citizen of the United States, and are not
> dependent upon his citizenship of any state. . . . They do not
> derive their existence from its legislation, and cannot be destroyed
> by its power. [95-96]

This laid them open to Miller's classic riposte affirming the peculiar neutral status of the federal judiciary in the federal system:

> In the early history of the organization of the government, its
> statesmen seem to have divided on the line which should separate
> the powers of the National government from those of the State
> governments, and though this line has never been very well
> defined in public opinion, such a division has continued from that
> day to this . . . Under the pressure of all the excited feeling grow-
> ing out of the war, our statesmen have still believed that the exis-
> tence of the States with powers for domestic and local govern-
> ment, including the regulation of civil rights—the rights of per-
> son and of property—was essential to the perfect working of our
> complex form of government, though they have thought proper
> to impose additional limitations on the States, and to confer addi-
> tional power on that of the Nation. . . .
>
> But whatever fluctuations may be seen in the history of public
> opinion on this subject during the period of our national existence,
> we think it will be found that this court, so far as its functions
> required, has always held with a steady and an even hand the bal-
> ance between State and Federal power, and we trust that such may
> continue to be the history of its relation to that subject so long as it

86   shall have duties to perform which demand of it a construction of
the Constitution or of any of its parts. [16 Wall. 81-82]

This was exactly the same attitude the Classical Court was to
strike, 30 or 40 years later, toward the problem of the "line which
should separate" the right of the individual from the "right of the
state" to regulate. The beginnings of that attitude, but only the
beginnings, appeared in the three *Slaughterhouse* dissents.

The dissenters were concerned to make their position as convincing as possible, and so made all the pre-Classical arguments,
and kept what was new masked behind them. For example, there
was a great deal in their opinions that suggested that the
Fourteenth Amendment federalized the vested rights doctrine,
rather than establishing legal rights of a novel kind. This was
the view of Cooley—it would have assimilated the Amendment
to the existing pattern of thought about constitutional limitations,
and followed the path of expansion of the definition of what
was "property" and what "vested," rather than breaking with the
past. Justice Field objected that the statute "restrains the butchers
in the freedom and liberty they previously had," [102] and argued
that the English common law, adopted into American constitutional law "declared void all special privileges, whereby others
could be deprived of any liberty which they previously had. . . ."
[107].

I pointed out earlier that the notion that the capacity to do *anything* legally, i.e., under the protection of the State, can be conceived as an abstract form of property. Field quoted Adam Smith
(1776) to the effect that "the property which every man has in his
own labor, as it is the original foundation of all other property, so
it is the most sacred and inviolable." Justice Swayne's dissent
baldly adopted this conception as the meaning of the "property"
of the due process clause: "Property is everything that has an
exchangeable value, and the right of property includes the power
to dispose of it according to the will of the owner. Labor is property and as such merits protection." [127] Bradley said that "a
calling, when chosen, is a man's property and right." [116]

The logical outcome of this line of attack is something like the unsuccessful argument in the early federal contracts clause cases, that everyone has a vested right to the set of values created for them by the body of law in existence at any given moment. *All* legislation then becomes a taking of property without compensation, and *all* legislation is also retroactive in the very special sense of destroying existing expectations. This kind of reasoning had great importance in the theoretical disputes of the 1920's, but the evolution of the Classical concept of rights got to it only by a circuitous route that started out in a different direction.

The striking characteristic of Classical rights is that they referred not to the maintenance of a body of pre-existing legal rules, but to areas of autonomy within which the individual was *free* of rules. Classical legal thinkers thought the essence of rights was freedom or liberty, a thing the law delimited and protected, but which was quite distinct from the law itself. Such a conception had definite implications, very different from the implications of the pre-Classical and modern conceptions, and Justices Bradley and Field began to work these out in their dissents.

Recall Miller's remark that forcing the butcher to slaughter on another's premises, and pay a fee for it, did not deprive him of "his right to labor in his occupation." Miller defended this proposition by pointing out that the states were constantly engaged both in regulating trades and in granting exclusive privileges. In other words, a pervasive practice of ordering the citizenry around, directing them and prohibiting them, was perfectly compatible with the existence of their "rights" to their callings. The rights did not represent autonomy, individual free choice to do what one would without government interference. They did not even represent some particular legal structure, minimal or maximal, that the citizen could rely on as defining the limit of government interference with his or her life. Because rights were quasi-legal, political entities, they were much vaguer than that. More, they were "natural;" what was legal, and so justiciable, was the body of the sovereign's regulations. A given regulation could be said to define a legal right, but only in the sense that until the regulation was changed, one could insist that it be enforced to one's advantage. There was a radical disjunction (mediated, it is true, by vested rights and implied limitations) between the mundane judicial activity of applying these laws, and the transcendent judicial duty to preserve a large political ideal.

Bradley and Field argued that the large political ideal was a legal concept, and that by reasoning legally from its existence, one could: first, define areas of individual autonomy and areas of state autonomy; second, specify what legislative rules were and what were not consistent with private autonomy (liberty, freedom). The first step was the claim that the privileges and immunities of *citizens in general* is but another phrase for "natural and inalienable rights," which "belong to the citizens of all free governments." [96-97] United States citizens therefore possess them. The Amendment is an express limitation on their abridgment. The judges must therefore enforce it as law. This involves defining these "natural and inalienable rights" as legal entities, and reasoning from the definitions to conclusions about what state laws are abridgments. It was implicit in this that the "right," e.g. "to acquire property and pursue happiness," [101] was a different, indeed an opposed legal concept to the law that "abridged" it, e.g., a monopoly statute.

The dissenters scheme for classifying a statute as an abridgment began by distinguishing a private and public sphere. They thereby disposed of Miller's argument about the prevalence of State granted monopolies: all of these had to do with the area of State autonomy, in which individuals acted only at the behest of the state; none referred to the area of private autonomy, i.e. of the exercise of a right.

The next question was what followed legally from the classification of butchering as an activity falling within the sphere of private autonomy. The answer was that anything that "hindered" [104] the butcher in the exercise of the trade was a restriction or abridgment of his freedom or liberty. "Hindrance" was defined in terms of the butcher's freedom of action, rather than in terms, say, of the welfare of the beneficiaries of the activity of butchering. "To compel a butcher...to slaughter [his] cattle in another person's slaughterhouse and pay him a toll therefore, is such a restriction upon the trade as materially to interfere with its prosecution."

[119] Since the right was the legalized version of the freedom, the hindrance abridged it, too.

This was the Classical structure very fully stated, very early. How different it was from the pre-Classical should already be apparent. Neither the opposition of public and private spheres nor the concept of reasoning from the character of a *legal* right to a conclusion about the validity of a legal rule existed in that system. Field and Bradley saw opposed legal entities, from *either* of which one could reason legally to conclusions about the other, where Miller saw a hierarchy.

Modern legal thought also, as we will see, rejects the concept of opposed realms of state and private autonomy—the "right-privilege distinction" so important to Classicism. It also rejects the notion that a regulatory scheme is *essentially* the imposition of legal coercion on legal freedom, the invasion of right by power. Modern critics of Classicism point insistently to the elaborate background of property and contract rules that heavily legalize the butcher's trade before anyone dreams of public slaughterhouses. The new statute should therefore have been conceived as an adjustment of a pre-existing framework rather than as a qualitatively new irruption of state interference.

One of the main purposes of developing the concept of legal consciousness is to explain how men like Field and Bradley could have failed to see things in the way that seems obvious to us. Surely they were both intensely aware that there were hundreds of legal rules, of varying degrees of specificity, that applied to every action of every butcher every day. Surely they realized that how much the butcher earned, how well he did in competition with others in the trade, the value of his property, and so forth, were all heavily conditioned by the existing regime of property, contract and tort. They also would have agreed that these legal rules were the product of sovereignty — that is, that the sovereign or his agents were responsible for promulgating and enforcing them. Yet they both seemed to feel that there was a self-evident difference between "hindrance" or "interference" of the kind involved here, and the "hindrance" or "interference" involved in forcing a man to respect a neighbor's boundaries and keep his promises.

Somehow, when Field and Bradley thought about rights against the state, *the common law background of rules of conduct the state enforces against private parties in their relations among themselves disappeared.* All that was left, if they disapproved, was a legislative invasion of private liberties. This in spite of the fact that, in cases like *Slaughterhouse*, the common law played a prominent role in the argument.

Justice Field, for example, put great emphasis on the English common law hostility toward monopolies that culminated in Coke's famous opinion nullifying a royal grant:

> The common law of England, as is thus seen, condemned all monopolies in any known trade or manufacture, and declared void all grants of special privileges whereby others could be deprived of any liberty which they previously had, or be hindered in their lawful trade. .
>
> The common law of England is the basis of the jurisprudence of the United States. It was brought to this country by the colonists, together with the English statutes, and was established here so far as it was applicable to their condition. That law ...[was] claimed by the Congress of the United Colonies in 1774 as a part of their "indubitable rights and liberties." . . . And when the Colonies separated from the mother country no privilege was more fully recognized or more completely incorporated into the fundamental law of the country than that every free subject in the British empire was entitled to pursue his happiness by following any of the known established trades and occupations of the country, subject only to such restraints as equally affected all others. The immortal document which proclaimed the independence of the country declared as self-evident truths that the Creator had endowed all men "with certain inalienable rights, and that among these are life, liberty, and the pursuit of happiness; and that to secure these rights governments are instituted among men."
>
> . . .[The Fourteenth Amendment] was intended to give practical effect to the declaration of 1776 of inalienable rights, rights which are the gift of the Creator, which the law does not confer, but only recognizes. If the trader in London could plead that he was a free citizen of that city against the enforcement to his injury

of monopolies, surely under the fourteenth amendment every cit- 91
izen of the United States should be able to plead his citizenship of
the republic as a protection against any similar invasion of his
privileges and immunities. [104-106]

Miller found this argument mystifying. It seemed to be possible to
answer it as follows:

> The great Case of Monopolies, reported by Coke, and so fully
> stated in the brief, was undoubtedly a contest of the commons
> against the monarch. The decision is based upon the ground that
> it was against common law, and the argument was aimed at the
> unlawful assumption of power by the crown; for whoever doubt-
> ed the authority of Parliament to change or modify the common
> law? [65]

For Field, the common law rules that form the background of legislation are not invisible at all. It is rather that, in our terms, they
have gone over to the enemy. They are not State imposed restrictions on liberty with which we can blend the new statute, but the
very essence of the liberty the statute invades. This attitude was
fanciful in 1872. I believe its implausibility had something to do
with the outcome of the case. But it more or less triumphed in
Justice Bradley's *Civil Rights Cases* opinion of 1883, and had triumphed fully by 1900. The rights the Fourteenth Amendment
guaranteed against state abridgment got their legal definition
from common law rules governing the relations of neighbors. My
argument is that this development was as much the result of the
evolution of the theory of common law rules as of the gradual
transformation of public law. In order to understand it, it is necessary to pass now to a sketch of the pre-Classical and Classical
conceptions of private law. The task was well stated by Corwin:

> The question is no longer how certain principles that ought to be
> restrictive of political authority took on a legal character or of the
> extent to which they did so, but rather how certain principles of a
> legal character in their origin assumed the further quality of prin-
> ciples entitled to control authority and to control it as law. In other
> words, the problem is not how the common law became law, but

how it became higher, without at the same time ceasing to be enforceable through the ordinary courts even within the field of its more exalted jurisdiction. [42 HLR 170].

CHAPTER III

Pre-Classical Private Law: Property

IN THE LAST CHAPTER, we mapped only the horizonal dimension of pre-Classical thinking about public law. We reviewed the legal concepts that served as a vocabulary for the statement and justification of legal rules, without discussing the methods of judicial reasoning the judges employed when faced with a choice about what rules to adopt. In this Chapter and the next, I will pursue a similar approach to private law theory. Once again the emphasis will be on the set of concepts used, and on their interrelationship, rather than on the process of legal reasoning by which the judges constructed a body of rules.

My purpose is to show that between 1850 and 1885 there was a transformation of the conceptual map of private law. This transformation paralleled that of public law. By 1885, there was such a marked similarity between the two fields that it was an easy matter for thinkers so inclined to put them together into a single integrated Classical theory of law. That process of integration is the subject of Chapter V.

As in the last chapter, I will use as a framework the notion that this structure of consciousness is an instrument for the mediation of the contradictions of experience. In other words, I will present the transition from the pre-Classical to the Classical mode as a transformation of a structure that allowed nineteenth century legal thinkers to deal with problems that seem to mid-twentieth century theorists insoluble. This presupposes that we do in fact experience private law as contradictory. The next section asserts more than it attempts to demonstrate that this is the case.

∾ 1 ∾

Modern theorizing about private law has left us with the sense that it is a mass of rules that cannot be understood as the rational working out of consistent general principles. It must rather be understood as the accumulation of the victories and defeats of two conflicting visions of the universe. Both judicial law making and judicial law application are indispensable to the working of the modern legal order, but both require the judge to engage himself in this battle of world views. To make things worse still, the typical member of the modern legal elite cannot claim to believe consistently in either of these ideologies. They define his discourse without compelling emotional involvement.

Short of the very abstract terms just used, there are many different ways to present the dilemma of private law. I have chosen a schema of four levels at which there exist readily accessible, stereotyped, pro and con positions for use in the construction of legal arguments. These are a kind of vocabulary that defines the possibilities of expression. The sense of contradiction arises as follows: all the different positions claim to describe the world accurately, and to prescribe for it rationally given obviously acceptable common goals; they cancel and refute each other; yet the private law system adopts all of them.

The first two problems have to do with the attitude the judge should adopt toward agreements or other undertakings of private parties. The judge must decide whether or not to give legal effect to some expression of intention or desire or decision, joint or individual. Arguments are presented to the effect that the expression is binding, and to the effect that he should ignore it. I have called these problems self-determination vs. paternalism and facilitation vs. regulation.

The third problem deals with the attitude the judge should 95
adopt when there is no expression of intention that he can appeal
to as establishing the appropriate structure for the parties' relationship. Either they are strangers or their undertakings have
failed of legal effect. In the absence of agreement, one party has
injured the other, or has appropriated benefits flowing from the
other's action, or has refused to participate in losses that have
resulted for the other party from some kind of joint action of the
two. The question the judge must answer is whether there exists a
legal duty of solidarity that requires one party to compensate, or
share gains or losses with the other. I have called this the problem
of autonomy vs. community.

The fourth problem concerns not the content or the objectives
of the law, but the form in which the lawmakers should cast the
rules that embody solutions to the previous problems. I have
called it formality vs. informality. This, like each of the others, is
a problem confronting the judge when his theory of his role tells
him that he has some leeway, in the sense of absence of directly or
intuitively obviously controlling precedent. He must consult, or at
least he feels free to consult "principle" and "policy." His problem is to decide what principle and what policy.

Problem #1: Self-Determination vs. Paternalism

(a) *The Self-Determination Position*
The parties are the best and the only legitimate judges of their
own interests. It is not a reason to refuse to enforce a transaction
that it would be better for one or both of the parties for such a
transaction not to occur. As long as the parties observe the
requirement that they not injure the rights of others, and have a
due regard for the good of the community as a whole, they can do
themselves "harm," behave "foolishly," and otherwise refuse to
accept any other person's views on what is the wisest course for
them.

(b) *The Paternalist Position*
The common law always has given and should continue to give
the judge tools by which he can protect people from their own

96   error and foolishness, and from subtle manipulation falling short of duress or fraud (e.g., advertising). The common law includes rules prohibiting or refusing to enforce particular agreements that are snares for the unwary, and requiring the courts to look after the interests of others even when the others don't want to be looked after.

Problem #2: Facilitation vs. Regulation

This problem is that of the legitimacy of bargaining power as the determinant of the distribution of income and the allocation of resources.

(a) *The Facilitative Position*

The rules as they were at some unspecified earlier point were a facilitative structure that allowed parties to act voluntarily to achieve their objectives. They allowed people to bind each other, and to keep each other off property, and they required compensation for injuries. Aside from that, they did not interfere to help one group at the expense of another. Nor did they attempt to induce one pattern or another of utilization of resources. The legislature has changed many of these rules to achieve particular allocative and distributive objectives. This is altogether fitting and proper, and the judges, of course, obey and cooperate with the legislature. Our problem is what to do when the legislature has not spoken. The answer is to develop the traditional common law policy of facilitating private action, which allocates resources and distributes income through the exercise of economic power within the neutral legal framework.

(b) *The Regulatory Position*

The common law rules represent the sovereign's will concerning issues of allocation and distribution. They are not facilitative, but rather expressive of an historical congeries of policy views about economic activity. Judges and legislators have collaborated in developing these policies and working them out in the form of particular rules of law. When the judge has to make law without legislative guidance, he should consult these policies, including *both* that in favor of private enterprise and that which mandates

governmental control of the use of economic power in circumstances where it poses a threat to the public interest.

Problem #3: Autonomy vs. Community

(a) *The Autonomy Position*

The legal rules ought to impose an absolute minimum of reciprocal duties on persons who have not entered into contractual
obligations defining their relationship. The sources of A's duties
to B are essentially two: voluntary undertaking by A to do something for B, and the moral rules of coexistence that dictate that A
should not deliberately or negligently injure B's interests. A has
no obligation to *support* B, and no obligation to share B's losses, so
long as A has neither agreed to do so nor been responsible for the
damage. Likewise, A is under no obligation to share his own good
fortune with B, even if B is in some measure its cause, so long as
he has made no agreement to do so.

(b) *The Communitarian Position*

The law does and ought to recognize many duties of mutual
solidarity, of willingness to share good and evil defined independently of contract, with those with whom one has entered
partnerships, joint ventures, long term contractual relationships,
short term contract transactions, pre-contractual negotiations,
relations of businessmen and invitees, and social relationships.
The duties imposed even on true strangers to look out for each
others' interests are constantly increasing.

Problem #4: Formality vs. Informality

The "problem of form" is that of the design of the "factual pred-
icates" or "triggers" that the judge must identify in applying a
rule; it equally concerns the definition of consequences that follow once the predicate is established. The problem arises regardless of whether one favors regulation or facilitation, paternalism
or self-determination, community or autonomy, although it
should be obvious that the way one feels about those issues will
influence the way one addresses it.

(a) *The Formalist Position*

The leeways that exist in the process of applying rules to facts are a serious weakness of the administration of justice because they make it possible for judges to subvert the policies embodied in the rules. The only way to deal with this problem is to accept that the rules must be designed as compromises between the policies that motivate them and the built in limits on effective legal action. In other words, we must accept that in order to use the system the rule maker must be deliberately inaccurate. The classic example is the use of the age of 18 or 21 as the definition of various kinds of legal capacity. The rule excludes some who have the actual capacity we care about, and includes others who lack it. But to put it in the hands of the judge to decide who has actual capacity would be disastrous. The hardships involved in maintaining a formally realizable rule system are usually less severe than in this case of fixing the age of capacity, because parties can usually adjust their behavior when they know in advance what mechanical standard will be applied. For example, the requirement of a writing for some kinds of contracts can be expected to do little harm, since parties who intend to be bound can easily comply with it.

(b) *The Informalist Position*

First, the search for objective criteria has proved illusory. Second, the victims made by the unexpected application of rigid but necessarily artificial rules are often sacrificed without any real increase in certainty, because the lay world refuses to learn to manipulate the technicalities of the system. Third, the demand for objective criteria imposes *substantive* limits on legal policy behind a formal smokescreen. The reason for this is that by definition a formal system cannot deal with wrongs that cannot be stated in terms of clear standards whose application can be accurately predicted in advance. The common law has always contained many undefined or loosely defined doctrines whose function is to be safety hatches through which the judge can pluck the innocent victims of the technicalities of the system. These should be developed rather than abolished.

The problematic character of private law theory is aggravated

by the historical fact that legal thinkers have tended to believe in 99
one or the other of two alignments of these positions:

Facilitation		Regulation
Autonomy	*vs.*	Community
Self-Determination		Paternalism
Formality		Informality

There is nothing *logically* necessary about either alignment. There
would be no logical contradiction involved in believing both in
rules securing a large measure of autonomy and in rules closely
regulating the exercise of bargaining power. There are, however,
two more abstract conflicts of legal philosophy that are relevant to
each problem. There has been a tendency for the disputants in
these more abstract debates to align the positions as I have just
done, and this explains the sense of polarization. The first is the
opposition between equity and efficiency: between the idea of justice as the resolution of disputes in such a way as to maximize the
welfare of the community over time, even at the expense of an
occasional injustice to individuals, and the idea of justice as
rewarding virtue and punishing vice in the particular case, without regard to the cost to the community.

The argument in favor of efficiency combines the positions
starting from the uncertainty and arbitrariness inherent in informal standards. Informality deters transaction and thereby stifle
economic progress because legal actors have no security that they
will be allowed to retain the benefits of their labors. But the ideals
of regulation (social justice), paternalism (protection of the individual against himself) and community (enforcing moral duties as
law) are inherently incapable of being framed in formal rules. If
the judges take them up as guides in their law making activities,
private parties will suffer paralyzing insecurity. Self-determination, facilitation and autonomy, by contrast are rendered determinate by their very absence of content. If they are adopted as
ideals, private energies will be released, and over the long run
everyone will be better off.

The response from the equitable position has two facets. One is

100   the simple argument that the cost of efficiently certain rules is too great, if the formal criteria require us to abandon the substantive goals of paternalism, regulation, community, as well as the procedural objective of justice in the individual case. A vague assurance that we will end up with all these things if we begin by vigorously renouncing them is not convincing. The other facet is an attack on the accuracy of the efficiency argument, beginning with the proposition that formality is more certain than informality. It may well be that the only way to achieve real certainty is to rely on the judge's intuition of community values. The parties are more likely to be able to predict and control these, than the technicalities that inevitably proliferate when an attempt is made to design a fully formal legal system.

The second way to link up self-determination, facilitation, autonomy and formality is through the idea of rights. The facilitative position can be justified on the ground that there is a fundamental moral/political imperative that private actors can do what they like unless they injure others. The whole idea of a right is that it is a guarantee of autonomy: within one's rights, one can injure the interest of others if that is necessary to pursue one's own way. Rights are also an alternative to efficiency as the foundation of the individual's refusal to let the state paternally define his best interests. And informality — the design of rule systems riddled with leeways for judicial discretion — is obviously a grave threat to any right dependent on judicial enforcement.

The answer from the perspective of public power is summed up in the word interdependence. The claim is that the proviso in the slogan "do anything you want so long as you don't hurt anybody" has long since swallowed the main clause. In a modern economy or society there is virtually total intertwining of cause and effect between all actions; rights no longer have any core of obvious meaning that we can use to construct political systems. Rights are no more than delegations of sovereign power for particular purposes. They are the legal outcome rather than the natural origin of the governmental system. The public interest may not be a highly determinate, operative concept with plain implications, but "rights" are totally illusory.

What I have been describing is a subsystem of thought, a part of the total system of legal consciousness. I believe that 90% of the "policy" arguments made in private law cases fit into one of the above categories. But this does not mean that the legal profession is divided into two camps, one composed of Group A and the other of Group B thinkers. The phenomenon of alignment of the positions on the four problems, and the continuing oppositions of efficiency vs. equity and rights vs. powers render legal thinking ideological without polarizing the legal community.

The system, as a part of consciousness, defines the universe of possible rules without dictating any rules in particular. It defines the universe of "legal philosophies" without requiring the adoption of any one in particular. Within a particular dispute, it defines the possible arguments on the issues presented without dictating even that the advocate stay consistently to the Group A or Group B side. For most of the participants, there are no "killer arguments" available within the system. None of the positions on any of the problems *in itself* disposes of any case. One moves from problem to problem without hope for decisive resolution. The arguments are pointers; they have "weight," more or less in different circumstances. That is all.

There are ways to make all the dilemmas go away: delegalization via the administrative process, as in "no fault" automobile insurance; informalization through institutions like family courts; detailed codification, as in Article 9 of the UCC. These expedients generate problems of their own. But what is important about them for us is that they represent abandonment of the enterprise of judge-made, common law ordering of economic and social life, rather than vanquishing of its contradictions. *Within* the common law premises, there is no escape.

Probably the single most common state of legal consciousness for non-theoretical lawyers forced into awareness of the dilemma is something like this. There is (1) a sense of all of the available rhetorical riffs for each of the problems, and willingness to use them ad hoc in the interest of one's client or of one's intuition of justice; (2) a rather indistinctly defined "general position," leaning toward one broad vision or the other; (3) a sense that each

102   position is untenable when pushed to extremes, and a willingness to acknowledge some validity to each on its strongest ground, so that "good judgment," rather than any mechanical analytic mode, is essential to find one's way through the maze of pros and cons; (4) a tendency to feel strongly that the arguments on one side or the other do cleanly resolve *some* issues, and inability to penetrate behind them to any other justificatory system.

For a subgroup within the legal elite, the problem presents itself much more sharply, in the form of an acute sense of the falseness of the pretensions of the legal order to rationality. These more sophisticated thinkers have, often, the sense of having discovered a social secret, like the "facts of life" for a child. They are initiates into the backstage world where the illusion of the rule of law is mounted, and must find a way to survive the loss of innocence.

The heightened awareness of contradiction may be a source of anguish, or frustration, or cynicism, or nostalgia. It may provide amusement, confirmation of world view, a sense of smug superior knowledge. One can believe that the contradiction is not important, given the overall "effectiveness" and "workability" of the system; or that the "gap between ideal and actuality" is narrowing, or is stable, or is widening, or is a part of the "nature of things," or is inevitable only under a liberal pluralist political and economic regime. One can regard the acceptance of contradiction as the badge of maturity, of corruption, of the "tragic view of life," or of the impotence of bourgeois intellectuals. The point is that the experience is close to universal among modern American legal thinkers.

It has been fashionable, among those who are both aware of contradiction and accepting of the political and economic status quo it represents, to draw an analogy to pre-Classical legal thought and a sharp contrast with the Classical period. The pre-Classical system supposedly acknowledged and confronted pragmatically the dilemmas that the Classics strove by various illegitimate expedients to suppress or deny. The rest of this Chapter explores the question of the relationship of the three periods, arguing that modern legal thought is the heir to the irreversible

Classical accomplishment of reconceiving all legal relationships.
The ultimate failure of that reconception defines our situation.
The modern form of disintegration resembles only in the most
superficial way that of the period immediately preceding the
grand synthetic effort.

~ 2 ~

The Classical approach to private law differed from the modern in
the following important particulars. First, the Classics believed
that each of the conflicting positions was entitled to full respect,
indeed to be accepted at face value, in resolving some issues, and
should be ignored in resolving others. Second, the boundary lines
of the areas of relevance of the different positions had been fixed
at a very abstract level through general principles. Third, the
judge could draw the line in particular cases by deductively elaborating the general principles into specific subrules.

The problems of individualism vs. paternalism and facilitation
vs. regulation the Classics handled mainly through the concept of
capacity, including duress. The law of capacity stated in general
terms that only "free will" should be enforced, but that those with
free will were entitled to enforcement to the hilt without judicial
second guessing or interference. Problems of autonomy vs. community and some of facilitation vs. regulation yielded to analysis
in terms of the contrasts between fiduciary relationship and arms
length dealing, between contract and quasi-contract, and between
family law and commercial law. The concept of estoppel came
into play to distinguish situations in which the benefits of formality were to be disregarded in favor of direct reference to the
understanding of the parties.

In public law, the Classics conceived the individual and state
spheres of action as opposed entities whose boundary the judge
delimited by deduction from general principles. In private law, it
would be more accurate to picture a sphere of individualism, facilitation, autonomy and formality surrounded by a periphery of
paternalism, regulation, community and informality. The boundary between the core and the periphery was defined by the con-

104   trast between capacity and incapacity, arms length dealing and fiduciary relation, and so forth. This boundary once passed, there was an abrupt, indeed a violent reversal of ethos.

What distinguishes the modern situation is the breakdown of the boundary between the core and the periphery, so that all the different conflicting positions are at least potentially relevant to all issues. Instead of a situation that permits consistent argument within one ethos or the other, with a few hard cases occurring at the border when it is necessary to draw a sharp line, we have a situation in which each conflicting vision claims universal relevance, but is unable to establish hegemony anywhere.

Yet, the disintegration of the boundary between the core and the periphery has not altered the basic conceptual vocabulary in which we discuss the now pervasive conflict of visions. Just as the Classics did, we perceive the issues through notions like individualism vs. paternalism, regulation vs. facilitation, and so forth. While the deductive method now looks like a Classical mistake, the fundamental categorical scheme of Classicism seems a part of the nature of things, a postulate of legal consciousness.

What this means is that the basic structure of private law theorizing has not changed since the High Classical period around the turn of the century. We share with the Classics the sense that the fundamental private law issue is the extent to which the wills of individuals, their "rights," should be recognized when the outcome violates the community's (the judge's) sense of justice or morality. We share with them also the sense that the key to the successful administration of the system of rights and powers, however they are finally adjusted, lies in designing rules that private legal actors can work with, without either paralyzing uncertainty about standards, or equally paralyzing fear of mechanical arbitrariness.

What *has* changed is our faith in legal reasoning as a way of dealing with these issues. Exactly as in public law, we are left with a sense that discretion, policy, politics, ideology, are all that remains of the "scientific" solutions of the Classics. And, as in public law, it is difficult to imagine any alternative to believing in or being disillusioned with the Classical scheme. My aim here is to persuade that there was a pre-Classical vision of the body of private law rules that was different.

∾ 3 ∽

The apparently ineradicable categories of Classicism came to dominate thinking about private law only in the 1870's, although they were given their first definition and some elaboration in the 1850's. The whole period between 1850 and 1885 was one of the reworking of legal rules so that they would fit harmoniously either into the core or into the periphery. We will examine this process by taking up a large number of changes in the substance of rules, in their phrasing, and in their organization into doctrinal fields.

It was the core organized around the ideals of self-determination, facilitation, autonomy and formality that dominated legal thought; we will consequently pay most attention to it, leaving the development of the periphery to a later chapter. It seems best to begin by developing a bit more fully the general characteristics that define the horizontal dimension of Classical private law theory, and then to pass directly to the transition from pre-Classical to Classical visions of actual rules.

Self-Determination and Facilitation: The Will Theory

In Classical legal thought, self-determination and facilitation were part of a more general tendency to conceive the judge as responsible for carrying out the will of some legal power holder. The notion, which I will call the will theory, was that legal rules should have the following content: they should designate an actor as a power holder; and they should instruct the judge to execute the will of the power holder. The will theory applied both to public and to private law, although in this chapter we will look only at its private law aspect. Because of this limitation of focus, it is important to guard against a misconception that is common when the totality of Classical legal thought is lost sight of.

Neither "laissez-faire" nor "individualism" are logically implicit in the will theory. It is as much a theory of statutory inter-

106   pretation and of the judge's proper attitude toward corporations as it is a theory of response to purely private intentions. Yet the will theory did have content. It told the judge to pick the legal actor whose will was authoritative in the particular situation and then enforce that will. It was implied that for each actor there was a set of actions for whose execution he could get judicial support. Other actions might be prohibited by the will of some other actor with authority in the premises. Still others might be open to the actor only so long as he could persuade another actor not to invoke state aid against him. These sets of actions constituted the "spheres" of absolute power.

At first for public law and later for private law as well, the image of spheres conveyed vividly and explicitly what was only suggested by the usual definition of the will theory: that the judge whose only function was the interpretation and enforcement of the commands of legal actors had a restricted choice of response to a demand for assistance. If the plaintiff was entitled to ask what he was asking, then the judge had no business making his own assessment of its reasonableness, conduciveness to the general welfare, or fairness to others involved. If the plaintiff was asking assistance to achieve an object that lay within the power of some other legal actor, then the judge must sit on his hands, no matter how equitable, useful or just the request might be.

Thus the will theory was neutral among substantive objectives of legal actors but not among institutional arrangements to carry them out. The will theory said nothing about the most desirable resolution of conflicts between state and citizen, federal and state governments, executive and legislative branches. The theory did say that the judiciary could participate in those quarrels only as the agent of someone else's will.

But this requirement of judicial passivity was more than a restraint on the judge: it was a restraint on public and private law makers as well. The judge must never slip into the attitude of arbitrator, of the voice of natural law or good morals; he must never confuse his function with that of the legislature or the private contracting party. They in turn must accept that the judge would either back them to the hilt or ignore them utterly. Their assurance that he would not slip into an active role was purchased at the price of renouncing any ability to force that role on him when it seemed appropriate, or vital to prevent a miscarriage of justice.

The will theory was thus a theory of the separation of powers *both* as between legislature and judiciary and as between private legal actors and judges. The judicial role was the same with respect to each. It consisted in deciding whose will, among those contending, the law entitled to protection, interpreting that will, and applying it to the facts at hand.

Objectivism as a Response to the Problem of Formality

Within the legal core, Classical legal thought was committed to formality. There was widespread acceptance of the proposition that legal rules should be framed in such a way that the judge would have little leeway in applying them, even if it was necessary to admit of a measure of crudity and arbitrariness in consequence. The Classical version of formality I will call objectivism, meaning the idea that the rules should attach legal consequences to actions when they were "reasonably" interpreted as manifesting a particular state of the will. What this program excluded was the "subjectivism" attributed to pre-Classical law, its concern with "actual" intent and its willingness to accept evidence meant to show the interior state of the willing party.

Objectivism meant a willingness to adhere to forms: to be valid a statute must be more than the will of the legislature — it must also have been formally enacted. It implied a respect for the literal words of statutes, conveyances and contracts — the "plain meaning" and parole evidence rules, for example. It also implied the search for the "reasonable man" as the standard of liability in tort, and the "objective" theory of the formation and interpretation of contracts.

Autonomy as a Strategy in Designing Rights

Before the parties can begin to exercise their wills with respect to the various objects of legal action, those objects must be given

108   some definition. The legal system must choose a set of rules that tell people what they can do to each other in the absence of agreement. Only then is there a basis on which they can deal.

The opposition of autonomy and community describes two general approaches to the problem of designing these pre-contractual groundrules. One strategy frames the rules so as to require people by law to live up to the highest moral standards of the community. This strategy legislates the "morality of aspiration," and requires people to compensate whenever they injure, to avoid the vice of thinking more of their own small gains than of others' large losses, to volunteer to share their own gains when another has contributed to them, and to share another's losses when they result from activities in common even though not contractual. This is the communal strategy.

The strategy of autonomy may be aimed at precisely the same outcomes as that of community. Its advocates may honestly believe that they are most likely to further the morality of aspiration by refusing to enforce it. Instead, they minimize extra-contractual obligation. There must be a floor of obligation represented by the criminal laws against force and fraud. But beyond that, the law tolerates many situations of "damnum absque injuria," meaning that there has been actual hurt but no legal redress for the innocent victim. This was the strategy the Classics adopted in framing the core of legal rules.

As with the will theory, there is danger of a misconception. It was no part of the theory that the legal system could not impose high moral obligations. Indeed, it was a common strategy for the judge to urge the legislatures to do just that. There would then be the will of the sovereign to substitute for the will of the parties, missing ex-hypothesis. The strategy of autonomy prescribes not the content of the total set of rules, but rather the principles the judge can use when he has to make new ones.

The notion of autonomy, moreover, is not tied to private law or to relations among private parties. It was the guide for the Classical theory of federalism and of rights against the state as well as of property, torts and contracts. It was much more abstract, more formal, than an idea like laissez-faire, and therefore

more widely applicable. Like the will theory and objectivism, it 109
had content and could affect substantive outcomes. But like the
other two characteristics, it did so by constraining the judge rather
than by directing him.

Will Theory, Objectivism and Autonomy
Were More than Just Policies

Classical legal thinkers defended the strategy of autonomy on
many different grounds. They sometimes claimed that autonomy
led to better moral results in the long run, but they also referred
to the "intrinsic nature" of legal as opposed to moral duties, to
the institutional incompetence of judges to make the judgments required in a communitarian system, and to the political
illegitimacy of their pretensions to do so. It is not possible to
understand the rise of the strategy without reference to the theory of judicial reasoning then coming into vogue. Many of the
most striking instances of preference for autonomy over community were justified as logical implications of more abstract concepts such as "property as absolute dominion," or "freedom of
contract."

Exactly the same complex web of causes lies behind both the
will theory and objectivism. The Classics only rarely discussed
their rationale, but when they did they were as likely to refer to the
"nature" of law, or of language or science or whatever, as to the
set of policies that now seem obvious motives. Furthermore the
will theory and objectivism fitted together with the deductive theory of legal reasoning into a whole whose coherent structure was
in itself a strong reason for clinging to each of its component
parts.

My objective in this chapter is strictly limited to setting the
stage for a description of that whole. To do so, it is essential to
establish the reality of the change toward will theory, objectivism
and autonomy even if we are not yet able to understand its causation. This requires a sketch, however superficial, of the characteristic pre-Classical modes of dealing with the contradictions of private law theory.

∿ 4 ൦

Pre-Classical legal thinkers organized the discussion of private law rules around the notion of a conflict between morality (or natural law, or natural justice) and "policy" (or utility, or the general good). One way in which this idea expressed itself was through the distinction between natural law and positive law. Counsel in the 1817 Supreme Court case of *Laidlaw v. Organ* defended his client's behavior as follows:

> Even admitting that his conduct was unlawful, in foro conscientiae, does that prove that it was so in the civil forum? Human laws are imperfect in this respect, and the sphere of morality is more extensive than the limits of civil jurisdiction. The maxim of caveat emptor could never have crept into the law, if the province of ethics had been co-extensive with it. [15 U.S. 178]

The private law distinction between moral rules and positive legal rules was like that between natural rights and legal rights in public law. What was legal, and so within the judge's jurisdiction, was something less than or narrower than, the full demands of morality. Positive civil law, as found by the judge, condoned evil doing. It thereby became not immoral, but simply less than *fully* moral. The explanation for this falling short was that reasons of policy militated against the fusion of law and morality. *Parsons on Contracts* (1853) contains a very perfect expression of the pre-Classical point of view on the subject. Parsons is discussing the law of fraud, and, in particular the distinction between:

> that kind and measure of craft and cunning which the law deems it impossible or inexpedient to detect and punish, and therefore leaves unrecognized, and that worse kind and higher degree of craft and cunning which the law prohibits, and of which it takes away all the advantage from him by whom it is practiced.
>
> The law of morality, which is the law of God, acknowledges but one principle, and that is the duty of doing to others as we would that others should do to us, and this principle absolutely excludes and prohibits all cunning; if we mean by this word any

astuteness practiced by any one for his own exclusive benefit. But this would be perfection; and the law of God requires it because it requires perfection; that is, it sets up a perfect standard, and requires a constant and continual effort to approach it. But human law, or municipal law, is the rule which men require each other to obey; and it is of its essence that it should have an effectual sanction, by itself providing that a certain punishment should be administered by men, or certain adverse consequences take place, as the direct effect of a breach of this law. If therefore the municipal law were identical with the law of God, or adopted all its requirements, one of three consequences must flow therefrom; either the law would become confessedly, and by a common understanding, powerless and dead as to a part of it; or society would be constantly employed in visiting all its members with punishment; or, if the law annulled whatever violated its principles, a very great part of human transactions would be rendered void. Therefore the municipal law leaves a vast proportion of unquestionable duty to motives, sanctions, and requirements very different from those which it supplies. And no man has any right to say, that whatever human law does not prohibit, that he has a right to do; for that only is right which violates no law, and there is another law besides human law. Nor, on the other hand, can any one reasonably insist, that whatever one should do or should abstain from doing, this may properly be made a part of the municipal law, for this law must necessarily fail to do all the great good that it can do and therefore should, if it attempts to do that which, while society and human nature remain what they are it cannot possibly accomplish.

There are numerous other issues that the pre-Classics cast in the same mold. I have already quoted from a discussion of the doctrine caveat emptor. Here are some further examples:

> *Negotiability*: It was common to argue that it was immoral to force the maker of a note to pay a holder in due course after failure of the consideration. The law was requiring the maker to pay for something he never got. Morality suggested loss splitting but policy dictated the cutting off of defenses.

Incorporation: It was a Jacksonian objection to incorporation that it allowed stockholders to escape liability for their share of the debts of the corporation. The law obliged partners to live up to their moral obligations, but allowed stockholders to behave dishonorably. The answer was the policy in favor of the pooling of resources.

Competitive Nuisance: Why should a mill owner who ruined his competitors by underselling them escape liability for damaging their businesses? He would have to pay for any other kind of deliberately inflicted injury, but the policy in favor of economic efficiency dictated an exemption there.

Consideration: The common law refused to enforce promises whose performance was dictated by the most solemn moral obligation when they lacked consideration. The reason was the policy against the multiplication of lawsuits and the legalization of family life.

Prescription and Statutes of Limitations: The law refused to punish plain wrongdoing or to provide redress to its victims when the wrong had gone stale. The reason was the policy of repose.

Vicarious Liability: The law imposed liability on the principal for the torts of his agent and on the master for those of his servant in cases where there was not the slightest fault in the person held. The reason was a policy of encouraging close supervision.

Absolute Liability of Common Carriers and Innkeepers: Common carriers and innkeepers may be ruined by liability for damage to property altogether beyond their control and wholly without fault on their part. The reason was the policy of discouraging fraudulent claims of goods having been destroyed accidentally when in fact the carrier had been negligent or dishonest.

Breaching Plaintiff's Suit for Restitution: Most courts refused to honor the breaching plaintiff's claim for restitution even when the result was a windfall unjust enrichment of the defendant. To allow recovery would have created a dangerous incentive to lax performance.

Bankruptcy: Bankruptcy laws sanctioned and even encouraged the dishonorable conduct of refusing to pay one's debts. The reason was the policy against demoralizing economic actors by eliminating the incentive of self-enrichment.

Remedies of Landlords: The exceptional remedy of distraint put it in the power of landlords to arbitrarily abuse honest tenants in difficulties. The reason was the necessity of providing an effective remedy against the dishonest tenants.

Damnum Absque Injuria in Easements: The law permitted landowners to inflict many kinds of uncompensable injuries on their neighbors. The reason was that a consistent and thorough policy of compensation would have deterred economic development.

It is easy to see in the conflict between morality and policy in pre-Classical legal thought the prototype of the elaborate contradictory structure we know today. Policy required that the individual just and moral solution, that responsive to the individual merits and demerits of the parties, should be disregarded so that, in Llewellyn's phrase, we could "get on with it." Morality, on the other hand, was uncompromisingly equitable and insensitive to questions of efficiency.

Morality was also concerned with the rights of the individual; indeed, it was another name for natural law or natural justice between individuals as it existed in an imagined state of nature without government. The whole point of policy, on the other hand, was that it was the pursuit of the regulatory interests of the state. National economic development, security of transaction, repose, the prevention of perjury, and so forth, were goals that could exist only within the context of a legal order. Their pursuit was part of official decision making. The very concept of policy presupposed a public role in the direction of private activity.

In spite of the implicit presence of the equity/efficiency and state/individual conflicts, pre-Classical private law theory seems strikingly innocent of the sense of contradiction. In public law, the problem of the relationship of natural right and sovereignty was both pervasive and urgent. Judges and theoreticians developed sharply contrasting positions, emphasizing positivism or transcendent reason, and attempted to apply them somewhat systematically to a range of issues. In private law, the conflict of morality and policy did not lead to a similar polarization. No one

114 seems to have doubted that both sources of law were legitimately available to the judge. No one seems to have doubted that judges had both a substantial measure of responsibility for creatively developing the body of common law rules, and that the legislature was ultimately empowered to resolve the issues as it saw fit.

There was a difference between the theory of public and of private law that goes some way, but no more than some way, toward explaining the unpolarized character of the former. In public law, positivism had an early and full elaboration. It may be true that:

> The attribution of supremacy to the Constitution on the ground solely of its rootage in popular will represents a comparatively late outgrowth of American constitutional theory. Earlier the supremacy accorded to the constitutions was ascribed less to their putative source than to the supposed content, to their embodiment of essential and unchanging justice. [Corwin, 42 Harv.L.Rev. 149, 152]

But by the second quarter of the 19th century legal positivism was the ideology of public law, and the judges made every effort to present themselves as doing the bidding of some sovereign, right up to the moment at which they rebelled in the name of natural rights.

In private law, by contrast, there was the theory of "found not made," inherited from Blackstone, but kept alive in opinions like *Swift v. Tyson* that distinguished radically between an artificial statute law and common law rules that were immanent in social life. My argument is that the "found not made" approach softened the conflict of policy and morality. Public law judges dealt with a specific, demanding, legislative sovereign opposed to a disembodied command of reason to honor natural rights. They had to choose which to obey. In private law, the exercise was less dramatic. Instead of a clash of commands, there was a problem of the ingredients discoverable in the mass of sources.

Today it is hard to believe that they took the idea of law finding seriously. If we do believe it, we tend to attribute it to a kind of pre-rational mind-set in which there are "brooding omnipresences." Nonetheless, there were concrete aspects of pre-Classical legal thought that made their vision plausible. The absence of these factors in public law helps to explain its greater positivism, and consequently more acute sense of contradiction.

The claim that the judge found the law was plausible in the private but not in the public system in part because the sources of law were so different. However "formative" it may have been, the body of pre-Classical private law was massive. From its first edition on, Kent's *Commentaries*, cited many thousands of cases. In the enormous mass of precedent and in the volumes of legal exegesis one might actually carry out something like a search for authority. By comparison, public law issues were constantly of first impression. The words of the Constitution were the only available source of legitimacy for judicial decisions that simply had no elaborate body of precedent to rely on.

The private law judge, moreover, could appeal to two vast sources of theory and practice altogether outside the domestic context. Both English and Roman legal doctrine were universally accepted as relevant, if not "controlling," no matter what the subject matter. In *Callender v. Marsh*, an 1823 Massachusetts case on consequential damages from digging down a road, counsel argued and the Court discussed at length the authority of Roman local officials with respect to the modification of highways. In this enormous web of *matter*, it was possible to argue forever without being forced to confront the fact of the judge's autonomous power to choose.

Finally, there was the tradition of technical legal reasoning, conceived by everyone, laymen and professionals alike, as infinitely difficult, obscure and inaccessible and as highly systematic, coherent and determinate, supposing that one understood it. The three most striking dimensions of technicality were:

1. The system of common law pleading, including the elaborate system of causes of action only very deviously connected to the substantive rights they protected; and the system of move and countermove by which issues were presented to the courts.

2. The interaction of legal and equitable rules, so that for much of the law of property, of partnership, of husband and wife, there were two quite coherent, wide ranging conceptual systems one must learn before one could hope to predict an outcome.

3. The subdivision of types of property and the association of each type with a distinct set of rules for alienation and involuntary transfer, so that there were literally hundreds of logically autonomous categories of doctrine to be learned by the conveyancer before he could hope to effectuate the will of his client.

One can understand the emergence of new private law doctrines after 1870 as responsive to the disappearance of the pre-Classical conditions just described. The "found not made" idea lost ground to the positivism that already held sway in public law. English and Roman *case law*, as opposed to theory, began to seem less relevant to America. The technicality of private law was radically reduced by the reform of procedure, the abolition of the English categories of estates in land, and the merger of law and equity. In a later chapter, we will examine the impact of these developments on the theory of the judicial role. For the moment, it is enough to note that they created intense awareness of the previously unsystematic character of private law theorizing, and opened the way for the discovery of contradiction.

Besides the contrasts, there were strong similarities between the public and private law systems. During the pre-Classical period, morality was thought of as prior to policy, as a set of principles of universal and transcendent validity, very like public law natural rights. Policy was much more mundane; like sovereignty in relation to natural right, it was hierarchically inferior to morality. But like sovereignty it controlled the extent to which the more exalted concept could achieve practical realization through positive law. As in public law, the judge often saw himself as obliged to make painful choices between the two most important ideals in his system.

In public law, various mediating devices (e.g., the hierarchical

ordering of concepts; the vested rights doctrine; and the doctrine
of implied limitations) reduced the sense of conflict. Similar and
sometimes identical structures prevented the conflict of morality
and policy from taking the form of insoluble contradiction. For
example, private law and public law judges distinguished between
rights and remedies in a way designed to reconcile natural rights
to sovereignty and morality to policy. In interpreting the
Contracts clause, the fundamental doctrine was that the legislature
could do what it would with contract remedies so long as it left the
right, here equated with the "obligation" alone. It was not uncommon to argue that limitations on compensation for eminent
domain takings were legitimate because they recognized the property right, through taking away any remedy for consequential
damages.

In private law, the same formula applied to nuisances: the law
took away the individual's remedy against a nuisance that was
public and gave it to the state, but did not in the process interfere
with the right. Statutes of limitation, of frauds, of bankruptcy,
took away remedies, for good policy reasons, but did not interfere
with the right which was founded on morality. The debt barred by
the statute of limitations was alive in the sense that it would justify the foreclosure of a lien or pledge, and justify the creditor in
retaining money paid in ignorance of the bar. Likewise for reasons
of policy, the law denied a remedy to the creditors of women
under coverture, minors and lunatics, but did not deny that
their unenforceable contracts sometimes gave rise to moral obligations. The rights corresponding to those obligations might
become enforceable if for some reason the policy ceased to be
applicable.

My notion is that the pre-Classical judges felt less conflict
between morality and policy because the distinction between right
and remedy could often be used to create relatively well-bounded
niches for each of the concepts. Policy confined its pretensions to
remedies, making no attack on the existence of moral obligation
and conceding that moral obligation created rights that would
once again have legal effect when the problem of policy disappeared. Morality claimed to be the one and only source of obliga-

118   tion and the guiding star in the formulation of all legal principles. It conceded, however, that it must sometimes confine itself to the theoretical domain of rights, allowing considerations of policy to curtail the remedies through which rights were implemented.

There were two other conceptual clusters that played similar but much more important roles in pre-Classical private law theorizing. The first of these was the descriptive dichotomy of "liberality" vs. "technicality." The second was the notion of rules founded on the "implied intent" of parties to stereotyped legal transactions. Each of these provided a way to mediate each of the fundamental dilemmas of private law: they blurred the contrast between the will of the state and the will of private parties (i.e., the opposition of rights and powers) and they obscured the necessity of choosing between the arbitrariness of rigid rules and the arbitrariness of flexible standards. My argument is that the presence of such mediators helps to explain why the acknowledged conflict between morality and policy did not develop into the acute contradiction we now experience.

I will take up the liberality/technicality distinction in the context of the law of real property, and the notion of implied intent will serve as an organizing theme for the discussion of the range of subjects pre-Classical thinkers classified under the general head of contract. In order to understand this approach, the reader must have some familiarity with the way in which categorical schemes of the whole private law system changed over the course of the 19th century.

The subject is unfamiliar because abstractions of the kind necessary to arrange all the doctrines seem meaningless to modern legal thinkers. As far as I know, the last American effort was Pound's table of all the "social interests" law protects, with appropriate doctrinal subdivisions annexed. Before Pound, however, classificatory schemes were an important part of legal thought. A review of the way they changed between 1800 and 1900 will give us an initial sense of the transformations of consciousness during the same period.

There were three classificatory phases during the 19th century. In the first, the dominant category was property law, with most of private law being seen as concerned either with objects or with the personal status of the possessors of objects. The second phase was that of contract: property law was reconceived as a specialized conveyancing discipline and virtually all of the rest of law seen as concerned with agreements. The third phase was the Classical, with the emphasis on will.

Blackstone (1765) and Kent (1825) were the great classifiers of the first phase. It requires a real empathic effort to understand their scheme of "law of persons"/"law of things." Here are the subjects that (apart from public law) comprise the law of persons:

1. Rules defining legal disabilities of aliens, lunatics and infants. These are involuntarily assumed "statuses."
2. Rules defining the mode of creation of and the rights and duties implied in the relationships of: husband and wife; parent and child; guardian and ward; master and servant.
3. The rules defining the special legal characteristics of corporations ("artificial persons").

The law of things included two major types of rules: those defining the various interests that a person could have in the various types of property, and those regulating the creation and transfer of interests. What is most striking from our perspective is that neither contracts nor torts was a separate heading in either Blackstone or Kent.

Most, although by no means all of contract and tort were *there*. They were distributed among the other categories as follows. First, contract law figured as an important formal category of the law of alienation of personal property. In other words, after dividing up all of property into real and personal, the question arose how one acquired title to the various types. Title to real property was by deed, by grant, by fine, etc. Title to personal property could be acquired by gift or by contract. There followed

120   a more (Kent) or less (Blackstone) detailed description of how one formed a valid contract transferring title to goods, and how the title might be defeated by such supervening events as a breach.

For us, such a classification seems bizarre because contract as a category is not tied to the transfer of title to goods. Indeed, the opposite is true. We now conceive the sales contract as a specialized subclass of the more general phenomenon of contract. This more generalized phenomenon never appears in Blackstone or Kent. Instead, various species of contract crop up here and there. For example, the modern category of employment contracts, including labor law, comes in under: the law of persons - status voluntarily undertaken - master and servant. Under bailments, defined as rules about temporary transfers of rights in property, it was possible to include the law of common carriers and innkeepers. Building contracts were contracts for the sale of an item of personal property, namely the finished building.

Another way in which relationships that we now see as part of the contract system could be assimilated to the property concept was through the *partial* abstraction of the idea of real property. Thus rents, easements and franchises were classified as "incorporeal hereditaments." The notion of the status-thing dichotomy could be maintained without excluding types of social arrangements that "really" involved neither.

Some deformation was involved in this; it is not generally true that there are *many* classificatory schemes all of which will accommodate a given body of material with equal ease. For example, many of the contracts of common carriers involve no property at all. They are simply contracts to carry a person. Innkeepers are involved with their guests' property, but have special duties unrelated to them. And there are many contract types that involve neither property nor employment (or another status), such as agency. The existence of "incorporeal" property that is nonetheless "real," although subject to different rules of definition and transfer than land, could serve as a type of unsatisfactory system building.

Kent wrote some lectures on the law of "injuries to the person" but decided that the subject was not important enough to include in his *Commentaries*. Blackstone dealt with what we would call torts in his section on Private Wrongs. Private wrongs were the different ways in which a person might violate another's basic rights. Injuries to the right of property were categorized according to the forms of action. These included trespass and case, but also types of wrong we would not classify as tortious. Breach of contract, under assumpsit, figured as the wrong of interfering with a property right acquired by contract. There was not the least suggestion of the existence of the modern category of general duty to observe a standard of care in one's relations with others in general.

The Blackstone/Kent schema suggested that the two main concerns of legal actors are the control of other members of a society with fixed social roles, and the control of physical objects that represent power, particularly land. In Blackstone's own time, it would have been absurd to describe English society in such terms. But it was not yet true that the main *conscious preoccupation* of the legal system was regulating the concerns of social strangers alternately contracting with and accidentally injuring one another. Tort and contract, as we see them, were perceived embedded in the elaborated social contexts of status and land holding. Because they were relatively unimportant *concepts*, they could be simply tacked onto the larger structure of the *Commentaries*.

By the time of Kent, this ordering had lost all of its autonomous intellectual power. Kent did not hesitate to construct what amounted to a general survey of all the basic commercial contractual relationships under "Title to Personal Property," although there were no property hooks for most of the contracts involved. After the contract for the sale of a chattel came Agency, Partnership, Negotiable Instruments and Marine Insurance. Bailment included a discussion of railroad law as it related to passengers. The placement of a subject within the contract category no longer suggested anything at all about its connection with the law of personal property. Kent preserved Blackstone's general scheme without any apparent belief that it was more than convenient.

Holmes remarked in 1872 that "generations of students must

122   have been puzzled that in Kent the law of master and servant [sta-
tus; law of persons] appeared several hundred pages away from
the law of principal and agent [contract; law of personal proper-
ty]." A review of a treatise on personal property pointed out that
many of the rules included "belonged rather to contract law." By
1872, it had already been clear for a full generation that the old
arrangement was inorganic. In fact, beginning in the 1840's, a
new total ordering around the concept of contract had begun to
emerge. The exemplars were Metcalf (1825), the little known
seminal thinker, W. W. Story (1848) and Parsons (1853), the writer
who summed up the tradition and represented it to posterity.

The basic idea of pre-Classical contractual classificatory
schemes was that virtually all legal relationships are contractual if
we consider that all legal obligation is, in a sense, the result of an
implied assent to be bound. The person-thing or status-property
dichotomy disappeared to be replaced by a contract-real property
dichotomy. The various status relations were restated as contracts.
Their implied rights and duties were treated as consensual. Their
main significance was that they made necessary a special contract
sub-category called "Parties," which included all of the special
rules of husband and wife, master and servant and so forth. At the
same time, the various commercial law specialties were liberated
from the "Title to Personal Property" rubric. They were treated
as the analogues of the old status relations in that they too
involved stereotyped relationships (partnership; bailment) and the
implication of assent to a set of judge-made rules.

This approach allowed the incorporation of all of the law
of injuries except that which governs strangers. In other words,
as part of each relationship he constructed, a writer like Parsons included an implied consent to a set of rules of liability
for injuries. The only injuries that such an approach dropped
out were those to real property and those personal injuries inflicted *outside* of a contractual relationship. Likewise, all of corporations was contractual: there was the law governing the
contract of formation and that governing the corporation as a
party.

The one body of law that was unequivocally distinguishable

from contracts was real property. Thus isolated, the law of real property was reformed. By the Civil War it had taken on most, although not all, of its most striking modern characteristics. It then exercised a profound influence—as an abstract model rather than as the core of an all-embracing doctrinal category.

The Post-Civil War development was the dissolution of the omnivorous law of contract and the reconstitution of its elements. The different parts of the Classical labor of rearrangement were thus accomplished at different times and with different degrees of rapidity and neatness. The most important elements were:

1. The reorganization of the law of alienation of property around the idea of respect for the will of the owner, subject to restraints imposed by the will of the sovereign in the public interest.
2. The attack on the corporeal-incorporeal distinction in property law, and its replacement with the idea of property as a right to protection of the will.
3. The sharp differentiation from contract law of types of obligation deriving from the will of the sovereign rather than from that of the parties to a transaction:
   (a) Tort
   (b) Status/Domestic Relations
   (c) Quasi-Contract
4. The reorganization of contract law around the idea of respect for the objective expression of the will of the parties subject to the restraint of the consideration doctrine.
5. The emergence of Torts as a field with its own internal structure of opposition between liability based on a defect of the will of the tortfeasor (intentional torts and negligence) and liability imposed by the sovereign without regard to the condition of the will.

It is this set of events that we will consider as reflected in the vicissitudes of the liberal/technical distinction and the notion of implied intent.

∾ 6 ∾

Pre-Classical legal thinkers classified legal rules as "liberal" or "strict and technical." Indeed, one of the most striking differences between the pre-and post-Civil War periods in American law is that the liberal/technical distinction was omnipresent in the earlier discussions. Today it is unfamiliar to the point of unintelligibility. References to the concepts can be culled by the dozens from the early reports, but it seems better to approach them as they appear in all their aspects in a single sustained work. What follows might be called the Romance of Liberality in Chancellor Kent's volume on the law of Real Property (1826).

Toward a Definition of Liberality

Kent began the final section of his work as follows:

> In passing from the subject of personal to that of real property, the student will immediately perceive that the latter is governed by rules of a distinct and peculiar character. The law concerning real property forms a technical and very artificial system; and though it has felt the influence of the free and commercial spirit of modern ages, it is still very much under the control of principles derived from the feudal policy. We have either never introduced into the jurisprudence of this country, or we have, in the course of improvements upon our municipal law abolished all the essential badges of the law of feuds; but the deep traces of that policy are visible in every part of the doctrine of real estates, and the technical language, and many of the technical rules and fictions of that system, are still retained. [III-593]

In the ensuing chapters, this theme recurred more consistently than any other. Indeed, the law of real property for Kent was

mainly an occasion to raise over and over the question of the relation of liberality and technicality.

Let me begin with a quotation from his discussion of the
requirement that, in order to convey a fee simple interest in land,
the deed must mention both the recipient and his heirs. Kent's
treatment suggests both the importance of the liberal/technical
distinction and its complexity.

If a man purchases lands to himself forever, or to him and to
his assignees forever, he takes but an estate for life. Though the
intent of the parties be ever so clearly expressed in the deed, a
fee cannot pass without the word heirs. The rule was founded
originally on principles of feudal policy, which no longer exist,
and it has now become entirely technical. A feudal grant was,
stricti juris, made in consideration of the personal abilities of
the feudatory, and his competency to render military service;
and it was consequently confined to the life of the donee,
unless there was an express provision that it should go to his
heirs.

But the rule has for a long time been controlled by a more liberal policy, and it is counteracted in practice by other rules, equally artificial in their nature, and technical in their application. It
does not apply to conveyances by fine, when the fine is in the
nature of an action, as the fine sur conuzance de droit, on account
of the efficacy and solemnity of the conveyance, and because a
prior feoffment in fee is implied . . . .

It is likewise understood, that a court of equity will supply the
omission of words of inheritance; and in contracts to convey, it
will sustain the right of the party to call for a conveyance in fee,
when it appears to have been the intention of the contract to convey a fee.

Thus stands the law of the land, without the aid of legislative
provision. But in this country the statute law of some of the
states has abolished the inflexible rule of the common law, which
had long survived the reason of its introduction, and rendered
the insertion of the word heirs no longer necessary. [IV-5]

126   Throughout the *Commentaries*, there are pitted against each other
       two teams, good guys and bad guys, most of whose members are
       brought together in the passage above:

The Strict, Technical Team:		*The Liberal, Progressive Team:*
Law	vs.	Equity
Common Law	vs.	Statute
Feudal Policy	vs.	Commercial Policy
English Law	vs.	American Law
Theoretical Consistency	vs.	Intuition of Justice

Even this list leaves out Common Law vs. Civil Law, and Artificiality
vs. Rationality, but their roles can be divined from the examples
which follow.

The underlying theme of the law of mortgages is set out in the
second paragraph of Kent's treatment:

> There is no branch of the law of real property which embraces a
> greater variety of important interests, or which is of more practical
> application. The different, and even conflicting views, which were
> taken of the subject by the courts of law and of equity, have given
> an abstruse and shifting character to the doctrine of mortgages. But
> the liberal minds and enlarged policy of such judges as Hardwicke
> and Mansfield gave expansion to principles, tested their soundness,
> dispersed anomalies, and assimilated the law of the different tri-
> bunals on this as well as on other heads of jurisprudence. The law
> of mortgage, under the process of forensic reasonings, has now
> become firmly established on the most rational foundations. [IV-
> 138]

The villain of mortgage law was the feudal common law, which,
in the absence of explicit provisions to the contrary, regarded the
mortgagee as the legal owner of the property, subject to the condition that it would revert to the mortgagor if he paid his debt on
time. "So rigorous a doctrine, and productive of such forbidding,
and, as it eventually proved, of such intolerable injustice" [IV-

142] led the equity courts to intervene, overlaying the common
law system with a whole new set of rules.

> In ascending to the view of a mortgage in the contemplation of a
> court of equity, we leave all these technical scruples and difficul-
> ties behind us. Not only the original severity of the common law,
> treating the mortgagor's interest as resting upon the exact per-
> formance of a condition, and holding the forfeiture or the breach
> of a condition to be absolute, by nonpayment or tender at the day,
> is entirely relaxed; but the narrow and precarious character of the
> mortgagor at law is changed, under the more enlarged and liberal
> jurisdiction of the courts of equity. Their influence has reached
> the courts of law, and the case of mortgages is one of the most
> splendid instances in the history of our jurisprudence, of the tri-
> umph of equitable principles over technical rules, and of the hom-
> age which those principles have received by their adoption in the
> courts of law. Without any prophetic anticipation we may well
> say, that "returning justice lifts aloft her scale." [IV-161-162]

The equitable treatment of mortgage had two salient aspects.
First, in contrast to the "strict technical principles of the common
law" it treated the mortgage according to "the true intent and
inherent nature of every such transaction." [IV-163] Second, the
equity courts imposed restraints on the terms of the mortgage in
favor of the mortgagor, and these could not be altered or removed
even by express agreement of the parties.

The two notions of responsiveness to intent and unwillingness
to countenance injustice recurred whenever there was a contrast
of equity and law. For example, in the discussion of when two
estates held by a single person will "merge" by operation of law,
Kent says:

> The rule at law is inflexible; but in equity it depends upon cir-
> cumstances, and is governed by the intention, either express
> or implied (if it be a just and fair intention), of the person in
> whom the estates unite, and the purposes of justice, whether
> the equitable estate shall merge or be kept in existence. [IV-
> 105]

128   Some other ideas associated with liberality were cultivation, refinement, complexity, plasticity, enlightenment and progress. Kent's vision of the rise of "uses," a whole system of equitable interests in land existing parallel to the common law system, is an example. Uses "were required by the advancing state of society and the growth of commerce. The simplicity and strictness of the common law would not admit of secret transfers of property, or of dispositions of it by will, or of those family settlements which become convenient and desirable. . . All such refinements were repugnant to the plain, direct mode of dealing, natural to simple manners and unlettered ages." [IV-298]

> Uses were well adapted to answer the various purposes to which estates at common law could not be made subservient, by means of the relation of trustee and cestui que use, and by the power of disposing of uses by will, and by means of shifting, secondary, contingent, springing, and resulting uses, and by the reservation of a power to revoke the uses of the estate and direct others. These were pliable qualities belonging to uses, and which were utterly unknown to the common law, and grew up under the more liberal and more cultivated principles of equity jurisprudence. [IV-299]

The trust was the modern equivalent, in Kent's time, of the medieval use, and, according to him different from it only in being the object of a "more liberal construction. . . and, at the same time, a more guarded care against abuse." This development was closely linked with progress in general:

> The advantages of trusts in the management, enjoyment, and security of property, for the multiplied purposes arising in the complicated concerns of life, and principally as it respects the separate estate of the wife, and the settlement of portions upon the children and the security of creditors, are constantly felt, and they keep increasing in importance as society enlarges and becomes refined. [IV-310-11]

On the legal, as opposed to equitable side, Kent's hero was Lord Mansfield, the most "liberal" of the English judges of the 18th

Century. Here also, the themes of intentionality, but also of the control of overreaching, were dominant. For example, Kent approved the Roman and English rules to the effect that tenancies "at will" should be construed as tenancies for a year with a requirement of notice of termination. After describing the Roman approach, he says:

> And when the sages at Westminster were called to the examination of the same doctrines, and with a strong, if not equally enlightened and liberal sense of justice, they were led to form similar conclusions, even though they had to contend, in the earlier period of the English law, when the doctrine was first introduced, with the overbearing claims of the feudal aristocracy, and the scrupulously technical rules of the common law. [IV-119]

Perhaps the quintessence of technicality was the English doctrine of wrongful disseisin. Without attempting to explain the content of the rules, we can gather something from the epithets Kent directs at the positions of the two sides in the debate. There were, on the one hand, "ancient and strict" notions on the question, which were also productive of "unreasonable and noxious" and "inequitable" consequences. On the other side, Lord Mansfield and his allies attempted to "disarm the doctrine of disseisin of much of its ancient severity and formidable application." They made everything turn on "the intention of the party, or...overt acts that leave no room to inquire about intention." This was the triumph of "good sense and liberal views" over an "old and exploded theory." [IV-534-35] In any case, none of this law applied in America, which had radically simplified and improved the whole system of conveyancing.

As a final illustration, consider the disposition of real property by will. There was an English rule that a disposition was revoked if the testator changed his interest in the property before his death, *even though* the change was temporary or purely formal, and he died in the same legal relation to the property as he had been in when he made the will. In Kent's opinion, this was "very strict and technical;" "shocking;" "had brought scandal upon the law;" was "hard and unreasonable." The courts were "holding

130   an act to be a revocation which was not so intended, and even when the intention was directly the contrary."[IV-58] Unfortunately, the American courts had adopted the rule, although avoiding "some of the excesses to which the English doctrine had been carried." The solution was a statute abolishing the whole doctrine:

> The simplicity and good sense of these amendments recommend them strongly to our judgment; and they relieve the law from a number of technical rules, which are overwhelmed in a labyrinth of cases; and when detected and defined, they are not entirely free from the imputation of harshness and absurdity. [584-85]

At this point, let me hazard a definition. Technicality meant to Kent three tendencies: (a) to attach particular legal meanings to words and acts and stick to those meanings in dealing with laymen who clearly meant something else by those words and acts; (b) the restriction of private transactions to a limited set each of which was defined by a set of judge-made rules rather than being a plastic reflection of the will of the parties; (c) the restriction of the judge to a relatively small number of remedial responses to disputes and wrongdoing, so that he must often choose between extreme treatments rather than tailoring the punishment to the wrong. Liberality meant adopting the opposite position on each point.

In a modern discussion of this program, we would be tempted to say that Kent grasped only a part of the problem of designing private law rules. His endorsement of the ideal of liberality was ideological, we might say, because it papered over rather than resolving the basic contradictions of private law theory. (1) It embraced the informal side of the dilemma of formality, ignoring the problems of uncertainty and arbitrariness that arise when the judge is invited to consider subjective intent. (2) It attempted to adopt simultaneously a position of judicial subordination to private will and of ad hoc judicial control of that will according to standards of morality and policy nowhere clearly stated. In other words, it attempted to embrace both sides of the conflicts between regulation and facilitation and between individualism and paternalism. (3) The ideal of liberality tells us nothing about what the groundrules of social life ought to be in the absence of agreement; it was unresponsive to the dilemma of autonomy vs. community.

I do not think that Kent would have found these objections at all convincing. For him, the ideal of liberality mediated successfully between the conflicting demands of morality and policy. This was possible because of an historical analysis that portrayed legal progress as moving from a particular brand of medieval technicality based on the peculiar conditions of medieval law toward a particular brand of modern liberality based on the peculiar conditions of early 19th century America. Because the opposition of liberality and technicality was also the opposition of modern America and feudal England, it lacked the hopelessly deadlocked quality of our present contradictions.

The Historical Analysis of Technicality

The medieval legal system had been characterized by a mode of thought—the "rigorous, simple, pure, strict" mode of the common law—unsuited to "civilization," "progress," "refinement, "cultivation," and "commerce." Moreover, the law had been designed to achieve the objectives of the feudal regime or "policy." These objectives included social hierarchy, collective military defense, self-sufficient agricultural economy, the organization of life around landed property, and hostility to all kinds of dynamism. The distinguishing marks of the feudal legal policy were two kinds of restraints on alienation: those imposed by testators through entails, and those imposed by the crown in favor of the lord at the expense of the tenant.[III-Ch. 53 passim]

The spirit and meaning of English legal history, according to Kent, lay in the "progress of the common law right of alienation from a state of servitude to freedom." The culmination of that progress was that "[e]very citizen of the U.S. is capable of taking and holding lands by descent, devise or purchase, and every person capable of holding lands, except [persons without legal capacity], may alien the same at his pleasure, under the regulations prescribed by law." [IV-475-76; see IV-269-70]

132   Technicality was a phase of this progression. The feudal restraints on alienation by tenants had once been highly rational, although not in accord with morality:

> The restrictions were perfectly in accordance with the doctrine of feuds, and proper and expedient in reference to that system, and to that system only. The whole feudal establishment proved itself eventually to be inconsistent with a civilized and pacific state of society; and wherever freedom, commerce, and the arts penetrated and shed their benign influence, the feudal fabric was gradually undermined, and all its proud and stately columns were successively prostrated in the dust. [IV-473]

Likewise, the system of entails arose from "the desire to preserve and perpetuate family influence and property," which "is very prevalent with mankind and deeply seated in the affections." The problem was that:

> Entailments are recommended in monarchical governments as a protection to the power and influence of the landed aristocracy; but such a policy has no application to republican establishments, where wealth does not form a permanent distinction, and under which every individual of every family has his equal rights, and is equally invited, by the genius of the institutions, to depend upon his own merit and exertions. [IV-18]

A major instrument in the struggle against the combination of the archaic form of common law reasoning and the feudal policy was, according to Kent, the judiciary. There consequently came into existence several layers of policy and several layers of rules, so that the inherent bizarreness of common law reasoning was worse confounded rather than alleviated. The great advantage of America was that it could import from England only the progressive net outcome of these struggles, rather than the total structure in which the English embodied them.

Technicality in the law of his own time Kent could therefore regard as essentially vestigial. It represented the object of an almost completed work of law reform that had been going on for generations, under the leadership of the equity courts, of Mansfield, and of the American courts and legislatures that had received English doctrine selectively rather than wholesale. Liberality on the other hand, was the spirit of the age. It represented the implication for law of the modern policy, which was progressive, commercial, contractual, individualist, egalitarian, rational and economically dynamic.

Technicality may appear to us to represent a viable counter-position to Kent's liberality. We sense that it might have been possible to defend it on the ground that it was at least certain, and that it prevented the judicial arbitrariness inherent in any system that allows the ad hoc review of private will according to the judge's notions of policy and fairness. But Kent believed that liberality was more rather than less certain than technicality, so that it could legitimately claim the virtues of both sides of the modern dilemma of formality. He also believed that liberality represented real freedom, as opposed to the arbitrariness of technicality; he did not see it as taking a side of the dilemma of regulation vs. facilitation.

The Uncertainty of Technicality

The theme of the uncertainty of technical systems of law is one of the most striking in the *Commentaries*, because it sharply contradicts modern notions on the subject. To look to intent on a case by case basis, to subordinate the structure of legal institutions to the actual practice of laymen, subject only to equitable restraint on overreaching—this program was designed to make law simple, clear, predictable and nondiscretionary. Here is a typical example from the law of mortgages:

> A very vexatious question has been agitated, and has distressed the English courts...as to the time at which money provided for children's portions may be raised by sale or mortgage of a reversionary term. The history of the question is worthy of a moment's attention, as a legal curiosity, and a sample of the perplexity and uncertainty with which complicated settlements "rolled in tangles," and subtle disputation, and eternal doubts, will

134   insensibly incumber and oppress a free and civilized system of
           jurisprudence. [IV-151]

Speaking of N.Y. statutory revision of the English and American
common law rules about remainders, Kent says that change "will
disperse a cloud of difficulties and a vast body of intricate learning relating to the subject." [IV-259] Of the law concerning the
mutual relations of tenants in common, he says:

> The ancient law raised this very artificial distinction, that tenants
> in common might deliver seisin to each other, but they could not
> convey to each other by release. A joint tenant could not enfeoff
> his companion, because they were both actually seised, but for that
> very reason they might release to each other; whereas, on the one
> hand, tenants in common might enfeoff each other, but they could
> not release to each other, because they were not jointly seised.
> Nothing contributes more to perplex and obscure the law of real
> property than such idle and unprofitable refinements. [IV-378]

On the practically important subject of the warranties accompanying the sale of real property, the "liberal" doctrine was to
reduce the buyer's protection by requiring a writing to establish
any obligation at all in the seller. The explanation was as follows:

> These provisions leave the indemnity of the purchaser for failure
> of title, in cases free from fraud, to rest upon the express
> covenants in the deed; and they have wisely reduced the law on
> this head to certainty and precision, and dismissed all the learning
> of warranties, which abounds in the old books, and was distin-
> guished for its abstruseness and subtle distinctions. It occupies a
> very large space in the commentaries of Lord Coke, and in the
> notes of Mr. Butler; and there was no part of the English law to
> which the ancient writers had more frequent recourse to explain
> and illustrate their legal doctrines. Lord Coke declared "the learn-
> ing of warranties to be one of the most curious and cunning learn-
> ings of the law;" but it is now admitted by Mr. Butler to have
> become, even in England, in most respects a matter of speculation
> rather than of use. [IV-513]

Statutory reforms in N.Y. had "swept away all the established rules of construction of wills, in respect to the quantity of interest conveyed," creating instead a set of presumptions that could be overcome by a showing of contrary intention. Kent approved: "These provisions relieve the courts in N.Y. from the study of a vast collection of cases, and from yielding obedience any longer to the authority of many ancient and settled rules, which were difficult to shake and dangerous to remove. Their tendency is to give increased certainty to the operation of a devise." [IV-590-91]

Liberality and the Dilemma of Formality

Nonetheless, even in Kent's *Commentaries* one can see the beginnings of the very different perception of the problem of formality that now afflicts us. To begin with, Kent was quite willing to recognize that the proper response to English technicality was sometimes a set of clear, simple but essentially arbitrary rules:

> Our registry acts, applicable to mortgages and conveyances, determine the rights and title of bona fide purchasers and mortgagees, by the date and priority of the record; and outstanding terms can have no operation when coming in collision with a registered deed. We appear to be fortunately relieved from the necessity of introducing the intricate machinery of attendant terms, which have been devised in England with so much labor and skill, to throw protection over estates of inheritance. Titles are more wisely guarded, by clear and certain rules, which may be cheaply discovered and easily understood; and it would be deeply to be regretted if we were obliged to adopt so complex and artificial a system as a branch of the institutes of real property law. [IV-94]

Second, Kent had a clear sense that in the argument about technicality there was a counterattack based on the uncertainty of liberality, with its associated danger of inefficiency and judicial usurpation:

> It is most desirable that there should be some fixed and stable rules even for the interpretation of wills; and whether those rules be

founded upon statute, or upon a series of judicial decisions, the beneficial result is the same, provided there be equal certainty and stability in the rule. There has been a strong disposition frequently discovered in this country to be relieved from all English adjudications on the subject of wills, and to hold the intention of the testator paramount to technical rules. The question still occurs, whether the settled rules of construction are not the best means employed to discover the intention. It is certain that the law will not suffer the intention to be defeated, merely because the testator has not clothed his ideas in technical language: But no enlightened judge will disregard a series of adjudged cases bearing on the point, even as to the construction of wills. Established rules, and an habitual reverence for judicial decisions, tend to avoid the mischiefs of uncertainty in the disposition of property, and the much greater mischief of leaving to the courts the exercise of a fluctuating and arbitrary discretion. The soundest sages of the law, and the solid dictates of wisdom, have recommended and enforced the authority of settled rules, in all the dispositions of property, in order to avoid the ebb and flow of the reason and fancy, the passions and prejudices of tribunals. [IV-592]

Finally, he did not blink the fact that his position implied the necessity of a residuum of pure technicality in a modern system. He was including himself when he said that: "All the great property lawyers justly insist upon the necessity and importance of stable rules; and they deplore the perplexity strife, litigation and distress which result from the pursuit of loose and conjectural intentions, brought forward to counteract the settled and determinate meaning of technical expressions." "Convenience and policy equally dictate adherence to [a particular] old and established doctrine." [IV-236-37] His comments on the abolition of equitable "uses" in N.Y. were typical of his style when he felt that the antitechnical position had been carried too far:

The operation of the statute of New York in respect to the doctrine of uses will have some slight effect upon the forms of conveyance, and it may give them more brevity and simplicity. But it would be quite visionary to suppose that the science of law, even in the department of conveyancing, will not continue to have its technical language, and its various, subtle, and profound learning, in common with every other branch of human science. The transfer of property assumes so many modifications, to meet the various exigencies of speculation, wealth, and refinement, and to supply family wants and wishes, that the doctrine of conveyancing must continue essentially technical, under the incessant operation of skill and invention. [IV-307-08]

At this point it may appear that Kent was simply an inconsistent thinker. From one point of view, this is quite true. He often felt it was enough to condemn a rule that it was strict or technical, but sometimes insisted that technicality was positively desirable. He provided no guide for deciding when one conclusion was more appropriate than the other.

Yet there is a passage in his discussion of the N.Y. statutory reform of the law of trusts that suggests that Kent had a highly sophisticated vision of the relation of liberality and technicality in a fully modern legal system. New York had enacted that there should be three, and only three kinds of express trusts and a fourth category of constructive trust. The claim was that the statute would "sweep away an immense mass of useless refinements and distinctions, relieve the law of real property, to a great extent, from its abstruseness and uncertainty, and render it, as a system, intelligible and consistent." Kent's response was as follows:

Nor can the law be effectually relieved from its "abstruseness and uncertainty," so long as it leaves undefiled and untouched that mysterious class of trusts "arising or resulting by implication of law." Those trusts depend entirely on judicial construction; and the law on this branch of trusts is left as uncertain and as debatable as ever. Implied trusts are liable to be extended, and pressed indefinitely, in cases where there may be no other way to recognize and enforce the obligations which justice imperiously demands. . . .It is in vain to think that an end can be put to the interminable nature of trusts arising in a great community, busy in the pursuit, anxious for the security, and blessed with the enjoyment of property in all its ideal and tangible modifications. . . . We cannot hope to check the enterprising spirit of gain, the pride of families, the anxieties of parents, the importunities of luxury, the fixedness of habits, the

138   subtleties of intellect. They are incessantly active in engendering distinctions calculated to elude, impair, or undermine the fairest and proudest models of legislation that can be matured in the closet, and ushered into the world, under the imposing forms of legislative sanction. [IV-325-26]

Kent regarded the essence of liberality as the control of technicality in the interests of morality and policy. He did not think it possible or desirable to *abolish* technicality, but neither did he treat it as an ideal parallel to or "in tension with" liberality. He turned it into a means. This made liberality a truly integrating, mediating concept: it was the guide for the "interminable" process of building up technical rules and then sweeping them away.

The essence of such an approach is its ambiguity. It refuses: (a) to admit that it will sometimes sacrifice to the judge's intuition of justice expectations of the parties about how the rules will be administered; and (b) to admit that it will sometimes sacrifice justice in the individual case to the preservation of the integrity of the system of rules. In other words, the ideal of liberality is a way to suppress the contradiction of formality and informality.

In Kent, the suppression was nearly complete. The reader gets the impression that Kent believed that there was *always* a solution, be it loose and equitable or strict and technical, that satisfactorily served the ends of a liberal administration of justice. In the typical situation, all that was required was good sense in order to see the *diritta via* between evils.

After Kent, for several decades, there seems to have been no theoretical work that overtly developed the problem of formality. But little by little it must have become apparent that feudal technicality was a straw man in 19th century America. The ancient doctrines succumbed one by one to the reformers, until what technicality there was in the law was clearly part of that residuum Kent had recognized and accepted as functional rather than vestigial. And at that point, there was no way to escape the question of how much and of what type was functional. Beginning with *Parsons on Contracts* and culminating with Holmes' lectures on criminal law and negligence, Classical theorists developed their answer in the

form of objectivism. We will take this up in the next chapter in the
discussion of contracts and torts.

The Will Theory in Property Law

A fundamental difficulty with Kent's theory of property law was that he believed *both* that freedom of alienation was the message of history, *and* that the state ought to restrain the freedom of alienation by refusing to recognize dispositions of property that contravened the liberal policy. Kent's treatment disguised what now seems an inconsistency by expedients we will presently examine. The Classics unmasked these as the evasions they "really" were.

I want to qualify and soften this schema. The law of property after the Civil War was more like what it had been before than was true of any other basic doctrinal field. Contract was shattered and rebuilt; torts came into existence; domestic relations changed in coverage and content; corporations underwent a conceptual revolution. Property concepts took their modern forms during the great statutory reforms of New York in the 1820's and 1840's.

More: the new property structure that emerged before the Civil War had profound influence on the post-war development of all those areas of law I have just mentioned. Property had included, in Blackstone and Kent, everything but status, and *real* property had been its core. But during the period between 1825 and 1870, real property ceased to play that role and became a "technical," specialized category not integrated into the new all-embracing concept of contract. During this period of exile, property law transformed itself. After 1870, its transformed state served as a paradigm or model for the construction of new fields out of the ruins of the empire of contract. Property played a role in private law similar to that of federalism in public law. Each was a precursor whose development before the Civil War turned out to have all sorts of implications for the Classical reconception of law in general.

There were two stages to the emergence of the will theory, each of which was well begun in property earlier than anywhere else. The first stage was the clear recognition that the outcomes of lawsuits are determined not by the intrinsic characteristics of the

140   legal "objects" involved, but by the application of rules that have
their origins in the desires of social actors. The vehicle for this
stage was the theory of liberality, with its critique of technicality
and its exaltation of rationality and intentionality.

The second stage was the focussing of attention on the specific identities and the claims to legitimacy of the different legal
actors among whose proposed rules the judge had to choose. The
second stage involved an attack on the ideal of liberality as an
inadequate because obscurantist criterion for deciding which
actors should have the power to make the rule in any particular situation. We can see each of these movements in Kent's treatment
of the central issue of restraints on alienation.

Technicality as a Restraint on Alienation

There is no need to repeat here the familiar story of the reduction
in the number and internal complexity of legally recognized interests in land, with the attendant reduction of the diverse modes of
conveying them to the omnipresent grant. Much of the description of liberality is a review of the different aspects of this
process. What we need to grasp is the radical conceptual transformation that was implicit in the attack on technicality.

Here are two examples of the phenomenon. Under the old system, it was *conceptually* impossible to convey an incorporeal
hereditament by livery of seisin, because there was no *thing* that
could be delivered. It followed that an actor who had intended to
grant an easement or assign a term for years, and who cast his
intention in the language of livery, had simply failed to alienate
his interest. [IV-537] Or take the problem of the effect of the
"nature" of remainders on attempts to convey them:

> There must be a particular estate to precede a remainder, for it
> necessarily implies that a part of the estate has been already carved
> out of it, and vested in immediate possession in some other person. The particular estate must be valid in law, and formed at the
> same time, and by the same instrument with the remainder. The
> latter cannot be created for a future time, without an intervening
> estate to support it. If it be an estate of freehold, it must take effect

Pre-Classical Private Law: Property

presently, either in possession or remainder; for at common law, no estate of freehold could pass without livery of seisin, which must operate either immediately or not at all. "If a man" said Lord Coke, (a) "makes a lease for life to begin at a day to come, he cannot make present livery to a future estate, and, therefore, in that case, nothing passeth." [IV-243]

The great occurrence of Kent's time was that all of this began to seem silly if not sinister. It came to seem obvious that the only reasons for distinguishing different modes of conveying different types of interest was a state policy in favor of greater formality in the more significant transactions. [IV-482; 539] It was only as a result of primitive thinking and historical accident that the different interests had seemed to require by their very nature different forms of transfer. A New York statute could simply declare that contingent remainders survived the determination of the precedent estate, and the only consequence would be an increase in the likelihood that private actors would succeed in carrying out their intentions. [IV-253]

Unfortunately, it soon became apparent that there was more to it than my two examples suggest. The intricate classification of estates and forms of conveyances had imposed dozens and dozens of restraints on alienation, in the sense that formal requirements are restraints. But there were also dozens of things that you just couldn't do with property, no matter what form you used, because to do them required saying or thinking things that were inconsistent with the imagery of the system. The structure of these constraints was the result of centuries of theorizing into which had been poured not only pre-scientific ideas about classification, but also all the political and economic issues of feudalism, mercantilism and emerging liberalism. In many cases, a particular restraint justified as no more than a logical consequence of the nature of the legal interest in question, served also to further a particular state policy that had nothing to do with the conceptual metaphysics. Let me illustrate this with two incomprehensible sentences from Kent's chapter on Powers:

The use declared by the appointment under the power is fed (to use the mysterious language of the conveyancers) by the seisin of the trustees to uses in the original conveyance. The consequence of this principle is, that the uses declared in the execution of the power must be such as would have been good if limited in the original deed; and *if they would have been void as being too remote, or tending to a perpetuity in the one case, they will be equally void in the other.* [IV-339 my emp.]

The abolition of technicality meant the placing of the courts at the disposition of the wills of private parties, subject only to those limitations that judges and legislators were willing to declare and enforce on their own merits. The state could no longer exercise an elaborate but politically invisible control through the expedient of nullifying transactions as incompatible with the "nature" of property.

The work of the ante-bellum property lawyers was both to dismantle the technical system, and to identify the policies that had been implicit in its structure, assess their usefulness in 19th century America, and work out the doctrinal implications of those found still serviceable. Property law was reconceived as a facility for the exercise of private will subject to limitations the state imposed on private will in order to protect larger interests of the community. This accomplishment was the indispensable precondition of Classical and modern theorizing about property, but it did not lead the ante-bellum thinkers themselves to anything more than a vague foreshadowing of the later approaches.

For Classics and moderns alike, the essential dilemma of the reconceived property system was that once it was recognized that the will of the sovereign could legitimately interfere with the alienation of property in order to achieve *some* community objectives, such as preventing the creation of family empires or keeping the wheels greased by preventing the creation of hidden encumbrances, the whole property structure was in danger of politicization. In public law, the question was: If it is constitutional to restrain the alienation of property for these purposes, can there be any objection to other kinds of legislative interference also motivated by the public interest? In private law, the problem was that of deciding when the judge should attempt to regulate and when he should conceive himself as merely a facilitator.

The Classical mode was to recognize a conflict between the will of the parties and the will of the sovereign, but to insist that it had been dealt with at a very high level of abstraction by the adoption of the policy against private restraints on alienation. This policy once adopted, it functioned like the requirement of consideration, as a fountain of deductions. Judges worked out its implications for all the different aspects of property law with no sense that they were personally or politically intervening to shape social and economic life. That had been done once and for all by the abstract principle that drew the line between the conflicting public and private wills. The moderns differ only in that they have lost faith in deduction, and so must carry out the accommodation through ad hoc interest balancing.

The pre-Classical mode was more complex. It had the following striking components:

(a) A limited recognition that there existed a perennial and irreconcilable conflict between private parties and the public interest, with the judges continually struggling against private restraints, sometimes in alliance with but sometimes opposed to the legislatures.

(b) The assertion of the existence of a solution of the judge's problem of what to do, in the form of:

(i) definitions of the various estates carefully phrased so as to render restraints on alienation "repugnant" to their"nature";

(ii) a general principle of hostility to "all" restraints on alienation, public or private, casting the judiciary in the role of the defender of the natural right of alienation against assaults from all sides; and

(iii) a general principal that private parties have an "absolute" control over the disposition of property, but no right at all to control the "form" or "nature" of property, whose definition is a state function.

144   (c) The retention within the law of real property of a large
residuum of unanalyzed technical doctrine still function-
ing to restrain private will but not yet recognized as anything more than a set of rules based on the nature of
things.

The Conflict Between the Courts and Family Pride

Kent took up restraints on alienation piecemeal in almost every
chapter on real property, but he had a general vision as well. That
vision "vibrated," as he might have put it, between the acknowl-
edgment and the suppression of conflict. He agreed with Coke
that the courts should refuse to enforce restraints imposed by private will because they are "repugnant to reason," and "unreasonable." [IV-136] He began his discussion of the then vast learning
of executory devises as follows:

> The history of executory devises presents an interesting view of
> the stable policy of the English common law, which abhorred per-
> petuities, and the determined spirit of the courts of justice to
> uphold that policy, and keep property free from the fetters of
> entailments, under whatever modification of form they might
> assume. Perpetuities, as applied to real estates, were conducive to
> the power and grandeur of ancient families, and gratifying to the
> pride of the aristocracy; but they were extremely disrelished, by
> the nation at large, as being inconsistent with the free and unfet-
> tered enjoyment of property. "The reluctant spirit of English lib-
> erty," said Lord Northington, "would not submit to the statute of
> entails; and Westminster Hall, siding with liberty, found means to
> evade it." Such perpetuities, said Lord Bacon, would bring in use
> the former inconveniences attached to entail; and he suggested
> that it was better for the sovereign and the subject, that men
> should be "in hazard of having their houses undone by unthrifty
> posterity, then be tied to the stake by such perpetuities." [IV-269-
> 70]

He concluded the same discussion with the remark that in spite of
"the constant dread of perpetuities, and the jealousy of executory

devises, as being an irregular and limited species of entail, a sense
of the convenience of such limitations in family settlements, has
enabled them, after a struggle of nearly two centuries, to come tri-
umphantly out of the contest." [IV-273] But his approach was far
more often to obscure this aspect behind a series of devices that
now seem no more than rhetorical.

Semantic Devices Reducing the Sense of Conflict

The notion of repugnancy seems today the most transparent. You
cannot attach a particular restraint to a particular estate because it
is part of the definition, i.e., the "nature," of that estate not to be
so limited. It just so happens that there does not exist, in the reper-
tory of estates, any capable of being qualified as you desire. It follows that you cannot achieve your objective, but no one has made
a policy or moral decision to thwart you. You simply can't get
there from here. [IV-4; 135-36]

A much more sophisticated approach was to claim that the
common law judges pursued a policy of securing the freedom of
citizens. The judges therefore opposed both attempts by the sovereign to limit the natural right of alienation and equally politically noxious attempts by individuals to do the same thing. Here
there was an attempt to turn the idea of freedom around, ignoring
the limitation on the exercise of private will and emphasizing that
the *recipients* of interests in property would be freer if unrestrained.
The first step in that argument was the characterization of the feudal restraints the sovereign had imposed on private landowners, in
favor of their overlords and their heirs respectively:

> A feoffment in fee did not originally pass an estate in the sense we
> now use it. It was only an estate to be enjoyed as a benefice, with-
> out the power of alienation, in prejudice of the heir or the lord;
> and the heir took it as a usufructuary interest, and in default of
> heirs, the tenure became extinct and the land reverted to the lord.
> The heir took by purchase, and independent of the ancestor, who
> could not alien, nor could the lord alien the seigniory without the
> consent of the tenant. This restraint on alienation was a violent
> and unnatural state of things, and contrary to the nature and value

146   of property, and the inherent and universal love of independence. It arose partly from favor to the heir, and partly from favor to the lord; and the genius of the feudal system was originally so strong in favor of restraint upon alienation, that by a general ordinance mentioned in the Book of Fiefs, the hand of him who knowingly wrote a deed of alienation was directed to be struck off. [III-779-80]

Kent took the second step in his "condensed view of the progress of the common law right of alienation from a state of servitude to freedom." [IV-475] After describing the various statutes and judicial decisions that eroded the feudal restraints in favor of lords and heirs, he proceeded, without transition of any kind, from the policy of the sovereign to that of individuals:

> In the time of Glanville, considerable relaxations as to the disposition of real property acquired by purchase, were tolerated. Conditional fees had been introduced by the policy of individuals, to impose further restraints upon alienation; but the tendency of public opinion in its favor induced the courts of justice, which had partaken of the same spirit, to give to conditional fees a construction inconsistent with their original intention. This led the feudal aristocracy to procure from Parliament the statute de donis of 13 Edw. I., which was intended to check the judicial construction, that had, in a great degree, discharged the conditional fee from the limitation imposed by the grant. Under that statute, fees conditional were changed into estates tail; and the contrivance which was afterwards resorted to and adopted by the courts, to elude the entailment and defeat the policy of the statute, by means of the fiction of a common recovery, has been already alluded to in a former part of the present volume. [IV-474]

The Distinction Between the Nature of Property and its Disposition

But the most interesting argument, and that which had by far the greatest influence on Classical legal thought, was one based on the distinction between the "nature" and the "disposition" of property. This distinction was at the very center of Kent's more general development of property as a right against the state:

> In England the right of alienation of land was long checked by the oppressive restraints of the feudal system, and the doctrine of entailments. All those embarrassments have been effectually removed in this country; and the right to acquire, to hold, to enjoy, to alien, to devise, and to transmit property by inheritance to one's descendants, in regular order and succession, is enjoyed in the fulness and perfection of the absolute right. Every individual has as much freedom in the acquisition, use, and disposition of his property, as is consistent with good order and the reciprocal rights of others....[T]he legislature has no right to limit the extent of the acquisition of property, as was suggested by some of the regulations in ancient Crete, Lacedaemon , and Athens; and has also been recommended in some modern utopian speculations. A state of equality as to property is impossible to be maintained, for it is against the laws of our nature; and if it could be reduced to practice, it would place the human race in a state of tasteless enjoyment and stupid inactivity, which would degrade the mind and destroy the happiness of social life. When the laws allow a free circulation to property by the abolition of perpetuities, entailments, the claims of primogeniture, and all inequalities of descent, the operation of the steady laws of nature will, of themselves, preserve a proper equilibrium, and dissipate the mounds of property as fast as they accumulate. [II-422-23]

Had the distinction occurred only in this passage, where its political function is transparent, one might doubt its reality as an aspect of the thought of the time. But Kent had not invented it to a special purpose; it was an established tool of analysis in conveyancing:

> Mr. Justice Buller observed, that if the testator made use of technical words only, the courts were bound to understand them in the legal sense. But if he used other words, manifestly indicating what his intention was, and that he did not mean what the technical words imported, the intention must prevail, if consistent with the

148 rules of law. That qualification applies only to the nature and operation of the estate devised, and not to the construction of the words. A man is not to be permitted by will to counteract the rules of law, and change the nature of property; and, therefore, he cannot create a perpetuity, or put the freehold in abeyance, or make a chattel descendible to heirs, or destroy the power of alienation by a tenant in fee or in tail. [IV-237]

Kent himself made it the key to the problem of liberality and technicality in the construction of wills:

> The intention of the testator is the first and great object of inquiry; and to this object technical rules are, to a certain extent, made subservient. The intention of the testator to be collected from the whole will, is to govern, provided it be not unlawful, or inconsistent with the rules of law. The control which is given to the intention by the rules of law is to be understood to apply, not to the construction of words, but to the nature of the estate—to such general regulations in respect to the estate as the law will not permit; as, for instance, to create an estate tail, to establish a perpetuity, to endow a corporation with real estate, to limit chattels and inheritances, to alter the character of real estate, by directing that it shall be considered as personal, or to annex a condition that the devisee in fee shall not alien. To allow the testator to interfere with the established rules of law, would be to permit every man to make a law for himself, and disturb the metes and bounds of property. [IV-586]

The Classical Approach

The Classical version of the problem, as represented by John Chipman Gray's small treatise on *Restraints on Alienation* (1883) is different in ways that reflect the transition from one consciousness to another, yet there is more continuity than will appear in the subjects taken up in the next chapter.

The striking innovation, as Gray was proud to point out, was the abstraction of the conflict between sovereign and individual will as a single problem capable of unified treatment:

Such errors as have risen in discussing restraints on alienation are largely due to the subject having been dealt with disconnectedly. If the restraint was in the form of a condition, it was treated with conditions. If it was in the form of a direction to a trustee, it was treated with trusts. Involuntary alienation, or liability for debts, has been considered without reference to voluntary transfers. It will be a gain to clear thought to bring the whole subject together. [Gray, Rest. 4-5]

The question was: "[U]nder what limitations, if any, does the law say it is against public policy to allow restraints to be put upon transfers which public policy does not forbid." [2] Once the disparate instances had been brought together, it became apparent that the various devices used to suppress the conflict had been mistaken: "The rule seems not to allow or call for any reason except public policy." [Id. 1-4]

The rule once justified on this basis, the remainder of the book works out its "logical" implications for the different kinds of estates. For example, Gray divided the whole into restraints in the form of conditions imposing forfeiture as a penalty for a forbidden alienation, and restraints in the form of limitations on the power of the grantee, without mention of forfeiture. Having established the rule against forfeiture in general on the ground of public policy, he introduced the discussion of simple limitations of power as follows:

As a gift over upon alienation by a tenant in fee simple, or one having the absolute interest in personalty, is void, so a fortiori any provision that such tenant or owner shall be seised or possessed of his property in spite of himself, that is, any provision against alienation, is void. [Id. 67]

Gray's book is a good example of the second stage of the will theory. He assumed that his readers were free of the kind of archaic thinking against which Kent battled interminably. The problem was to identify clearly the conflicting wills of the relevant legal actors, and to resolve that conflict deductively by reference to general principles. Indeed, he wrote at a time when the triumph of the rationalizing spirit had rendered the traditional learning irrelevant. The world of legal theory seemed on the brink of dramat-

150   ic advances in the formulation and elaboration of such principles. It was possible for an American analytical jurist writing in 1883 to begin his chapter on property, thus:

> In our law the most conspicuous division of property rights is into real and personal. This division is largely accidental. Though in any system of law property in immovable and in movable things cannot be treated exactly alike, yet the exaggerated importance which our law attaches to the difference is indefensible on any rational grounds. Still more absurd is the classification of the lesser estates in land, under the incongruous name of "chattels real," with rights in movables instead of with the other rights in land. How this came to be done can be explained by reference to certain historical facts which were its causes, but it cannot be reconciled with any principle of arrangement which ought to be resorted to in a system of modern law. I propose therefore in this chapter to lay out the subject on a somewhat different plan, bringing into greatest prominence those resemblances and differences which are of the greatest intrinsic importance. Tenure, which is theoretically extinct in some of the United States and practically so in all, and of no great importance in England, I shall pass over without notice;... [Terry 369]

Kent, by contrast, still paid homage to the "clearness," "accuracy" and "elegance of style" of Blackstone. [III-593; IV-4] Both the opportunities and what proved the insurmountable difficulties of the Classics were obscured for him by the continued viability of the old categorical scheme. Gray's confident generalization could come only after the critical spirit Kent had applied here and there to technicality had worked its solvent effect on the whole structure of imaginary property entities. Holmes' analysis of the law of easements, covenants and privity is one of the most striking examples of this process, as well as of the second stage of focus on the conflict of wills.

Extirpating the Residuum of Technicality

What Holmes did in his 1872 annotations to Kent's Commentaries was to show that two sets of rules Kent treated as mechanical derivations from the nature of particular property concepts ought to be understood as attempts to implement a basic policy. The first set of rules was that about easements. Their peculiarity was that they were a closed class of incorporeal hereditaments giving the owner of a dominant tenement the right to demand that the owner of the servient tenement suffer some interference with his power to use his land. Covenants, which Kent treated 420 pages further on, were promises made by one land owner to another respecting the two properties. Their peculiarity was stated by Kent as follows:

> The distinction between the covenants that are in gross and covenants that run with the land (and which are covenants real, annexed to or connected with the estate, and beneficial to the owner of it, and to him only) would seem to rest principally on this ground, that to make a covenant run with the land, there must be a subsisting privity of estate between the covenanting parties. [IV-517]

Holmes argued that both sets of rules were designed to prevent the creation of complex burdens that would "tie up land." One could not justify the rules that defeated the intentions of the grantor of the easement, or of the covenantor who intended to permanently modify the legal relationship of the owners of two pieces of land, on the "narrow ground" of privity, or on the ground that there are only so many "kinds" of easement "known to the law." "The law" was willing to restrain private will in particular in order to retain economic flexibility in general. "[T]he question of liability ought, in the United States, to be determined by considerations of policy...and a test of such doubtful meaning as privity between the parties should be abandoned." [IV-526]

He then considered the policy. His conclusion seems to have been that the modern trend toward making covenants run with the land, when the parties so intended and the covenant was meaningfully related to it was a good thing. [IV-526-28] In any case, by rejecting Kent's technical formulation, he made it possible to get at the policy overtly. And when he and Gray did go at the policies, they rejected the formula of liberality. They tended to see the

152 problem in terms of the sacrifice of the individual to the group rather than in the more rosy hue of conflicts overcome, and they were proud of their clear-sighted tough-mindedness (as they seem to have thought it).

This brings us to a final aspect of the emergence of Classical property law: the growth of the idea that, the landowner's rights being absolute so long as he acts within the boundaries of his lands, he is entitled to inflict various kinds of damages on his neighbor without having to pay any compensation. It was here that the tough-mindedness of the young appeared to contrast most starkly to the question begging liberality of the old.

The Strategy of Autonomy in Property Law

The emergence of the will theory meant that the question of what rules should govern private interaction presented itself in terms of a conflict of private and public will. But the will theory did not answer the question of what policy the judges should pursue when they had the power to shape the rules themselves. There was, however, a bias associated with the will theory——that in favor of autonomy.

In the context of property law, autonomy had two meanings. First, it meant an effort to prevent "dormant encumbrances" (Kent's description of dower), perpetuities, and complex inter-relations of estates that would reduce the marketability of land. The program aimed at a situation in which each piece of land would be under the control of a single legal actor with a power to develop it or sell it that was both complete and easy to establish to the satisfaction of others. The second meaning of autonomy was that adjoining landowners should have a minimum of power to control each other's use of property. In practice, this meant the elimination or attenuation of the rights of "quiet enjoyment" which an owner could assert to prevent a neighbor from engaging in activities that disturbed him.

Autonomy was one of the strands of liberality, one of the characteristics that distinguished it from technicality. Kent's position on restraints on alienation and other complex encumbrances such as dower was a first attempt to generalize a version of autonomy to all estates in land. During the second quarter of the 19th century, the courts went much further than he would have in the piecemeal implementation of this vision. Gray and Holmes, the Classical successors, did not do much more than to precipitate out a general theory and show it to be more pervasively relevant than even Kent had thought.

Pre-Classical thinkers seem to have been less self-conscious about the constriction of the landowner's rights of quiet enjoyment. Fortunately for us, Morton Horwitz has collected and analyzed the mass of cases. I will limit myself to a summary of his conclusions, which provide a striking confirmation of the general description of Classical legal thought.

Horwitz distinguished three phases in the law of easements. The doctrine of 1800, heavily influenced by England, amounted to a proliferation of easements so as to give the owner relief against almost anything a neighbor might do in the way of damage. This liability was based on the idea that ownership meant a right to compensation for injuries, rather than on any theory of fault or negligence in the other party, and it was prototypically "technical." The trend in the other direction began with *Thurston v. Hancock*, a Massachusetts case of 1815, which held that, if he exercised due care, Ebenezer Hancock could excavate on his Beacon Hill building lot right up to his boundary line, even though this caused a house built on a neighboring lot to fall. *Thurston* came to represent the general idea of treating injuries caused by what an owner did within his own boundaries as *damnum absque injuria*.

At first, the courts replaced the "quiet enjoyment" emphasis of 18th century law with "reasonableness" tests. For example, in the law of riparian rights, the old doctrine gave an owner an absolute right to existing flows. The intermediate phase was one in which the courts allowed mill owners, for example, to make reasonable diversions and interferences without liability to those injured. Similarly, in 1836, in interpreting the *Thurston* rule, the Massachusetts court spoke of the "absolute dominion" of the excavating landowner, his right to "consult his own convenience," but nonetheless stated clearly that "malice" would render an undermining excavation legally actionable. This was

154 the phase of the ideal of liberality, with its tendency to fuzz the issues behind appeals to progress and immanent social rationality.

In the third phase, beginning in the 1850's and continuing through the Civil War, the courts began to cut off cleanly the owner's rights to protection against damage caused by what neighbors did within the boundaries of their land. Counsel in an 1855 New York case summed up this development: "There is much vulgar error touching rights supposed to exist beyond the line of the lot owner's boundary. Much of it has been exploded in this country." He then cited cases restricting riparian rights, ancient lights, support from adjoining land, and the right to existing unobstructed prospect.

The New York courts held that by erecting a barrier on his own land, an owner could divert the flow of draining surface water onto his neighbor's land. Moreover, he could drain his neighbor's well, so long as he tapped the underground water by a shaft on his own land. At the same time, the courts began to argue that the absoluteness of rights precluded any inquiry either into the subjective malice or the objective reasonableness of their exercise.

The constriction of easements corresponded in time to the rise of the general principle of liability for negligence, which we will examine in the next chapter. As the owner lost his right to be compensated for injuries regardless of his neighbor's state of mind in inflicting them, he acquired a right to insist that whatever his neighbor did, he do it with reasonable care. The owner therefore retained some power to control adjoining property. The point is that there was a sharp reduction in the legal recognition of interdependence. Horwitz summed up the total evolution in a passage that deserves full quotation:

> There were essentially three stages in the development of American law relating to conflicting uses of property. In the first stage, which continued until roughly 1825, the dominant theme was expressed by the maxim sic utere. Dominion over land was defined primarily as the right to prevent others from using their property in an injurious manner, regardless of the social utility of a particular course of conduct. This system began to break down

in the second quarter of the nineteenth century as it became clear not only that common law doctrines led to anti-competitive results, but that the burdens on economic growth under such a system might prove overwhelming. With the limitations imposed on the scope of the nuisance doctrine as well as the emergence of the negligence principle, and the riparian doctrine of reasonable use, courts began to strike a balance between competing land uses, freeing many economically desirable but injurious activities from legal liability if exercised with due care. Thus, in a second stage which crystalized by the middle of the nineteenth century, property law had come largely to be based on a set of reciprocal rights and duties whose enforcement required courts to perform the "social engineering" function of balancing the utility of economically productive activity against the harm that would accrue.

In the two decades before the Civil War, however, one detects an increasing tendency by judges to apply the balancing test in such a way as to presume that any productive activity was reasonable regardless of the harm that resulted. And out of this intellectual climate, a third stage began to emerge which self-confidently announced that there were no legal restraints at all on certain kinds of injurious activities. In a number of new and economically important areas, courts began to hold that there were no reciprocal duties between property owners; that courts would not even attempt to strike a balance between the harm and the utility of particular courses of conduct. While this trend only reached its culmination after the Civil War, its roots nevertheless were deep in an antebellum change in the conception of property. For dominion over land had begun to be regarded as an absolute right to engage in any conduct on one's property regardless of its economic value. And with this shift in attitudes, judges began to withdraw to some extent from their role of regulating the type and degree of economic activity that could be undertaken, and the mercantilist character of American property law was diluted by an emerging laissez-faire ideology. [p. 74-76]

In this chapter we are concerned only with the substance of the changes in legal rules and concepts during the period of the emergence of Classicism. When we have a full picture of the shift in

156   the map of legal consciousness, we will examine various explana-
tory hypotheses. Different writers have invoked concrete economic interests, theories or strategies of national economic development, ideas like mercantilism and laissez-faire, belief in the
"natural right" of property, and what appeared to be the internal
logic of fundamental legal conceptions. It is enough to say that all
of these quite obviously played a part in the emergence of the
strategy of autonomy in property law, and that any attempt to
explain the evolution of legal thought must recognize the complexity and ambiguity of their interrelationships.

What is important for our present purposes is that liberality,
here taking the form of a "reasonableness" test by which judges
regulated conflicting land uses, was not an adequate response to
the dilemma of autonomy vs. community. Just as liberality
seemed to dodge the issues of formality and of the confrontation
of sovereign and individual will, it suppressed the problem of
autonomy rather than admitting or transcending it. The Classics
resolved it at an abstract level through absoluteness; the moderns
confront it piecemeal, as did the ante-bellum writers, but without
any sense that particular resolutions are more than the contingent
outcome of the balancing of local interests.

There is a striking parallel between the emerging ante-bellum
ideas of a property owner absolute within the boundaries of his
land and of a state absolute within its borders. These two conceptions are the source of the "powers absolute within their spheres"
imagery of Classical legal thought. The accomplishment of the
later thinkers was to abstract and generalize the fundamental
notion, and to show that the entire legal system could be analyzed
into a structure of complexly interlocked, everchanging absolute-
nesses. But before we can take up this process, we must complete
our review of the structure of pre-Classical private law thinking
by examining the use of the concept of "implied intent" as an
alternative to liberality. In the process, we will survey substantive
areas of law that underwent a much greater transformation
through Classicism than did real property.

CHAPTER IV

Pre-Classical Private Law:
The Transformation of Contract

THIS CHAPTER DESCRIBES the breakup of the pre-Classical vision of all of legal obligation as essentially contractual, and the emergence of the Classical vision of law as concerned with establishing spheres of autonomy for the wills of legal actors. It seems worth repeating that we are still concerned with the horizontal dimension of legal consciousness, with describing the ways in which an existing mass of legal rules were integrated into subsystems. In the next chapter, the addition of the vertical dimension, within which rules and principles are linked hierarchically, will make it possible to address Classical legal thought as a whole.

~ 1 ~

Beside the ideal of liberality, the second important mediating concept within pre-Classical legal thought was "implied intent." When pre-Classical thinkers had to justify a rule, or explain an area of doctrine, they often appealed to the "justice and policy" of the situation. They also referred constantly to the intent of the parties, meaning the actual desires and goals and understandings of the particular legal actors involved. Implied intent was a cate-

158   gory situated at about an equal distance from these three justifying ideas of morality, policy and actual intent.

Like liberality, implied intent was a child of 18th century enlightment, and specifically of the law reforming enthusiasm of Lord Mansfield. As with liberality, the idea had a powerful appeal to Chancellor Kent. His discussion of the revocation of wills contained a typical use of the concept:

> A will may be revoked by implication or inference of law; and these revocations are not within the purview of the statute [requiring wills to be executed formally]; and they have given rise to some of the most difficult and interesting discussions existing on the subject of wills. They are founded upon the reasonable presumption of an alteration of the testator's mind, arising from circumstances since the making of the will, producing a change in his previous obligations and duties. [IV-572-73]

In the context of wills, the concept blurred the distinction between what people actually intend and what they ought to intend. Another problem for which implied intent provided a solution was that of making people intend what convenience or policy would like to have as the rule. For example, in rationalizing a particular pattern of easements, Kent said:

> Sergeant Williams is of opinion, that the right of way when claimed by necessity, is founded entirely upon grant, and derives its force and origin from it. It is either created by express words, or it is created by operation of law, as incident to the grant; so that, in both cases, the grant is the foundation to the title. If this be a sound construction of the rule, then it follows, that, in the cases I have mentioned, the right of the grantor to a way over the land he has sold, to his remaining land, must be founded upon an implied restriction, incident to the grant, and that it cannot be supposed the grantor meant to deprive himself of all use of his remaining land. This would be placing the right upon a reasonable foundation, and one consistent with the general principles of law. [III -424]

Lord Mansfield attempted to use implied intent to reconstruct the law of contracts on an overtly ethical basis unencumbered by technical concepts of formation and consideration. His famous opinion in the case of *Moses v. Macpherlan* contained the following language:

> If the defendant be under an obligation, from the ties of natural justice, to refund, the law implies a debt, and gives this action [indebitatus assumpsit], founded in the equity of the plaintiff"s case, as it were upon a contract (quasi ex contractu, as the Roman Law expresses it).

Contract students sometimes get the impression that this was the first case recognizing the existence of a distinction between a cause of action on the contract for expectation damages and a cause of action in quasi-contract for restitution of benefits conferred. This is incorrect. What Mansfield did was to suggest not a new cause of action for restitution, but a new general theory of the basis of contractual liability. This theory fused individual intention with community morality and commercial policy. In this respect, it differed sharply from the Classical and modern theories, with their insistence on carefully discriminating these elements. It differed no less from the approach of the traditional common lawyers, who offered lists of the requirements of success in the actions of debt and/or assumpsit rather than justifications of the phenomenon of liability.

The particular rules Mansfield proposed to instantiate his theory were, in many cases, rejected, and the common law forms of action endured in America another 70 years. But Mansfield"s approach to intent was the basis of the emergence of contract in place of property as the main organizing concept of mid-nineteenth century law. We have already referred to *Parsons on Contracts* as representative of this vision. Here are the opening paragraphs of the work:

> The Law of Contracts, in its widest extent, may be regarded as including nearly all the law which regulates the relations of human life. Indeed, it may be looked upon as the basis of human society. All social life presumes it, and rests upon it; for out of contracts, express or implied, declared or understood, grow all rights, all duties, all obligations, and all law. Almost the whole

procedure of human life implies, or, rather, is, the continual fulfilment of contracts...

It would be easy to go farther, and show that, in all the relations of social life, its good order and prosperity depend upon the due fulfilment of the contracts which bind all to all. Sometimes these contracts are deliberately expressed with all the precision of law, and are armed with all its sanctions. More frequently they are, though still expressed, simpler in form and more general in language, and leave more to the intelligence, the justice, and honesty of all the parties. Far more frequently they are not expressed at all; and for their definition and extent we must look to the common principles which all are supposed to understand and acknowledge. In this sense, contract is coordinate and commensurate with duty; and it is a familiar principle of the law, of which we shall have much to say hereafter, and which has a wide though not a universal application, that whatsoever it is certain a man ought to do, that the law supposes him to have promised to do. "Implied contracts," says Blackstone (Vol. ii, p. 443,) "are such as reason and justice dictate, and which, therefore, the law presumes that every man undertakes to perform." These contracts form the web and woof of actual life. If they were wholly disregarded, the movement of society would be arrested. And in so far as they are disregarded, that movement is impeded or disordered. [I - 3-4]

The most striking of the uses of implied intent to contract was in the treatment as contractual of family law subjects previously classified under the "Law of Persons." Parsons was aware that this posed difficulties.

Even those duties, or those acts of kindness and affection which may seem most remote from contract or compulsion of any kind, are nevertheless within the scope of the obligation of contracts. The parental love which provides for the infant when, in the beginning of its life, it can do nothing for itself, nor care for itself, would seem to be so pure an offering of affection, that the idea of a contract would in no way belong to it. But even here, although these duties are generally discharged from a feeling which borrows no strength from a sense of obligation, there is still such an

obligation. It is implied by the cares of the past, which have per-
petuated society from generation to generation; by that absolute
necessity which makes the performance of these duties the condition of the preservation of human life; and by the implied obligation on the part of the unconscious objects of this care, that when,
by its means, they shall have grown into strength, and age has
brought weakness upon those to whom they are thus indebted,
they will acknowledge and repay the debt. Indeed, the law recognizes and enforces this obligation to a certain degree, on both
sides, as will be shown hereafter. [I - 3-4]

The chapter on infants illustrates the use of implied intent as a
mediator of the conflict of morality and policy. The question was
the liability of parents to pay debts contracted for necessaries by
their children.

The obligation of the father to maintain the child is and always
has been recognized in some way and in some degree, in all civilized countries. The infant cannot support himself. Others must
therefore supply him with the means of subsistence; and the only
question is, whether the public (that is, the State), shall do this, or
shall his parent. And justice, equally with the best affections of
our nature, answer that it is the duty of the parent. But it is a very
difficult question how far this duty is made a legal obligation, by
the common law.

In England, after much questioning, and perhaps a tendency to
hold the father liable for necessaries supplied to the child, on the
ground of moral obligation and duty, it seems to be, on the whole,
settled that this moral obligation is not a legal one; and indeed it
has been recently peremptorily decided that no such legal obligation exists in the case of contracts made by the child for necessaries. The father's liability is nevertheless admitted in many
English cases, but is now put on the ground of agency; and the
authority of the infant to bind the father by contracts for necessaries is inferred, both in England and in this country, from very
slight evidence. [I - 247-50]

American law exhibited the same movement from direct appeal to
moral obligation toward the agency idea. The plasticity of the

162   concept of agency as Parsons was using it was very great. It was designed to do justice, and Parsons was unwilling to accept it as a constraint. This became clear when he considered the situations in which there would be no liability if we took agency seriously:

> If we take the case of necessaries supplied to an infant actually incapacitated by want of age, or by disease of mind or body, from making any contract, or acting in any way as the agent of any person, the father cannot be made liable excepting on the ground of his parental obligation; and some of the cases cited in the two last notes indicate, perhaps, that the question would be decided in England in favor of this liability on his part. It will be noticed, that where it is most distinctly denied that this moral obligation of the parent constitutes a legal obligation the denial is confined to a liability for the contracts of the child. The reason is said to be, the danger of permitting a father to be bound in this way, and it is variously illustrated in the cases; but this reason fails where the infant can make no contracts, and must be supplied or suffer. [I - 250-251]

What this meant was that the implied agency idea was a means of justifying a compromise between the moral obligation to support and the policy against encouraging false or frivolous claims against parents. When this policy became irrelevant, the court ought to discard the mediating concept.

Parsons treated the case where the father clearly had no intention of authorizing his child as agent as follows:

> So far as the duty of support certainly belongs to the parent as a legal obligation, and is neglected, any other person may perform it, and will be regarded as performing it for him; and, on general principles, the law will raise a promise on the part of the parent, to compensate the party who thus did for him what he was bound by law to do. [I - 254]

Where the father went so far as to formalize his intention not to be responsible, Parsons had at last to abandon his obfuscatory language:

It is very common in this country to see in the newspapers an advertisement signed by a father, stating that he has given to his minor son "his time" and that he will make no future claim on his services or for his wages, and will pay no debts of his contracting. But if a stranger supplied a son, at a distance from his home, with suitable necessaries, in ignorance of such arrangement, there is no sufficient reason for holding that it would bar his claim against the father. And we think that he might recover from the father for strict necessaries, even if he knew this arrangement. On what ground could the father discharge himself from his liability by such a contract? Even if the father had paid the son a consideration for the release of all further obligation, it would be a contract with an infant, and void or voidable, because certainly not for necessaries. And the whole policy and reason of the law of infancy would seem to be opposed to permitting a father to cast his son in this way upon the public, and relieve himself from the obligation of maintenance. [I - 258]

The net effect of the use of the implication idea was that except in the case of express disclaimer, the discussion of the obligation of the parent to support the infant never directly confronted the conflict of morality and policy. The infant's claim might have compelling moral force. But the recognition of it would embroil the legal system in the regulation of fragile relationships to the detriment of both courts and families. But so long as we speak only of agency and the "raising" of promises, this problem can be kept on the periphery.

The use of a mediating concept like implied intent does *not* imply unconsciousness or ignorance of the conflicts mediated. It affects our perception of their importance, their pressingness, their pervasiveness, without concealing or resolving them. It makes it possible to admit, in a *few* cases, what we could not admit everywhere. So at the end of a discussion of the husband's duty to support his wife that paralleled that of parent and child, Parsons could openly acknowledge the limits of implied intent. The particular question was the husband's liability for the wife's necessaries purchased against his express prohibition:

164   It seems, however, absurd to say that a man who has driven his wife
from his house and his presence and manifested by extreme cruelty
his utter hatred of her, was all the time constituting her his agent, and
investing her with authority to bind him and his property. And if we
suppose the case, where a wife perfectly incapacitated by infirmity of
body or mind from making any contract at all, is supplied with necessaries by one who finds her driven from home and ready to perish,
and who now comes to her husband for indemnity, we cannot doubt
that he would recover. But the proposition would seem too absurd
even to take its place among the fictions of law, that the wife, when
she received this aid, promised in the husband's name that he would
pay for it, and that he had given her a sufficient authority to make this
promise for him. For these and other reasons, courts now show a tendency to rest the responsibility of the husband for necessaries supplied to the wife, on the duty which grows out of the marital relation.
He is her husband; he is the stronger, she the weaker; all that she has
is his; the act of marriage destroys her capacity to pay for a loaf with
her own money; and all she then possesses, and all she may afterwards
acquire, are his during life and marriage; upon him must rest, with
equal fulness, if the law would not be the absolute opposite of justice,
the duty of maintaining her and supplying all her wants according to
his ability. And we think this plain rule of common sense and common morality is becoming a rule of the common law. [I - 290-291]

The notion of implied intent played just as great a role in commercial as in family law. There, too, there was a constant perception of a conflict between morality and policy, and a constant
search for formulae that would reduce the acuteness of that conflict. For example, Parsons acknowledged that the institution of
negotiability had been seen as involving concessions granted by
morality to policy: the cutting off of equitable defenses had to be
justified. Here is how he did it:

It is generally said that the law of bills and notes is exceptional;
that they are choses in action, which, by the policy of the law mer-
chant, and to satisfy the necessities of trade and business, are permitted to be assigned as other choses in action cannot be. But the
law of negotiable paper may be considered as resting on other

grounds. If A. owes B. one hundred dollars, and gives him a 165
promissory note wherein he promises to pay that sum to him,
(without any words extending the promise to another,) this note is
not negotiable; and if it be assigned it is so under the general rule
of law, and is subject in the hands of the assignee to all equitable
defenses. But if A. in his note promises to pay B. or his order, then
the original promise is in the alternative, and it is this which makes
the note negotiable. The promise is to pay either B. or some one
else to whom B. shall direct the payment to be made. And when B.
orders the payment to be made to C., then C. may demand it
under the original promise. He may say that the promise was
made to B., but it was a promise to pay C. as soon as he should
come within the condition that is, as soon as he should become the
payee by order of B. [I - 202-03]

The doctrine of respondeat superior provides a somewhat more
complicated example. The problem was to explain why the law
held the master when the master had neither been negligent nor
given instructions to be negligent. Parsons' solution was as follows:

> The responsibility of the master grows out of, is measured by, and
> begins and ends with his control of the servant. It is true that the
> policy of holding a master to a reasonable care and discretion in
> the choice of a servant may cause a liberal construction of the rule
> in respect to an injured party, and may therefore be satisfied in
> some instances with a slight degree of actual control; but, of the
> soundness and general applicability of the principle itself, we do
> not doubt; nor do we see any greater difficulty in the application
> of the principle than may always be apprehended from the variety
> and complexity of the facts to which this and other legal principles
> may be applied. The master is responsible for what is done by one
> who is in his constant control, and may direct him from time to
> time as he sees fit; and therefore the acts of the servant are the acts
> of the master because the servant is at all times only an instru-
> ment; and one is not liable for a person who is a servant only by
> construction, excepting so far as this essential element of control
> and direction exists between them. [I - 87-88]

166   A few pages later, Parsons began to substitute "power of directing" for actual control [I - 90-91] and finally pointed that the matter of control was for the jury. [I - 92] The master's control was
inherently fictional. It was a basis for imputing responsibility that
obscured the difficulty involved in imposing liability without fault.
        By far the longest section of Parsons' discussion of considera-
tion doctrine concerned the "many nice questions" that arise when
a claim is made that plaintiff has benefited defendant without any
contemporaneous promise of reimbursement. The general rule
was that "a past or executed consideration is not sufficient to sustain a [subsequent] promise founded upon it, unless there was a
request for the consideration previous to its being done or made."
But the reader who stopped with the general rule risked serious
misconception since:

> This previous request need not always be expressed, or proved,
> because it is often implied. As, ... where one accepts or retains the
> beneficial result of such voluntary service. Here, the law general-
> ly implies both a previous request and a subsequent promise of
> repayment.

        Language of this kind occurs in modern treatises and judicial
opinions but it has lost all persuasive effect. Implied intent is
meaningless. We have substituted (a) tort liability based on fault
or the policy calculus of liability without fault, (b) the objective
theory of contracts based on the "reasonable man" standard, and
(c) quasi-contracts or estoppel arguments appealing directly to the
judges responsibility for distributive justice between the parties. It
is hard for us to believe that the addition of fudging categories and
language such as "he makes it his own" add anything. The explanation of our attitude lies in the devastating assault Classical legal
thinkers leveled at the approach Parsons typified.
        That assault was aimed at more than the ambiguities of the
concept of implication. The fudging of the distinctions between
the actual intentions of the party and the intentions of the judge
based on morality or policy had been part of a larger vision of the
legal order. As Pound pointed out in 1918, the key to that attitude
was the idea of relationship.

Parsons' book was organized on the premise that there were four requirements for the creation of a contract: parties, consideration, mutual assent, and a subject matter. The sections on consideration and assent comprise about 60 pages; those on parties, 350; and those on subject matter, about 300. The initial 350 pages on parties contains the following divisions:

Agents	Parties by Novation
Factors & Brokers	Parties by Assignment
Servants	Parties to Negotiable Instruments
Attorneys	Infants
Trustees	Married Women
Executors & Administrators	Bankrupts & Insolvents
Guardians	Lunatics
Corporations	Aliens
Joint Stock Co.'s	Slaves
Partnerships	Outlaws

The subject matters were the following:

Sale of Real Estate	Hiring of Persons
Hiring of Real Estate	Service Contracts Generally
Sale of Goods	Marriage
Warranty	Bailment
Hiring of Goods	

Each of these categories represented for Parsons a social entity with its own positive body of expectations of the parties and its own set of moral obligations tempered by policy. This is *not* to say that there was no general theory of contract. The general theory of contract was the body of principles that governed the interaction of morality, policy, actual intent and implied intent in the different relationships that define social life. These are ideas like pacta sunt servanda, estoppel against denying things after others have relied on one, the presumption that people intend to perform their moral duty, the desirability of encour-

168   aging transactions. The development or rationalization of a body of contract rules meant showing that within the context of a particular relationship the rules comported with these principles.

The importance of context dominated the organization of the book. For example, the discussion of infants includes both the question of the parent's obligation to support and a discussion of the validity of the infant's contracts on his own behalf. It also raises the question of the infant's duty to support his parent and the parent's responsibility for the infant's contracts for necessaries. In the discussion of partnership, Parsons found it "convenient" to deal with the organization and internal arrangement of the institution as an adjunct of the discussion of the special character of partners as parties in contracts with third persons.

The chapter on Bailment began by referring to "systematic arrangement" and "profound and accurate investigation into its principles," and defined the subject in terms of the delivery of property by one to another for a special purpose. It included the "rights and duties of the parties in relation to the property and to each other." [I - 569] But of the 150 pages he devoted to this subject, no fewer than 90 in fact concerned the law of common carriers. Parsons described their liabilities for the carriage of passengers with no reference at all to property bailed and included a detailed review of duty of care under different circumstances, and even some paragraphs on the law of railroad injuries to pure strangers. Bailment, the legal category, was a pretext for a discussion of all the legal aspects of the social and economic category.

The idea of relationship was important if not essential to the plausibility of the idea of implication because it provided a source for the intentions and duties the judge imposed on the parties. Parsons spoke constantly of reasonable expectations in the situation of agent, or broker, or guardian, or innkeeper. These standards he never clearly imputed to actual intent, to morality, or to policy. They were "there" in the relationship without a sharp need to identify their source.

In light of this, it would be more accurate to identify as the

mediating concept an amalgam: the process of implication of   169
intent based on reasonableness within the context of one of the
basic social-legal relationships. The judge working within such a
conceptual frame of reference could feel that he was carrying out
an objective judicial task that did not require him to confront
directly the problem of conflict between morality and policy that
pervaded private law as he experienced it. Implied intent without
a belief in the background of conventionally defined relationships
might have seemed open to arbitrary manipulation. Relationship
without the imputation of assent and assumption of responsibility
might have seemed pure judicial imposition.

The two taken together bear an interesting relationship to the
notion of implied limitations in constitutional law. The implied
limitations concept allowed the judge to draw on the elaborate
context of natural rights philosophy and political theory without
abandoning the claim that he was a positivist carrying out the will
of the constitutional sovereign. Implied limitations therefore
could mediate the contradiction of sovereignty and natural right
without pretending to resolve it. Implied intent permitted the
same kind of reference to ideals and usages without abandonment
of the claim that the obligations imposed had been voluntarily
assumed.

Implied intent was also a part of the program of liberality,
rather than an altogether separate concept. The liberal notion that
law could abandon the "rigorous, artificial, strict, and technical"
forms of the feudal common law was implausible, unless one
could point to alternative sources, both of content for rules, and
of objectively determinable facts on which to found judicial
action. Implied intent provided a solution wherever the quarreling
parties were linked by a socially defined relationship. The liberal
program called for flexible interpretation of words and acts, for
the recognition of intent, and for flexible judicial remedial
response to abuses. All of these were achieved in an apparently
certain and non-arbitrary way when the judge appealed to implied
intent for standards of reasonable expectations and behavior. The
concept gave him access to morals, policy and actual intent, but
required no discussion of any of them.

Parsons thought of his work as part of a trend. In his Introduction, he pointed out that Blackstone had devoted only a single chapter, called "Of title by gift, grant, and contract" to his subject matter. He remarked that of the many treatises since published, "the latest are the largest." "But", he went on, "I have thought that a work of still wider extent, that is, embracing some topics not usually presented in these treatises, and exhibiting the principles of law upon many subjects more fully, would be useful to the student and practitioner." [I-vii] Treatises continued to grow larger, but the theory Parsons used to annex all of substantive law except real property to contracts was superseded by the quite different organizational scheme of the Classics. The rest of this chapter deals with the impact of will theory, absoluteness and objectivism on the elements that constituted contracts in 1850. This section describes the implications of will theory for the organization of legal rules into distinct doctrinal fields.

Parsons almost never referred to the "will" of the parties or even of the state; nor did Kent or Story. For them, the crucial category had been "intention." The change in the dominant word after 1870 was more than formal. It signified a new preoccupation with locating a legal actor whose wishes would control the judge. "Will" suggested that controlling actor's dominance; it suggested that he was empowered by the legal order to determine the outcome, and acted with that power in mind. The category of intention, by contrast, suggested the whole pre-Classical apparatus based on the process of judicial implication, stereotyped social relationships, and the norm of reasonable behavior.

The pre-Classical approach blurred the distinctions between parties and judge, actual intent and moral duty, privately desired outcomes and socially desired outcomes. The essence of will was that it was on uncompromisingly *positive* concept. It represented a self-conscious decision to avoid fuzzing policy, morality and actual intention, and to avoid ambiguity about *whose* will was involved in any particular situation. Will was also positiv*ist*, in the sense that those who used it were insisting that the judge was always at the beck of some lawmaker, the sovereign or the holder of a legal right derived from the Constitution. The judge's task was to do that actor's bidding, not to twist or interpret his bidding into something compatible with the judge's view of policy or morality.

The adoption of the will theory was manifested in (a) the dismantling of contracts by the spinning off of Quasi-Contract and Tort; (b) the rise in jurisprudence of an ordering of private law based on two distinctions: rights against the world versus rights against individuals; and rights arising from private agreement vs. those created by the state; (c) the emergence of the concept of status to deal with legal relationships organized in a way inconsistent with this scheme; (d) the reordering of the residuum of pure contract in terms of the will of the parties and the will of the sovereign; and (e) the organization of the brand new field of tort law into intentional tort, negligence and absolute liability.

The Emergence of Quasi-Contract

Parsons assumed that his readers were familiar with two forms of action, both loosely called contractual: an action "on the contract" or in "special assumpsit," and an action of "general assumpsit" based not on the express terms of the parties agreement but on the duties arising out of their relationship. This pleading distinction was *not* the basis of a distinction between contract and quasi-contract as we understand them. The category of general assumpsit included both what we would call contracts "implied in fact," or based on an inference of actual intent from conduct, and obligations imposed by law regardless of intent. Parsons treated recoveries in general assumpsit, where an express contract was void, as "contractual," even where we see them as not consensual at all. [I-57-58]

Take the case of the infant who receives goods, and then repudiates his promise to pay for them. Everyone agreed that an executory contract between an infant and an adult was void, but could the infant retain the goods while refusing to pay? There was a strong argument, based on the simple proposition that general

172 assumpsit was a contract action, that the infant could do exactly that. It was even possibly the case that an infant who rescinded his own contract ipso facto cut off his own restitutionary remedy for his uncompensated part performance. The opposition to these results rested on the "equity" of allowing general assumpsit in the particular circumstances, rather than on appeal to a recognized cause of action for unjust enrichment. [I-265-268]. Somewhat similar problems arose with breaching plaintiffs in employment contracts. [I-522-526]

The lumping of implied-in-fact with implied-in-law contracts has struck classical and modern legal thinkers as supremely irrational. The tendency has been to attribute it either simply to "confusion" or to archaic thinking controlled by the forms of action. But what we have said already about the concept of implied intent should make it clear that the category is typically pre-Classical. The suppression of the sharp distinction between the will of the state and that of the individual was a general principle rather than an aberration.

The emergence of the modern notion began with the Pennsylvania case of *Hertzog v. Hertzog*, decided in 1856. The court drew the distinction as follows:

> There is some looseness of thought in supposing that reason and justice ever dictate any contracts between parties, or impose such upon them. All contracts grow out of the intentions of the parties to transactions, and are dictated only by their mutual and accordant wills. When this intention is expressed, we call the contract an express one. When it is not expressed, it may be inferred, implied, or presumed, from circumstances as really existing, and then the contract, thus ascertained, is called an implied one. The instances given by Blackstone are an illustration of this.
>
> But it appears in another place, 3 Comm. 159-66, that Blackstone introduces this thought about reason and justice dictating contracts, in order to embrace, under his definition of an implied contract, another large class of relations, which involve no intention to contract at all, though they may be treated as if they did. Thus, whenever, not our variant notions of reason and justice, but the common sense and common justice of the country,

and therefore the common law or statute law imposed upon any one a duty, irrespective of contract, and allow it to be enforced by a contract remedy, he calls this a case of implied contract. . . . The latter class are merely constructive contracts, while the former are truly implied ones. In one case the contract is mere fiction, a form imposed in order to adapt the case to a given remedy; in the other it is a fact legitimately inferred. In one, the intention is disregarded; in the other it is ascertained and enforced. [K&G - 122]

As far as I am able to determine, this is the first American case to make the distinction. In *all* previous cases, the protection of the restitutionary interest through the general assumpsit form of action is carried out without allusion to any distinction between private and public will. *Hertzog* is conventionally the earliest case cited in opinions of the 1870-1910 period.

In the early 1860's a second, much enlarged edition of Austin's *Jurisprudence* was published, and quickly acquired a readership far larger than Austin had been able to command when he wrote and lectured in the 1830's. This book and Maine's *Ancient Law* (1861) created a whole new area of learning for American legal thinkers. They began to study not the masses of Roman and medieval *rules* that had been the mark of erudition for the older generation, but rather pure Roman law *theory*. The distinction between the will of the parties and the will of the state played an important part in that theory, and Austin (in lectures only included in the later edition) and Maine discussed it. The second American reference to quasi-contract was by Justice Field in *Pacific-Steamship Co. v. Joliff*, decided in 1864, citing Maine and a California case not in point. *Leake on Contracts* referred prominently to the concept in 1867. The third American allusion appears to have been a sentence by Holmes in his first legal article in the American Law Review in 1871. In the next year, he brought out his 12th edition of Kent's *Commentaries*. No earlier edition of the work mentioned the distinction. All Holmes did was to append the following footnote to the initial definition of a contract:

The student should take notice that the phrase implied contract means two things, which have no connection with each other. It is

174 applied in the first place to those contracts, properly express, where the promise is signified by other means than by words, as when a man orders goods at a shop, and says nothing further. Austin on Jurisp. 3d. ed. 325. Secondly, to a class of cases which are not contracts at all, but which the law by a fiction treats as contracts, implying, as it is said, the request, consideration, or promise in order to render the common law forms of action ex-contractu available. This fiction has always been a source of confusion, and is not needed where forms of action are abolished, and a recovery may be had on a simple statement of facts. See *Hertzog v. Hertzog*, 29 Penn. St. 465; [Holmes in] 5 Am. Law Rev. 11, 12. [II-608]

After 1870, the progress of the idea was rapid. The question of whether or not to distinguish arose whenever statutes prescribed particular procedures for actions "sounding in contract" as opposed to others. It arose also in the case of the supply of necessaries to legal incompetents who refused to pay for them and then pleaded the invalidity of the contract of sale. In New Hampshire in 1872 and New York in 1879 these situations led to rather elaborate disquisitions on the importance of keeping the will of the sovereign clear of the will of the parties. In Bishop and Page, the leading treatises after Parsons and before Williston, much introductory space was devoted to the distinction in order to set up very clearly that the theme of contracts proper was utterly distinct from that of quasi-contract. In 1893, Keener completed the development by publishing a *Treatise on the Law of Quasi-Contracts*, summarizing and systematizing what had happened since *Hertzog v. Hertzog*. Keener began by stating the division of contracts into Express, Implied in Fact and Implied in Law, thereby showing that, by 1893, the essential distinction did not need preliminary explanations. He continued as follows:

> This treatment of Quasi-Contracts is, in the opinion of the writer, not only unscientific, and therefore theoretically wrong, but is also destructive of clear thinking, and therefore vicious in practice.

> It needs no argument to establish the proposition that it is not 175
> scientific to treat as one and the same thing, an obligation that
> exists in every case because of the assent of the defendant, and an
> obligation that not only does not depend in any case upon his
> assent, but in many cases exists not-withstanding his dissent. And
> yet with this wide difference between simple contracts and quasi-
> contracts, the latter are generally treated to-day as a species of
> simple contract. [K-3]

He then constructed the first comprehensive list of subjects that
belonged to quasi-contract and not to contract. The list included
the following items treated by Parsons as contractual: obligations
of common carriers and innkeepers; obligations of incapacitated
persons to pay for benefits; obligations of parents to children and
of husbands to wives; liability for benefits received under voided
express contracts; liability for money paid by mistake. [K-16-25]
This subtraction from the domain of contract was justified on the
basis of a general principle against unjust enrichment. Keener was
clear that he was dealing with a separate cause of action with its
own rules rather than with a pleading category. This view is universally accepted today. For example, the A.L.I. Restatements
placed quasi contracts with the constructive trust in a separate volume on Restitution, restricting contracts to the class of obligations
supposedly essentially voluntary.

The Emergence of Torts

In Parsons, what we would now call torts figured as an important
aspect of every subject considered. I have already mentioned that
his discussion of bailment involved the issue of the duty of care of
a railroad company to trespassers on its tracks. In each relationship he took up, Parsons dealt with the standards of behavior the
law imposed on the participants. A trustee "is held not only to
careful management of the trust property, so that it shall not be
wasted or diminished, but he is bound to secure its reasonable pro-
ductiveness and increase." [I-103] Details followed. Parsons took
up the liability of an agent for deliberately or negligently misleading as to the scope of his authority, respondeat superior, and

176   the responsibility of husbands and fathers for the tortious acts of
wives and children. The torts of fraud and breach of warranty
were the subjects of separate chapters.

One of the functions of the implied intent concept was to blur
the question whether these duties of care were properly contractual or properly imposed by the sovereign. (The treatment of a
father's attempt to disclaim liability for a son's debts is one of the
very few cases in the whole treatise in which Parsons squarely
considered the problem of contractual modification of legal liabilities.) The Classical reaction against what had come to seem his
obfuscation was naturally concerned with rectifying this state of
affairs. One of the consequences was the initial attempt to define
a field of torts.

It is a familiar "startling" fact that the first treatise on Torts, by
Hilliard, an American, appeared only in 1859. Prior to that time,
the learning of torts was contained only in works on evidence, on
"nisi prius," and on pleading and practice. Hilliard's objection to
this treatment was based on the proposition that "Contracts, Torts
and Crimes, [make] up, in their broadest interpretation, an entire
corpus juris civilis." [i] The fragmentary treatment of Torts was
"not the mode demanded by the nature and importance of the
general subject." [ii] In the earlier treatments, "remedies have
been substituted for wrongs." [vi]

Hilliard's program seemed to mark a departure: "in first looking at the wrong itself, its nature, its subject, its author, its recipient or victim, and subordinately its remedy; I have, at least to my
own partial satisfaction, evolved a series of principles, far less
fragmentary and disconnected, than they have always appeared to
me when stated in connection with mere forms of action." [vii]
The ultimate goal was to "consolidate private wrongs into one
great subject, the unity of whose nature both admits and demands
unity of treatment." [ix]

Neither this book, nor Addison's, published in England a year
later, came close to fulfilling this promise. They began with a
broad distinction, derived from the Roman law, between obligations *ex contractu* and obligations *ex delictu*. They had as well the
conventional division of all the forms of action into contract writs

and tort writs. Their books proceeded to enumerate different   177
kinds of rights (personal security, possession, property, reputation, etc.) and then to describe the remedies the tort writs gave for
violation of those rights. The limits of the subject were defined
without reference to any general principle, and the only internal
ordering produced, albeit an advance, was the list of rights, each
of which was treated according to the same taxonomic scheme of
content, types of injury, etc.

It is striking that Hilliard's first two chapters are called "Torts
as Connected With Contracts," and "Torts and Crimes." But the
first of these does not distinguish contract and tort at all. It is a
description of the situations in which actions undertaken in a contractual situation can give rise to liability in forms of action classified as tortious, such as fraud and breach of warranty. Likewise
with torts and crimes. The definitions of a tort in the early books
were of no more help. Addison's was "every invasion of a legal
right...every neglect of a legal duty, every injury to the person,
character or reputation of another." [iv]

Markby (1871), the first of the analytical jurists after Austin,
was also the first to see this procedure as problematical. He began
by defining contract as a legal obligation whose content the sovereign defined according to the intentions of the parties. The
problem arose in defining torts:

> I know nothing more difficult to grasp than the distinction on
> which this classification [of actions as tort or contract] is founded.
> Indeed, if we accept some accounts of that distinction, it is diffi-
> cult to believe that it exists at all.
>
> If, for instance, we turn to the description of torts by a very
> modern writer, what we are there told is, that a tort or a wrong,
> independent of contract, involves the idea of the infringement of
> a legal right or the violation of a legal duty. But is not a breach of
> contract both an infringement of a legal right and a violation of a
> legal duty? Further on we are told that one class of actions of tort
> are founded on infractions of some private compact, or of some
> private duty or obligation, productive of damage. But are not
> actions for breach of contract founded on that, which is at once

178   the infraction of a private duty or obligation, and also of a compact? Again, though we are reminded that tort differs essentially from contract, yet I have in vain endeavoured to discern what the essential difference is. On the contrary, I find it stated, that the same transaction may give rise to an action of tort and an action of contract. True, it is said that an action of tort cannot be maintained for a breach of contract, but only where the tort complained of flows from a contract. But what sort of special connection is expressed by the word "flowing" I am unable to conceive. [Id. 179-80, p. 87-88.]

Beside the problem of apparent over-inclusiveness, there was the problem that no one called violation of a civil duty to pay taxes, or of quasi-contractual obligation, a tort.

Markby proceeded to an extraordinary discussion of tort liability, one that we will take up in a later chapter. But he had nothing further to say about the classificatory dilemma he had posed. The Classical answer was propounded by Holmes two years later in his anonymous article on the "Theory of Torts" (1873):

Torts have been thought to be infractions of rights availing against all the world. This may prove too narrow a definition, although the title includes all such rights. It contains in the first place duties of all the world; that is, duties of subjects generally to subjects generally, irrespective of any more special circumstances on either side than such as make it possible to incur a legal liability. For instance, the duty not to commit an assault and battery is imposed on all persons not excepted from ordinary rules in favor of all persons upon whom a battery is possible. The fact of possibility is merely a condition precedent, not a defined state of facts to which a peculiar rule of law attaches. A second class of duties, equally general as regards the persons on whom they are imposed, are owed, not to every member of the community, but only to persons in particular situations of fact; that is, to persons distinguished from the rest of the community by certain definite marks. Such, for example, are the duties of all the world to a possessor, a patentee, or a master. The rights corresponding to both of these enumerated classes are, of course, rights availing against all the world, but there are other cases which are harder to deal with. There are some instances, undoubtedly, in which the duty seems to arise out of a special relation between the parties. Take the case of a vendor of an article known to have a secret tendency to do damage if applied to the contemplated use. It would seem, at first sight, that the duty was a consequence attached by the law to the special relation of vendor and purchaser. But the same duty would arise out of the relation of bailor and bailee, and we think reflection would show that, although the relation of the parties afforded the occasion, the duty in question was capable of being generalized into a form irrespective of the particular relation. . . .Take again fraud in the making a contract. The breach of duty is only complete when the contract is made, but the duty not to defraud is logically anterior to the contract, and seems to be recognized as being so by the option given the defrauded party to sue in tort for the fraud. . . .There are, however, some truly special liabilities arising out of special relations of fact other than contract, which, as they are not enforced by actions ex contractu, are included in books on torts; for instance, the duties of a tenant for life to the remainder-man. But although such duties cannot be resolved into contracts, it is believed that together with contracts they fall under a distinct generalization: viz., duties of persons in a particular situation of fact to persons in a particular situation of fact; or, perhaps, more concisely, duties of the parties to a particular relation of fact to each other.

This arrangement is a particularly detailed and innovative example of the general classificatory pattern of the late nineteenth century, as we will see in a moment. It also immediately influenced the field it described. In 1875, Melville Bigelow of the Boston University Law School brought out a casebook on Torts, in the Langdellian manner, and in 1878 he published the first *short* book on Torts. He organized both as Holmes had suggested, acknowledging his debt [T-V]. The text opened as follows:

The substantive law of torts treats of the civil aspect of duties, and, by consequence, of the breach of duties, which govern the relations of individuals to each other (1) as mere members of the

180   State; or (2) as occupying some special situation towards each other not produced by agreement inter sese; or (3) as occupying some special situation of agreement inter sese which affords occasion for breaches of duty between them that need not be treated as breaches of contract.

Bigelow was attempting to carry out the basic program of the group of young legal scholars who published the American Law Review, particularly Holmes, Gray and Thayer. Their constantly repeated demand was for a "philosophical" arrangement of the law, rather than one based on purely utilitarian or accidental properties (the Law of Telegraphs being a favorite example). It is to the larger program that we now turn.

The New Classification of Legal Doctrines

The Parsonian vision of a relationally organized corpus juris within which implied intent would be the crucial integrating concept does not seem to have had any theoretical exponents. In 1870, the problem of arrangement was to take the pieces that writers like Parsons had fitted together and distribute them in a scheme that would overcome what seemed the manifest inconvenience and irrationality of Blackstone and Kent. Beginning with the posthumous publication of the extended version of Austin's *Lectures,* and with Maine, there seems to have been a general consensus both on the criticism of the old system and that the new should take the *in rem* vs. *in personam* distinction as its starting point. Markby was representative:

> Laws which concern, or which chiefly concern the rights, duties, and obligations of persons in respect of persons, have been sometimes classed together and called the law of persons; and laws which concern, or which chiefly concern, the rights, duties, and obligations of persons in respect of things, have been likewise classed together and called the law of things.
>
> I cannot discover that this classification of law has been turned to much purpose, and it would have been scarcely worth while to mention it, had it not been that by slightly changing the terms in

which this classification is expressed, Blackstone has introduced an egregious error. He speaks not of the law of persons and of the law of things, but of rights of persons and of rights of things. Rights of persons there are undoubtedly; for all rights are such. There may be also rights over things, and rights over persons; but rights of, that is, belonging to, things, as opposed to rights of, that is, belonging to, persons, there cannot be.

In English law, at any rate, the law of persons and the law of things is so mixed up, that no use can be made of this classification so long as our law retains its present form. [Markby 133-34, pp. 63-64]

He then offered the following instead:

Sometimes a right exists only as against one or more individuals, capable of being named and ascertained; sometimes it exists generally against all persons, members of the same political society as the person to whom the right belongs; or, as is commonly said, somewhat arrogantly, it exists against the world at large. Thus in the case of a contract between A and B, the right of A exists against B only; whereas in the case of ownership, the right to hold and enjoy the property exists against persons generally. This distinction between rights is marked by the use of terms derived from the Latin: the former are called rights in rem; the latter are called rights in personam. [Id. 136, pp. 63-64]

In two unsigned articles appearing in the American Law Review in 1872 and 73, Holmes significantly elaborated this scheme. He distinguished six categories:

1. Duties of all to the sovereign (e.g. not to be guilty of contempt of court);
2. Duties of all to all (e.g., to respect personal security and reputation);
3. Duties of all to those in particular positions (e.g., to respect the property and contract rights of others);
4. Duties of those in particular situations to the sovereign (e.g. Markby's case of the duty to pay one's taxes);
5. Duties of those in particular situations to all (e.g., duty of master to compensate for torts of his servant; liability for inherently dangerous instrumentalities);

6. Duties of those in particular situations to others likewise
particularly situated (e.g., duty to perform one's contracts; familial duties). [7-46; 7-652]

Some variant of these distinctions was the primary basis of every
arrangement of private law that I know of for the late nineteenth
century period. [e.g. Holland, Amos, Terry, Salmond] Yet there
was little if any discussion in the books of the reason why this
distinction was expected to be so useful and accepted as eminent-
ly "natural." It seems likely that it is best understood as a further
manifestation of the will theory. So long as the crucial fact about
the legal system was that it was made up of legal actors each of
those wills had a sphere of power, one of the crucial descriptive
tasks was to identify, for each right, those against whom it could
be exerted, and to distinguish them from those not bound. A passage from Holland at least suggests this conclusion:

> A right which is at rest requires to be studied with reference to its
> 'orbit' and its 'infringement.' By its 'orbit,' we mean the sum, or
> extent, of the advantages which are conferred by its enjoyment.
> By its 'infringement,' we mean an act, in the strict sense of the
> term, which interferes with the enjoyment of those advantages....
> It is obvious that to know the whole extent of the advantage con-
> ferred by the enjoyment of a right is the same thing as to know
> what acts are infringements of it. Thus the right may be such as to
> exact from the world an abstention only from any deliberate inter-
> ference with it, or it may be such as to exact an abstention even
> from such an infraction of it as may result from want of care.
> [Holland 2nd p. 112]

The notion of a right "at rest," by contrast with a "right in motion"
was Holland's way of stating the contrast between what we would
call the content of a right and the means of origination, transfer or
extinction of it. A second major dimension of classification during
the Classical period was according to whether these changes took
place by the will of the parties or by the will of the sovereign.
Holland, for example, began his discussion of rights in personam
as follows:

[R]ights 'in personam' are divisible, according to the investitive fact to which they owe their origin, into two great classes. Such rights either arise or do not arise out of a contract. In the latter case, since they arise from facts of various kinds to which it pleases the Law to affix similar results, we shall describe them as rights 'ex lege;' and it will be convenient to consider the rights which arise thus variously before treating of those which arise solely from contract. [id. pp. 182-83; see also Holmes 77 and Terry 480]

We have already seen the very powerful solvent effect that attention to the question: Will of the parties or will of the Sovereign? had on the pre-Classical classificatory schemes. The combination of this distinction with that between rights *in rem* and rights *in personam* gave Classical legal thinkers the sense that they had reordered the whole in a way that was more rational, and more responsive to the ends of law, than what had gone before. But it took a surprisingly long time for the two distinctions to be combined as a matter of course. For example, Wigmore, in an 1894 article on torts, had no directly relevant authority to cite for the following taxonomy:

Private law, then, deals with the relations between members of the community regarded as being ultimately enforceable by the pol-itical power. Such a single relation may be termed a Nexus; . . . For the first and broadest division it seems best to distinguish according as the Duty has inhered in the Obligor (1) without reference to his wish or assent, or (2) in consequence of some volition or intention of his to be clothed with it. The former we may term Irrecusable, ——having reference to the immateriality of the attitude of the obligor in respect to consent or refusal; the latter, Recusable, ——for the same reason. The latter sort includes Contracts (in the narrow sense), and some few varieties not here important. The former includes Torts (so called), Enrichment (a part of Quasi-Contracts as now treated), and a few minor ones. The permanent justification for this division, it may be said, will be found in the deep-rooted instinct of the Anglo-American legal spirit, which is strikingly backward in imposing or enlarging an

184   irrecusable nexus, but gives the freest scope for the voluntary
       assumption (Recusable) of nexus of any content. Dividing further
       the former sort, we find (a) many imposed universally, i.e., on all
       other members of the community in favor of myself; and (b) a
       few imposed on particular classes of persons by reason of special
       circumstances. Of the latter sort the duty of a child to support a
       parent, as recognized in Continental and other law, is an example;
       but the most important group is found in parts at least of the sub-
       ject known. . . as Quasi-Contract. . . .The subject of Tort, then,
       deals with the large group of relations here termed Universal
       Irrecusable Nexus. [8 Harv. L. Rev. 200-201]

The isolation of tort and quasi-contract in the categories of
irrecusable rights in rem and irrecusable rights in personam was a
manifestations of the will theory. It was an assertion that the crucial question in these areas was to determine the will of the sovereign; the will of the parties was irrelevant by definition, at least as
a source of obligation. But this alone does not tell us very much.
First, as we will see, the will theory had significance in the internal
working out both of torts and of quasi-contract. Second, once we
know we are dealing with obligations imposed by the sovereign,
we must go on to find out how the actual rules dealt with the dilemmas of autonomy vs. community and formality vs. informality.
These inquiries seem best deferred, however, until we have said
something of the contractual core that survived the amputations
just described.

∾ 3 ∽

In the last chapter, I suggested that Classical legal thought dealt
with the contradictions of private law theory by the creation of a
mediating structure. There was a core of fully legal, highly salient
relationships ruled by the ideals of Will Theory, autonomy and
objectivism. There was also a periphery of relationships ruled by
regulatory, paternalist, communitarian and informal ideals. The
extrusion of quasi-contract and tort from the body of contract
doctrine was an incident in the creation of this structure. But, as I
said at the end of the last section, the mere fact of regrouping did

not imply the victory of any set of ideals within the new subject matters.

Nor was there any logical necessity that the remaining core of contract should be organized to reflect facilitation, self-determination, autonomy and formality. This did, however, occur. And in order for it to occur, it was necessary for the Classical theorists to deal with the fact that even after the expulsions I have mentioned there were a large number of contract rules that appeared to be direct reflections of regulation, paternalism, community and informality. There were two doctrinal developments that together solved this problem:

1. The undermining and eventual rejection of the ideas of "status," "relation," and "condition" as the operative sources of the great mass of contract rules.
2. The emergence of a specialized law of persons, and of a new category of status, that grouped together and explained the peculiar character of rules incompatible with the new vision of the nature of "real" contracts.

Status as an Operative Legal Category

In the discussion of Blackstone in the last chapter, I mentioned his dichotomy of the law of persons and the law of things, and illustrated the former with subjects like master and servant, husband and wife, corporations, aliens, and so forth. That listing understated the centrality of the idea of a social role as the operative, organizing concept in Blackstone, because it was restricted to private law subjects. In fact, Blackstone included, in an indiscriminate mixture with the categories I mentioned, clergymen, soldiers, sailors, attorneys, justices of the peace and members of Parliament.

Under each category, Blackstone included some or all of the following kinds of rules:

(a) special formalities governing entry into the status (e.g. official solemnization of marriage);

(b) limitations of legal capacity "flowing" from the status (wife cannot make binding contract);

    (c) special duties to others within relationships (as of husband to wife) whether subject to contractual modification or not;

    (d) special duties to or rights against strangers flowing from the status (husband must pay debts of wife for necessaries; husband can bring action against stranger for alienation of affection);

    (e) limitations on withdrawal from the status (divorce, etc.).

Now one of the striking facts about both Blackstone and Kent (who followed his arrangement) is that they included no general discussion of the private law legal rights and powers of persons who occupied no status at all. They did include important sections on the rights of subjects—e.g. property, personal security—but these were oriented to the question of the legitimacy of state interference with vested rights. They assumed, without ever explicitly discussing, some set of private law rules somehow corresponding to the public law rights.

In Blackstone, one finds out about the law of contract and tort as they apply to persons occupying no special status by consulting the Law of Wrongs. Here one learns substantive private law by studying the forms of action. In Kent, there was no tort law, but all the various commercial law specialties were grouped under Title to Personal Property.

There was no direct movement from this toward the Classical and modern categorization. Instead, the contractualist theoreticians, Metcalf, W.W. Story and Parsons, created the system we examined at the beginning of this chapter. The statuses of clergyman, soldier, justice of the peace, and member of Parliament disappeared, along with the form of social life that produced them as political/legal/economic institutions. But the contractualists put together the remnants of the ancient law of status and the new commercial relationships not dependent on any legal peculiarity of the actor. The result was a new version of the law of persons as the master category, contrasting with that of real property.

The internal organization of the legal discussion in these books resembled that of Blackstone and Kent. Starting from the "nature" of the status, condition or relation, the author developed a set of rules governing capacity, duties to strangers, termination, and so forth. There were still only very minimal "general parts" dealing explicitly with the rights and powers of an individual seen as existing outside of any one of those situations listed in the massive sections on "Parties" and "Subject Matter of Contract."

No one suggested that the judge could *deduce* the various legal aspects of a status from its nature. The categories were not experienced as operative in the very powerfully controlling manner of the Classical legal concepts like property or police power. Yet it is equally clear that there was a felt connection among the elements assembled under husband and wife, and that that connection had to do with what seemed plain and undisputable characteristics of the relationship as it existed in social life. The wife's inability to contract was a function of the "nature" of marriage, and so was the husband's duty of support.

Likewise in partnership, it was a consequence of the nature of the relationship that partners were held to the highest duties of good faith, *both* inter se and in respect to their collective obligations. In short, the different categories of relationship gave rise to legal concepts of an intermediate operative power, somewhere between that of mere conventional pigeonholes and that of logical implication.

The Concept of Status as Role Loses its Operativeness

The first striking manifestation of the declining operativeness of this conception of status was Austin's treatment of the subject in lectures delivered in the 1830's but not published until the 1860's. He was describing the distinction between the law of persons and the law of things. He seems to have taken it for granted that if such a division was desirable, the law of persons, or of status should include all the different indicia I have mentioned, including both the peculiarities involved in entering and leaving the status, the rights and duties toward others within or with respect to a relationship like marriage or wardship, and the special capacities and incapacities of occupants of the status.

Austin devoted a whole lecture, one that nicely illustrates the argumentative style of the early utilitarians, to the question

188   whether the various elements lumped together as a status could be
said to be implicit in its nature:

> According to a definition of status, which now (I think) is explod-
> ed, but which was formerly current with modern civilians, "Status
> est qualitas, cujus ratione homines diverso jure utuntur."
> "Exempli gratia," (adds Heineccius,) "alio jure utitur liber homo;
> alio, servus; alio, civis; alio, peregrinus."
>
> Now a given person bears a given condition, (or, in other
> words, belongs to a given class,) by virtue of the rights or duties,
> the capacities or incapacities, which are peculiar to persons of that
> given kind or sort. Those rights or duties, capacities or incapaci-
> ties, are the condition or status with which the person is clothed.
> They are considered as forming a complex whole: And, as form-
> ing a complex whole, they are said to constitute a status which the
> person occupies, or a condition, character, or person, which the
> person bears.
>
> But, according to the definition which I now am considering,
> the rights or duties, capacities or incapacities, are not themselves
> the status: but the status is a quality which lies or inheres in the
> given person, and of which the rights or duties, capacities or inca-
> pacities, are merely products or consequences.
>
> The definition (it is manifest) is merely a case of the once cur-
> rent jargon about occult qualities. Wherever phenomena were
> connected in the way of cause and effect, (or of customary
> antecedence and sequence, or customary coexistence,) it was usual
> to impute the so-called effect, (not to the customary antecedent, or
> to the customary coexistent,) but to an occult quality, or occult
> property, which was supposed to intervene in the business of cau-
> sation. [Jur.II-720]
>
> . . . The supposition that a status is a quality inhering in the
> party who bears it, has every fault which can possibly belong to a
> figment. The supposed quality is merely fictitious. And, admitting
> the fiction, it will not serve to characterise the object, for the pur-
> pose of distinguishing which, the fictitious quality was devised.
>
> It is remarkable that Bentham (who has cleared the moral sci-
> ences from loads of the like rubbish) adopts this occult quality
> under a different name. In the chapter in the Traite de Legislation,

which treats of Etats (or of status or conditions), he defines a status thus: "Un etat domestique ou civil n'est qu'une base ideale, autour de laquelle se rangent des droits et des devoirs, et quelquefois des incapacities."

Now this base ideale (which is distinct from the rights or duties constituting the condition, and also from the fact or event by which the condition is engendered) is clearly the fictitious quality (expressed in another shape), which, according to the scholastic jurists, forms the status. [Id. 722]

Austin's conclusion about the logical status of the word status as it was used in legal thought in his time was unequivocal:

The sets of rights and duties called condition or status have no common generic character which determines what a status or condition is. Certain sets of rights and duties are detached for convenience from the body of the legal system, and these sets of rights and duties are styled status or conditions. [Id.-710]

The justification for the use of the concept for *purposes of arrangement* was that it made it possible to highlight what writers like Blackstone and Parsons had suppressed: the existence, at the core of the legal order, of the private law of persons having no peculiarities of status at all:

The main advantages of this division seem to me to be these.

First: in the Law of Things, or the Law of Things Incorporeal, or the Law of Rights and Duties, or The Law generally, all which can be affirmed of rights and duties considered generally, or as abstracted from status or condition, is stated once for all. One advantage, therefore, of the division is that it is productive of brevity: again, the general rules and principles with which the Law of Things is properly or directly concerned, are preserved detached and abstracted from everything peculiarly relating to particular classes or persons; they are, therefore, presented more clearly than if they were interspersed with that more special matter. Each rule or principle is apprehended more easily and distinctly than if the modifications which it receives from that more special matter, were appended or annexed to it. Being

190   brought together more closely, their mutual relation and dependency is more easily perceived. The brevity, therefore, which this division of the corpus juris produces, tends also to its clearness.[713-14]

Austin's approach became the premise of the way law was organized, written about, taught, practiced and understood during the Classical period, and it is hardly less influential today. The division between the abstract core and the "exceptional" periphery is almost never discussed. When it is, it seems enough to justify it on the basis of "convenience." Yet it has the most profound consequence for the substantive content of legal rules.

The reason for this is that the particular rules that characterize the relationships that constitute the law of status are those that most clearly embody the ideals of regulation, paternalism, community and informality. In the arrangement of Blackstone and Parsons, these rules were at the center of attention. Everything from the table of contents to the footnotes emphasized that the Law in General is constantly concerned with the ideals that motivate them. The exceptional category was that of relations so "abstracted" from any well defined social context that the equitable ideal was irrelevant. Indeed, this category was so exceptional that it was not even formally recognized as worthy of separate analysis.

The Austinian arrangement was then much more than an affair of convenience. It was part of a refocussing that made it possible to shift *analytic* effort from the development of one general vision to the development of another. But the change was by no means complete with Austin. He still, for example, found it so obvious as not to merit discussion that the legal category of a status ought to include *both* peculiarities of capacity and special rights and duties arising out of social role. He thus recognized, though only on unstated grounds of convenience, that there was something viable in the notion of relationship.

Holland (1880) went a step further:

The 'Ius quod ad personas pertinet' aptly enough expresses the law as to those variations in rights which arise from varieties in the Persons who are connected with them. But it is unfortunately also used by the Roman jurists to express what the Germans call 'Familienrecht;' i.e. to express, not only the variation in rights which is caused by certain special variations in personality, but also the special rights which belong to certain personal relationships. Not merely, for instance, the legal exemptions and disabilities of infants and femes covert, but also the rights of a father over his son, a husband over his wife, and a guardian over his ward.

Such questions, however, as how far a woman's capacity for contracting is affected by coverture, and what are the mutual rights of husband and wife, are radically different in character. [2nd ed. 99]

On this ground, Holland classified all the special duties involved in relationships like marriage and parenthood under quasi-contract. The various rules of vicarious liability for the torts of children and servants found a place in the category "rights in rem created by the will of the sovereign" rather than of individuals. Status he restricted to variations in capacity. Since nothing was left of the Law of Persons, but the rules about the legal disabilities of married women, children, lunatics, drunkards and spendthrifts, he proposed a change in terminology: the law of persons became the law of "abnormal" persons. [id. 101-03] It was to be treated in a strictly segregated part of the rationally organized corpus juris, where it could have no contaminating effect on contracts "proper." [See Terry 614-619]

Thus the old concept of status underwent two vicissitudes. First, it came to exist in opposition to rights in the abstract, rather than as the medium for the organization and exposition of rights in particular. Second, the elements composing particular statuses were fragmented and dispersed, rather than treated as the elements of operative wholes. Both of these developments were influenced by, and also appeared to confirm Maine's famous generalization that "the movement of the progressive societies has hitherto been a movement from status to contract." [100]

Yet having said this much, an ambiguity arises, and one with a good deal of significance for Classical legal thought. The catego-

192   ry of status did not disappear from legal consciousness. Quite the
contrary. As the particular relations lost their ability to explain
existing rules and generate new ones, the general category gained
in importance.

Status as a Relationship Controlled by the State

Maine's generalization is the culmination of his description of the
process of transition from ancient to modern society. Ancient law

> is full, in all its provinces, of the clearest indications that society in
> primitive times was not what it is assumed to be at present, a col-
> lection of individuals. In fact, and in the view of the men who
> composed it, it was an aggregation of families. The contrast may
> be most forcibly expressed by saying that the unit of an ancient
> society was the Family, of a modern society the Individual.
> [Maine 74]

Maine defined status "agreeably with the usage of the best
writers," to signify "personal conditions" connected with the
"powers and privileges anciently residing in the Family," and contrasted it with "such conditions as are the immediate or remote
result of agreement." [100] His argument concerned the disappearance of the Roman *patria postestas*, the expanding legal capacity of sons and women, the abolition of slavery, and the reduction
of guardianship to a purely protective, rather than a proprietary
institution. In short, it had to do with the decline of the power of
heads of households to dictate to their dependents.

> Ancient law is scanty, because it is supplemented by the despotic
> commands of the heads of households. It is ceremonious, because
> the transactions to which it pays regard resemble international
> concerns much more than the quick play of intercourse between
> individuals. Above all it has a peculiarity of which the full impor-
> tance cannot be shown at present. It takes a view of life wholly
> unlike any which appears in developed jurisprudence....The moral
> elevation and moral debasement of the individual appear to be
> confounded with, or postponed to, the merits and offences of the
> group to which the individual belongs. If the community sins, its

guilt is much more than the sum of the offences committed by its members; the crime is a corporate act, and extends in its consequences to many more persons than have shared in its actual perpetration. If, on the other hand, the individual is conspicuously guilty, it is his children, his kinsfolk, his tribesmen, or his fellow-citizens, who suffer with him, and sometimes for him. [Id. 74-75]

When Austin, and the analytical jurists who followed him, argued for the relegation of the law of persons to the peripheral categories of "abnormal persons," quasi-contract, and special instances of tort liability, they reflected the conviction that the family relations were no longer either conceptually or practically central to law. The "scanty" law of the "international relations" between heads of households had become the more and more fully developed law of contractual dealings between autonomous individuals.

The ambiguity arose as follows. What interested Maine was the decline of despotic paternal power. The categories the analytical jurists purged from the legal core had to do with the relationships once governed by that despotic power. But at the time of the purging, the actual rules involved embodied not the idea of arbitrary power but that of communal solidarity. The specific provisions concerning parental obligations of support or the master's liability for the torts of servants were state *limitations* on arbitrariness. "Such conditions as are the immediate or remote result of agreement" came to be contrasted, through the undiscriminating use of the word status, with relations within which the state imposed a particularly demanding rather than a particularly lax moral standard of conduct.

Thus wrenched from its content, Maine's law of progress became a slogan of laissez-faire. The important thing was not the opposition of the law of persons to abstract contract law, but that of legal relations whose terms the parties controlled to legal relations the state treated in a regulatory, paternalist, communal and informal manner. Once the situation was described and understood in these terms, it followed as a matter of course, unless one was a socialist, that the category of pure contract, ruled by ideals of facilitation, self-determination, autonomy

194 and formality, was the norm, and the end of historical development.

Both the earlier and the later uses are oddly juxtaposed in Holland (1882). I have already referred to his extended discussion of the distinction between the law of abnormal persons and the abstract core of legal rights. He there reduced the concept of status to variation in legal capacity. As far as one can tell from the index, he never used the word in any other fashion.

Nonetheless, there is an unindexed reference that gives the word an altogether different meaning:

> It may appear questionable whether the rights of husband and wife can be reckoned among those which arise by operation of law rather than out of contract. It is however submitted that this is the true view. The matrimonial status is indeed entered upon, in modern times, in pursuance of an agreement between the parties, accompanied by certain religious or civil formalities; but its personal incidents are wholly attached to it by uniform rules of law, in no sense depending on the agreement of the parties, either at the time of the marriage or subsequently. The effect of the contract, coupled with the other acts required by law, in producing a status, to which rights of definite kinds are incident, closely resembles that of a sale of property. In the one case, as in the other, the contractual act is complete, so far as its direct effects are concerned, when the status has been produced or the ownership changed. The necessarily resulting rights of the person newly invested with the status, or newly become owner of the property respectively, are the creatures not of the will of the parties but of fixed rules of law. [2nd 184]

The question whether marriage was a contract or a status had little significance in England, except for rare problems of the conflicts of laws. In America, it was or became crucial. Thirty years before Holland wrote it was already an issue, and provided an early occasion for the emergence of the will theory as a mode of dealing with the contradictions of private law theory.

In his discussion of divorce, Chancellor Kent said:

> The first inquiry, is, how far has the legislature of a state the right under the Constitution of the United States, to interfere with the marriage contract and allow of divorces between its own citizens, and within its own jurisdiction? The question has never been judicially raised and it has generally been considered that the state governments have complete control and discretion in the case. In the case of Dartmouth College v. Woodward, the point was incidentally alluded to; and the chief justice observed, that the Constitution of the United States had never been understood to restrict the general right of the legislatures of the states to legislate on the subject of divorces; and the object of state laws of divorce was to enable some tribunal, not to impair a marriage contract, but to liberate one of the parties, because it had been broken by the other. It would be in time to inquire into the constitutionality of their acts, when the state legislatures should undertake to annul all marriage contracts, or to allow either party to annul it at the pleasure of the other. Another of the judges of the Supreme Court, [Story] spoke to the same effect. He said that a general law regulating divorces was not necessarily a law impairing the obligation of such a contract. A law punishing a breach of contract by imposing a forfeiture of the rights acquired under it, or dissolving it, because the mutual obligations were no longer observed, was not a law impairing the obligation of contracts. But he was not prepared to admit a power in the state legislatures to dissolve a marriage contract without any cause of default, and against the wish of the parties, and without a judicial inquiry to ascertain the breach of the contract. [II-128-29]

Up to 1850, most of those who argued that the Contracts Clause did *not* apply to marriage did so on the basis of a vision of marriage as profoundly contractual, as Story's argument that divorce is recission for breach vividly suggests. It was also argued that the mere fact of the long history of legislative divorces showed that the Convention could not have intended to treat them as impair-

196 ment of contracts. When marriage was distinguished from contracts in general, it was often on the ground that it was in a class
wholly by itself, sometimes on the ground of its "non pecuniary"
character. There were, however, at least three cases that stated
very clearly that it was because marriage was a "relation," like
master and servant or guardian and ward, that the clause did not
apply. These cases deduced from this categorization that the legislature had unusually broad powers to modify the terms and even
the existence of marriage contracts. [16 Me. 481; 7 Dana 181; 5
Barb.474]

This minority view received a great boost with the introduction of the contract/status dichotomy, beginning with the publication of Bishop's treatise on *Marriage and Divorce* in 1852. His
definitions were as follows:

> The word marriage is used to signify either the act of entering into
> the marital condition, or the condition itself. In the latter and more
> frequent legal sense, it is a civil status, existing in one man and one
> woman, legally united for life, for those civil and social purposes
> which are founded in the distinction of sex. Its source is the law of
> nature, whence it has flowed into the municipal laws of every civ-
> ilized country, and into the general law of nations.... While the
> contract remains executory, that is, an agreement to marry, it dif-
> fers in no essential particulars from other civil contracts, and an
> action for damages may be maintained on a violation of it. But
> when it becomes executed in what the law recognizes as a valid
> marriage, its nature as a contract is merged in the higher nature of
> the status. And, though the new relation may retain some simili-
> tudes to remind us of its origin, the contract does in truth no
> longer exist, but the parties are governed by the law of husband
> and wife.
>
> Various definitions have been given of marriage; and the fore-
> going is not in the language of any former one. It is believed to be
> free from some of the objections which may well be urged against
> all former definitions, whatever defects it may have of its own. [B
> 1st, p. 25-26]

He summarized the objections to the old definition as follows:

In England and continental Europe, little inconvenience can result from making use of the word contract, rather than status, as applied to an executed marriage; for the jurists of those countries are not troubled with many of the peculiar questions of constitutional law, and the conflict of laws relating to divorce, which, arising under the constitutions of the United States and of the several States of this Union, have proved more embarrassing than almost any others to our courts, and have led to irreconcilable diversities of decision. No one can read the conflicting decisions of American tribunals on this subject, without perceiving, that the chief embarrassment has arisen from the tendency to apply the rules governing contracts to the status of marriage, owing to the fact of marriage having been so commonly defined by courts and jurists as a contract. . . . Thus to say, that marriage is a contract, when speaking of the marital condition, and not of the agreement to assume it, is, as we have seen, according to the general current of authorities, inaccurate; since they further declare, that it differs in many particulars from other contracts. And when the differences are pointed out, we perceive that they have covered every quality of the marriage, and left nothing of the contract. To term it, therefore, a contract, is as great a practical inconvenience as to call a certain well-known engine for propelling railroad cars "horse," adding, "but it differs from other horses in several important particulars," and then to explain the particulars. It would be more convenient to use at once the word locomotive. [Id. S.41, p. 34-35]

Bishop felt that his definition alone was enough to preclude application of the Contracts Clause to legislative divorces, and his views were immediately influential. Nonetheless, some courts preferred to concede contract and then deny impairment. A Pennsylvania case from 1867 illustrated the typical analytic mode of pre-Classical legal thought when it argued as follows: in normal contracts, the parties can dissolve their relationship by mutual agreement; this comports with the natural justice of the situation; for reasons of policy, the legislature abolishes this power in the case of marriage, a contract the parties cannot dissolve at will;

198   when the legislature relents in a particular case by granting a
divorce, it is *restoring* rather than impairing the normal operation
of the law of contracts; the Contracts Clause is therefore inapplicable.

The trend was the other way. It was reflected in the note
Holmes appended in 1872 to the passage from Kent quoted a-
bove:

> Constitutional Law. Marriage, although beginning in contract, is
> a legal status which may be modified from time to time by law.
> Hence, a legislative divorce has been held constitutional; or a law
> authorizing divorces for causes which accrued before the passage
> of the act. Carson v. Carson, 40 Miss. 349; contra, Clark v. Clark,
> 10 N.H. 380.

By 1888, when the Supreme Court finally took up the question of
whether legislative divorce violated the Contracts Clause, the
issue was close to moot because most states had instituted strictly
judicial systems based on fault. Yet Justice Field's review of
the authorities is interesting. It emphasized the historical argument for legislative power, then quoted at length from the
cases defining marriage as a status. There was no mention at all
of the various arguments to the effect that, though marriage
is a contract, the constitutional clause is inapplicable, because
divorce does not impair it. The status/contract distinction had
won the day.

Bishop brought out a fully revised edition of his treatise in
1891, and took the occasion to crow:

> Bishop on Marriage and Divorce—was published in 1852. In it the
> author, it is believed for the first time in any legal treatise or judi-
> cial opinion, broke away from the old shackles, and defined mar-
> riage as a status. The result has been already stated, citing many
> subsequent cases, the forms of expression from the bench have
> been gradually modified, until now those earlier ones above quot-
> ed would seem quite antiquated. [IB 2nd p. 13-14]

I remarked earlier that the point of the will theory was the suppression of intermediate terms, and this applied within the law of marriage. The married state lost its contractual character and came to be defined as within the sphere of official definition and regulation. Individuals lost their claims to have rights against state modification of the relationship. But, at the same time, an opposite evolution occurred in the law governing the act of marrying. This is illustrated by the fate of the doctrine of marriage *per verba de futuro cum copula*, or of marriage executed by the making of mutual promises of future marriage followed by intercourse.

The notes to Reeve's treatise on domestic relations, published in 1846, state the doctrine "adopted by most if not all of the United States" as follows:

> The consent of parties, without any peculiar forms or ceremonies, is all that is required to its valid celebration. The Roman lawyers, (says Ch. J. Kent, 2K C. 89,) strongly inculcated the doctrine, that the very foundation and essence of the contract, consisted in consent, freely given, by parties competent to contract; Nihil prodent signasse tabulas, si mentem matrimonii non fuisse constabit. Nuptias, non concubitas sed consensus facit. The common law requires no ecclesiastical sanction, to render it valid, and considers it merely in the light of a civil contract; if it be made per verba de praesenti, and is not followed by cohabitation or per verba de futuro, and followed by consummation, it amounts to a marriage, which the parties cannot dissolve, if they are competent as to age and consent, and is just as binding as though made in facie ecclesia.

This passage asserts both that consent is required and that the mere act of intercourse executes a marriage if there was a previous promise of future marriage. The doctrine was a typical pre-Classical case of implied intent, with the typical ambiguity concerning the primacy of the will of the sovereign or the will of the parties. Bishop, who was the first to insist that the married state

200   was a status, was also one of the first to insist on the purely voluntary character of the act of marriage. This required him to enter somewhat more carefully than had been habitual with pre-Classical writers into the effect of the *copula* on the prior promises:

> When there is a contract of future marriage, we shall see a little further on, and the parties have sexual intercourse, the law usually presumes the intercourse to have been lawful, the parties having changed their future into a present consent. Hence it is said, that marriage may be contracted per verba de praesenti, merely, or per verba de futuro cum copula.
>
> The copula, however, is no part of the marriage; it only serves, to some extent, as evidence of marriage. It was a maxim of the civil law, and it has become equally so of the ecclesiastical, of the common, and indeed of all law, that "Consensus, non concubitus, facit matrimonium." [B 1st p. 53-54]

In the 1850's, New York and Ohio cases rejected the doctrine altogether, refusing even to admit the copula as evidence of intent. Other courts, at least in dicta, accepted it in the form of a "conclusive presumption" not rebuttable by showing of contrary intent. The first case to put the matter clearly was *Robertson v. State*, 42 Ala. 509 (1868):

> There are many authorities that sustain the proposition, that in the absence of statutory restraints, a marriage may be had *per verba de futuro cum copula*, but this doctrine is only reasonable upon the idea, that the *copula* was *prima facie* evidence of an acceleration of the espousals. Where this idea is negatived, . . .to regard the marriage as consummate . . .would substitute the copula for the consent as the constituent of the marriage. . . . [T]o infer the consent would be in contravention of an established fact. [42 Ala. 509 (1868)]

This position gained support through the 1870's and 1880's. Nonetheless, in 1891, Bishop's second edition had to admit that "doubt more or less prevails" on the question whether the presumption of intent from copula was conclusive or might be rebutted. He did claim that all but three states accepted his "true view:"

The True View—is believed to be, that the copula after promise establishes marriage prima facie, yet no further; that this prima facie case may be rebutted by evidence, for which purpose circumstantial evidence is as good as any other; that thus a question of fact is raised, to be decided on presumption and testimony combined, and this question is, under instructions from the court, for the jury. All the circumstances of the case may be looked into, including the conduct of the parties both before and after the relied-on copula. And if they did not regard themselves after it as married, the marriage presumption is weakened. [IB 2nd p. 149]

By 1922, commentators had begun to deny that the doctrine had ever existed in America outside of dicta [Koegel].

The distribution of rules about marriage into a formation category and a status category was a typical instance of the classical strategy of resolving contradictions through a kind of conceptual segregation. For this reason, it is wrong to view the new concept of status as no more than a tool in the attack on regulation. It could be used, as in this example, to strengthen state power in areas where pre-Classical contractualism had weakened it. The classification of marriage as a status simply eliminated a whole set of problems that would have arisen if the courts had attempted to subject it to Fourteenth Amendment freedom of contract theories.

The point is a more difficult one. The effect of segregation was to make it appear a datum of legal logic that contract law was the domain of the ideals of laissez-faire. Analogies from the laws of marriage were not available for the development of contract rules because marriage was not a contract. The ideals that marriage rules embodied could find their way into contracts only sub rosa, and subject always to suspicion as non-legal.

The completion of the separation affected both sides to it. In other words, the categories status and contract took on a whole new kind of operative power. Placement of a subject within the corpus juris came to affect dramatically the rules applicable to it. Enlistment contracts will serve as an illustration.

Enlistment Contracts as Creating a Status

Throughout the 19th century there was litigation on the question whether minors' enlistments were valid. The question typically arose when a soldier charged with a crime before a military tribunal denied the court's jurisdiction on the ground his induction had been void or voidable. The federal statute set a minimum age of 16, with a requirement of parental consent up to the age of 18. The most frequent claim was that the recruiter had neglected to get this consent. The question was whether Congress could authorize minors over 18 to make enlistments which would be valid (a) without parental assent, and (b) in spite of the infant's subsequent repudiation. Justice Story decided the question on circuit in 1816, with an opinion that brings together many of the strands of pre-Classical legal thought.

He began by characterizing the common law powers of parents to control their children as "rights depending upon the mere municipal rules of the state [which] may be enlarged, restrained and limited as the wisdom or policy of the times may dictate." [24 Fed. Cas. 949] He then adduced elaborate policy arguments in favor of making minors available for naval service. "And if this exercise [of the power to enlist] should sometimes trench upon supposed private rights [of parents] or private convenience, it is to be enumerated among the sacrifices, which the very order of society exacts from its members in furtherance of the public welfare." [950] This is a good example of the positivist manner of treating rights against the state that constituted half of the pre-Classical repertoire.

It remained to consider whether the infant could take advantage of his common law disability to void the contract once entered. Story declared the law to be that the infant's power of avoidance did not exist in cases where the contract was beneficial to him, as in contracts for necessaries. The argument from that point was as follows:

> And whenever any disability, enacted by the common law, is removed by the enactment of a statute, the competency of the infant to do all acts within the purview of such statute, is as com-

plete as that of a person of full age. And whenever a statute has   203
authorized a contract for the public service, which from its nature
or objects, is manifestly intended to be performed by infants, such
a contract must, in point of law, be deemed to be for their benefit,
and for the public benefit; so that when bona fide made, it is neither void nor voidable, but is strictly obligatory upon them. [U.S.
v. Bainbridge, 1 Mason 71, 24 Fed. Cas. 946 (1816)].

This opinion did not settle the issue. For the next 75 years, both
state and federal courts held on many occasions that because
enlistments were contracts like any others, they could be voided
by minors. There was a good deal of confusion, which need not
concern us here. The important thing is that the first person who
seems to have thought to apply the status notion was Horace
Gray, serving his first term on the Massachusetts Supreme Judicial
Court, in 1864, the year after the publication of *Ancient Law.* He
pointed out, in a dispute about the moment at which a recruit
became bound, that:

> The question before us is no ordinary one of the force, construc-
> tion or validity of a contract-whether the plaintiff has made an
> agreement and broken it, and is liable in damage for the breach;
> but of a change of *status*—whether by signing a particular paper
> or by any other act, the plaintiff has changed his condition, given
> up some of the rights of a private citizen, and become amenable
> to military discipline. [Tyler v. Pomeroy, 90 Mass. (8 Allen) 480,
> 485-86 (1864)]

By the time the Supreme Court considered its first enlistment contract cases in 1890, the status-contract distinction had become a
tool of analysis customary to the point it needed no citations.
Justice Brewer first addressed the case of a man who wanted to
escape the jurisdiction of a court martial on the ground he had
been over the maximum age when he signed up. The Court rejected the argument:

> But in this transaction something more is involved than the mak-
> ing of a contract, whose breach exposes to an action for damages.
> Enlistment is a contract; but it is one of those contracts which

changes the status: and, where that is changed, no breach of the contract destroys the new status or relieves from the obligations which its existence imposes. Marriage is a contract; but it is one which creates a status. Its contract obligations are mutual faithfulness; but a breach of those obligations does not destroy the status or change the relation of the parties to each other. The parties remain husband and wife, no matter what their conduct to each other—no matter how great their disregard of marital obligations. It is true that courts have power, under the statutes of most States, to terminate those contract obligations, and put an end to the marital relations. But this is never done at the instance of the wrongdoer. The injured party, and the injured party alone, can obtain relief and a change of status by judicial action. So, also, a foreigner by naturalization enters into new obligations. More than that, he thereby changes his status; he ceases to be an alien, and becomes a citizen, and when that change is once accomplished, no disloyalty on his part, no breach of the obligation of citizenship, of itself, destroys his citizenship. In other words, it is a general rule accompanying a change of status, that when once accomplished it is not destroyed by the mere misconduct of one of the parties, and the guilty party cannot plead his own wrong as working a termination and destruction thereof. [137 U.S.151-52]

In the next case, Brewer dealt with a minor who had enlisted without parental consent, in violation of the statute, and then deserted. The distinction between status and contract was now enough to explain what Story had put on grounds of a presumption "in point of law" that the contract was beneficial:

An enlistment is not a contract only, but effects a change of status. Grimley's Case, ante, 147. It is not, therefore, like an ordinary contract, voidable by the infant. [137 U.S. 159]

Status in Classical Contracts Books

Given such a dichotomy, it made no sense to attempt to integrate statuses into the core of pure contract doctrine. In most of the Classical treatises, this is too obvious to merit discussion. But in

one of the first of these, Anson's *Principles*, published in 1879, the
author took the trouble to make his assumptions explicit. He
began with a broad definition of obligation, which he then nar-
rowed by excluding transactions that were "not such as we ordi-
narily term Contracts." Among these were "[a]greements which
affect a change of status immediately upon the expression of the
consent of the parties, such as marriage, which, when consent is
expressed before a competent authority, alters at once the legal
relations of the parties in many ways." [1st ed. 3]

This was enough to explain why a contracts book should not
include subjects like the infant's right to support, or even the
mutual obligations of partners, which had figured so prominently
in the pre-Classical treatises. But Anson was also interested in the
question of which variations in contractual capacity should figure
as part of the subject matter. This brought him up against the
problem of defining the proper scope of the law of persons. He
remarked in a footnote on the need to "help the student out of the
difficulties which Austin's discussion of the subject of status tends
to increase rather than diminish." His solution typifies the shift
from status as a derivative of paternal arbitrariness to status as a
derivative of sovereign rather than individual will:

> In dealing with parties to contracts it seems right to limit that
> branch of the subject to the Capacity of Parties as affected by
> *Status*, and not to introduce limitations or modifications of con-
> tracting power, which, as in the case of Agency, spring from con-
> tract.
>
> For Agency is not a *Status*. The essential feature of a *Status* is
> that the rights and liabilities affecting the class which constitutes
> each particular status are such as no member of the class can vary
> by contract while he remains a member of the class. An infant, for
> instance, can by no possibility contract himself out of the Infant's
> Relief Act, nor can a soldier contract himself out of the Mutiny
> Act. [1st ed. 328-29]

By far the most delicate issue of status and contract was that concerning the relation of "master and servant," or employer and
employee. The very sharp distinction between two types of legal

206 relationship had obvious political implications when applied to industrial relations. If the employment relation was a status, there could be no objection to extensive public regulation of its terms. The whole point about statuses was that because of their public importance, it was not open to the parties to redesign them at will. But if employment was a status, it was also, according to the dichotomy that dominated Classical legal thought, "feudal, regressive, paternalistic," and so demeaning to the laborer. To say that "laborer" was a special status was to say that workers lacked full legal capacity; they were, like women, lunatics and aliens, presumed unable to look after their own affairs.

We will discuss the war of words that grew up around this position in a later chapter. For the moment, it is enough to note that the basic modernist strategy was to break down the sharp classical dichotomies so that the regulatory, paternalist, communal and informal ideals of the law of persons would be made relevant to the situations of employees and small businessmen. Anson's *Principles* happens to provide an example.

The first American edition of this book appeared in 1930, edited by Arthur Corbin, the first modern American contract theorist. He appended a note to Anson's paragraph banishing status relations from contract law. By that time, the text I quoted above had gone through several transformations, but it still used marriage as an example of an agreement that "effects a change of status" and "creates legal relations between the parties . . .which they themselves do not contemplate." Corbin's comment was that:

> The ceremony creates a multitude of legal relations between the parties. . .many of which they did not foresee or intend. The same is true of many business contracts, the difference being one of degree. [1st Amer. ed. 6]

4

The remainder of this chapter describes the impact of Classicism —meaning will theory, objectivism and autonomy—on contract, quasi-contract, and tort law. The Classical version of each will be the subject of considerable discussion in later chapters. Here my purpose is to illustrate the process of transition from one consciousness to another as it played itself out within the contours of concrete doctrinal subject matters.

In 1867, there was no Anglo-American literature on the theory of contract. Between 1867 and 1880 there appeared books by Leake, Langdell, Pollock, and Anson, along with Holmes' three lectures in *The Common Law*, and important discussions by Markby and Holland in books on jurisprudence. These works created the Classical field, which the moderns have disintegrated but have not restructured.

The Classics created, as we have seen, by subtraction. It was these authors of the 1870's who purged quasi-contract, status and tort from the subject. In place of the imperialistic claims of Parsons, they began with elaborate descriptions of all the things that "contract" was *not*. They created also by abstraction, by asserting and then trying to show that there had been an essence hidden at the core of the pre-Classical hodgepodge. Martin Leake stated this program in the preface to the first of the new books (1867):

> The present work professes to treat of the elementary rules and principles of the law of contracts, exclusively of the detailed application of that law to specific matters; such applications of the law being referred to only occasionally, as subsidiary to the main object of the work, for the purposes of proof, argument, and illustration.
>
> It is in this respect essentially different from all those treatises on the law of contracts which treat exclusively or primarily, and either collectively or separately, of the applications of the law to the various specific matters of contract; such as the treatises on the law of vendors and purchasers of land, the sale of goods, landlord and tenant, carriers, insurance, bills of exchange and the like; and though all such works occasionally, in connection with their immediate practical object, deal in some degree with the general rules and principles of the law, the writer of the present treatise is

not aware of any English work undertaken with the exclusive object of treating the law of contracts in its general and abstract form, apart from its specific practical application. [Leake K-i]

Will Theory Within Contract

What was left after subtraction and abstraction was the idea of an agreement of the parties, an agreement that they intended to create an executory legal obligation. There followed immediately an extended discussion of the elements of agreement, namely offer and acceptance. Gone were the interminable listing of all the different kinds of parties and kinds of subject matters of contract. What had been half of the total law of the subject either disappeared altogether or was sliced up and distributed in small pieces in chapters on subjects like "Capacity" appearing toward the end of the story.

The essential question in the new books was never what type of relationship the parties had entered. For pre-Classical legal thought this had been important because the judges would impute different standards of reasonableness, appeal to different moralities, according to whether they were dealing with sale, partnership, a trust or marriage. The Classical focus was on the total autonomy of the will of the parties, their power to shape the relationship they created in any way they wanted. It followed that the essential question was *whether* there was a contract, rather than what type.

Offer and acceptance became a larger and much more difficult at the same time that it became a more fundamental subject. The judges had, as we will see, renounced much of their power to control conduct by regulating the terms of relationships once entered. There was a corresponding temptation to avoid having to do the will of the parties by denying the existence of a contract. The Classical answer to the problem of judicial discretion in this area was objectivism, which created its own host of technical difficulties. The result was that almost as many pages came to be devoted to the apparently trivial question of offer and acceptance as had once been sacrificed to the equally anomalous subject of Parties.

The other great gainer from the rise of the will theory was the consideration doctrine. It represented the will of the sovereign on the subject of what promises should be enforced. In pre-Classical legal thought it had figured as a pleading requirement that functioned in aid of a policy against enforcing promises to make gifts. But the doctrine was not sharply defined as a pervasive test of legal enforceability. As Pound showed in a famous article, it was treated in radically different ways at law and in equity and according to the social character of the relationship between the parties. Concepts like "moral consideration" allowed pre-Classical judges flexibility in adjusting its impact to particularized ideas of the just outcome.

Classical consideration was a different matter altogether. It was formalized in a series of definitions, which the Classics applied systematically to all promises enforceable at common law. Where there appeared no way to square the common law practice with the definition, there was pressure to change the older rules to make them consistent with "principle." For example, the Classics developed the view that past and moral consideration were not worthy of the name, so that the pre-classical doctrines were anomalies and exceptions, held up as examples of the inferiority of earlier styles of judicial reasoning. Needless to say, the same increase in extent and difficulty as had occurred in offer and acceptance doctrine occurred likewise for consideration.

This parallel growth in doctrines supposed to reflect the will of the parties and the will of the sovereign should serve as a reminder that in itself the will theory was neither "individualist" nor associated with laizzez-faire. It represented the judges' commitment to finding a determinate legal actor to obey, a refusal to interject himself or to arbitrate. The adoption of that approach did not it itself settle the question which it put at the center of inquiry. For example, the rise of will theory meant an increase in the number of situations in which the doctrine of duress was at least theoretically available to a defendant. The older rules requiring a showing of one or another specific type of unacceptable conduct gave way to abstract statements about "free will" being "overborn."

Objectivism

The Classical version of the history of objectivism in contract law was laid out by Williston in a famous 1920 article:

> The point of dispute is whether actual mental assent of the parties is a legal prerequisite, or merely such an expression by them as would normally indicate assent, whatever may have been in the minds of the parties. Is the test objective or subjective?
>
> . . . [N]ear the end of the eighteenth century, and for the ensuing half century, the prevalent theory of contract evidently involved as a necessary element   actual mental assent. External acts were merely necessary evidence to prove or disprove the requisite state of mind.
>
> This is shown most clearly in the assumption that an offer to sell specific property was necessarily revoked by the sale of the property to a third person, though the offeree had no knowledge of the sale and accepted the offer within the limit of time fixed by it. . . . The terms coming into use at this time of "meeting of minds," and "notice" of acceptance and of revocation contain the same implication that the attitude of mind of the parties is the ultimate fact to be proved, and that their acts are merely evidence of it.
>
> At the present time courts of law at least—more clearly perhaps in America than in England—have generally turned from this theory of contracts which was emphasized during the half century or more following the year 1790, and have expressed or by implication asserted that the words and acts of the parties are themselves the basis of contractual liability, and not merely evidence of a mental attitude required by the law. In other words, that an expression of mutual assent, and not the assent itself, is the essential element of contractual liability. [14 Ill.L.Rev. 525-27 (1920)]

There are two distinct aspects to the objectivist position:
(a) In deciding what meaning to attribute to the behavior of a party, the judge inquires not into his actual mental state as it is suggested by all the evidence available at the time

of judgment, but rather into the meaning which a reasonable man in the other party's position would have imputed to his partner's behavior at the time.

(b) The rules of formation and interpretation of contract are then applied to this imputed meaning, and neither party is allowed to bring in his deviant actual intentions, or deviant actual understanding of the other party's behavior, even if the deviation was:

(i) altogether without fault on his part and

(ii) caused the other party no injury.

The result of the application of the objective theory is that the deviations of actual intent or understanding from what the judge finds to be the objective meaning of actions leads from time to time to arbitrary redistributions of contractual gains and losses. For example, parties who thought they had entered — who fully intended to enter — contracts that afterwards turn out badly, discover that their lawyers can get them out of their losses by showing that the objective manifestations did not meet the requirements of the rules of contract formation.

Both the partisans and the foes of objectivism agree that the main alternative is a "subjective" theory, looking to real rather than manifested intent, combined with the application of tort doctrine to compensate the victims of those who negligently misrepresent their own intent, and to equitably adjust the losses where no one is at fault. It is also common ground that this was the pre-Classical approach. Whittier set out the modernist position to this effect in a strong article published in 1929:

> It will probably be admitted by everybody that in the making of most contracts there is actual assent communicated by each party to the other. Professor Williston himself says: "An outward manifestation of assent to the express terms of a contract almost invariably connotes mental assent." It is only in the very exceptional case, therefore, that any doctrine other than that of mutual assent communicated is made necessary by the decisions.
>
> As Professor Williston pointed out in his strong article on Mutual Assent in the Formation of Contracts, no new doctrine for

exceptional cases appeared until about 1850 and then chiefly as a misapplication of the principal of estoppel. The substance of the new doctrine which was adopted seems to have been that one who did not actually assent to the contract may be held to it if he carelessly led the other party to reasonably think that there was assent.

As an original proposition the wisdom of the innovation may well be doubted. It would have simplified our law of contracts if actual meeting of the minds mutually communicated had remained essential. The liability for carelessly misleading the other party into the reasonable belief that there was assent might well have been held to be in tort. With such a liability in tort the danger that one could falsely claim that he did not assent and so escape the contract would be rendered insubstantial. In most cases the triers of the fact would not be misled by his false evidence of non-assent. If they concluded that he truly did not assent then there would be liability in tort unless his mistake was also found to have been non-negligent or to have resulted in no damage. Under the present law the non-consenting party is liable on the contract itself if careless. The chief unfortunate result of this state of the law is that he is bound to the contract though the other party is notified of the mistake before the latter has changed his position or suffered any damages. [17 Cal.L.Rev. 441-42 (1929)]

Today, the problem of choosing between Whittier and Williston presents itself as follows: Objectivism justifies its arbitrariness on the ground of certainty of judicial administration. The predictability of rules based on the application of a reasonable man standard to the outward manifestations of intent should be great. By contrast, subjectivism requires the judge to combine a hopelessly obscure inquiry into actual intent with the uncertain value judgments about fault and equity that are inevitable in tort law. Tort law is fine when dealing with accidents, because accidents are unplanned. To introduce its uncertainties into contract would deter transaction.

The familiar responses both deny that subjective intent and tort standards of fairness are less certain than an intrinsically illusory objectivism, and assert that it is simply wrong to shoot hostages to preserve a hollow appearance of judicial impersonality. The problem of objectivism in contracts is a paradigm of the

emergence of the modern contradiction of formality vs. infor-   213
mality.

Nothing like this contradiction existed until the birth of modernism after 1900:

(a) Under the general term objectivism, we now refer to a
congeries of problems that were treated, before the Civil
War, under different rubrics: there was no pre-Classical
perception of a pervading issue.

(b) The process of integration by which the elements of the
modern problem were brought together proceeded
piecemeal over a thirty year period between 1850 and
1880: the integrated Classical treatment of the issue
emerged not at mid-century, but between 1870 and 1880.

(c) The Classical treatment put much emphasis on the "logical necessity" of objectivism given overt premises about
the "nature" of contract and covert ones about the nature
of the judicial role; the "policy" conflict between formality and informality was a subsidiary, though not
insignificant theme (except in Holmes).

In modern legal thought, the category of objectivism is relevant to at least the following array of contract issues:

1. *Formation*
   (a) *Meeting of the Minds*
      (i) do the offer and acceptance have that degree of
      correspondence necessary for the existence of a con-
      tract?
      (ii) is the agreement sufficiently definite to be legally
      binding?
      (iii) did each party promise to the other something
      sufficiently substantial to constitute consideration?
   (b) *Contract by Correspondence*
      (i) is an acceptance by mail legally effective on deposit
      in the mailbox, or on receipt?
      (ii) is the revocation of an offer effective on mailing,
      or on receipt by the offeree?
      (iii) what is the effect of the uncommunicated death of
      the offeror on a subsequent acceptance by an unwit-
      ting offeree?

(c)   Does *unilateral mistake* void a contract? If negligent? If without fault?

2. *Interpretation*: Is the judge attempting to determine the subjective intent of the parties, or is he trying to determine objectively the meaning of their verbal or non-verbal communications?

In spite of the modern pervasiveness of the problem, Williston, in the article already quoted, could not cite a single pre-Civil War discussion of the *general issue*. He inferred the existence of a subjectivist approach from the treatment in judicial opinions of a small number of the issues just listed, particularly the contract by correspondence. These cases state it as an axiom that contract depends on a "meeting of the minds," but so do virtually all Classical and modern opinions. The most important single piece of evidence of subjectivism was that the early writers seemed to feel that proof positive that the offeror had changed his mind before the unwitting offeree accepted destroyed the contract. The evidence is sparse to say the least.

The reason for this is that formation in general played only a minuscule part in the theoretical literature. As we have seen, doctrinal writing was dominated by the concepts of relationship and implied intent. It was only after the emergence of the will theory, with its insistence on a sharp distinction between judge and litigant, implied in fact and implied in law, that writers began their treatises with long chapters on offer and acceptance. Problems of definiteness, contract by correspondence, and unilateral mistake were discussed, but often separately, and never in the context of a few powerful generalizations, whether subjectivist, objectivist, both, or neither. Interpretation of existing contracts was an altogether distinct subject, and it was possible to treat it according to principles bearing little or no relation to those of formation.

Parsons may serve once more as an example, perhaps most appropriately here, since Langdell was his research assistant, Holmes his student and Williston the editor of the last edition of his treatise. Moreover, his second volume (1854) contained what seems to have been the first attempt at a somewhat general state-

ment of the problem of form. As was often the case with the pre-
scient insights of the 1850's, what was new was encased and
obscured in a mass of typically pre-Classical analysis.

Pound chose the following from Parsons' chapter on
Construction as the archtypical statement of the ideal of "security" in law:

> If any one contract is properly construed, justice is done to the
> parties directly interested therein. But the rectitude, consistency,
> and uniformity of all construction enables all parties to do justice
> to themselves. For then all parties, before they enter into con-
> tracts, or make or accept instruments, may know the force and
> effect of the words they employ, of the precautions they use, and
> of the provisions which they make in their own behalf, or permit
> to be made by other parties.
>
> It is obvious that this consistency and uniformity of construc-
> tion can exist only so far as construction is governed by fixed prin-
> ciples, or, in other words, is matter of law. [IIP2d 4]

After asserting that the rule of construction was the same in law
and in equity, Parsons stated his alternative to the orthodox position (e.g., II Kent 760; IV Kent 107-08) that the actual intent of the
parties will control contrary contractual language:

> The first point is, to ascertain what the parties themselves meant
> and understood. But however important this inquiry may be, it is
> often insufficient to decide the whole question. The rule of law is
> not that the court will always construe a contract to mean that
> which the parties to it meant; but rather that the court will give to
> the contract the construction which will bring it as near to the
> actual meaning of the parties as the words they saw fit to employ,
> when properly construed, and the rules of law, will permit. In
> other words, courts cannot adopt a construction of any legal
> instrument which shall do violence to the rules of language, or to
> the rules of law. [Id. 6]

What made Parsons' accomplishment extraordinary was that he
abstracted the analysis of the interpretation of existing contracts
to cover the distinct situation in which the interpretation process

216   determines the prior question of formation. Parsons was certainly the first to go this far:

> This desire of the law to effectuate rather than defeat a contract, is wise, just, and beneficial. But it may be too strong. And in some instances language is used in reference to this subject which itself needs construction, and a construction which shall greatly qualify its meaning. Thus, Lord C. J. Hobart said: ——"I do exceedingly commend the judges that are curious and almost subtle, astute, (which is the word used in the Proverbs of Solomon in a good sense when it is to a good end,) to invent reasons and means to make acts according to the just intent of the parties, and to avoid wrong and injury, which by rigid rules might be wrought out of the act." Lord Hale quotes and approves these words, and Willes, C. J., quoting Hale's approbation, adds his own. And yet this cannot be sound doctrine; it cannot be the duty of a court that sits to administer the law, and for no other purpose, to be curious and subtle, or astute, or to invent reasons and make acts, in order to escape from rigid rules. All that can be true or wise in this doctrine is, that courts should effectuate a contract or an instrument wherever this can be done by a perfectly fair and entirely rational construction of the language actually used. To do more than this would be to sacrifice to the apparent right of one party in one case, that steadfast adherence to law and principle, which constitutes the only protection and defence of all rights, and all parties.

Yet even this statement is far from the degree of abstraction of Classical objectivism. It did not embrace all of contract law, not to speak of the generalization of the position to tort and to public law. Parsons saw his model of interpretation within the pre-Classical frame of reference as a conflict between morality and policy, as one of the endless series of particular illustrations of the most general of pre-Classical legal categories:

> It may be true ethically, that a party is bound by the meaning which he knew the other party to intend, or to believe that he himself intended; but certainly this is not always legally true. Thus, in the cases already supposed, he who was to give might know that

the party who was to receive, (a foreigner perhaps, unacquainted with our language,) believed that the promise was for "oxen," when the word "horses" was used; but nevertheless an action on this contract could not be sustained for "oxen." So if he who was to pay money knew that the payee expected compound interest, this would not make him liable for compound interest as such, although the specific sums payable were made less, because they were to bear compound interest. In all these cases, it is one question whether an action may be maintained on the contract so explained, and another very different question, whether the contract may not be entirely set aside, because it fails to express the meaning of the parties, or is tainted with fraud; and being so avoided, the parties are left to fall back upon the rights and remedies that may belong to their mutual relations and responsibilities. [Id. 9-10]

And on this general issue, Parsons was, exactly like Kent, unwilling to commit himself *either* to the virtues of "technicality" represented here by objectivism, *or* to an unbuttoned liberality. Exactly like Kent, he acknowledged not just that the law must sometimes appeal directly to subjective intent and to morality, but that there was at least sometimes a necessity for standards that flatly contradicted the whole idea of objectivity. I quoted at the beginning of the last chapter from his description of the law of fraud as a compromise of morality and policy. Here is what he said about the framing of the concrete legal doctrines implementing that compromise:

It follows that a certain amount of selfish cunning passes unrecognized by the law; that any man may procure to himself, in his dealings with other men, some advantages to which he has no moral right, and yet succeed perfectly in establishing his legal right to them. But it follows also, that if any one carries this too far; if by craft and selfish contrivance he inflicts injury upon his neighbor and acquires a benefit to himself, beyond a certain point, the law steps in, and annuls all that he has done, as a violation of law. The practical question, then, is, where is this point; and to this question the law gives no specific answer. And it is somewhat

218   noticeable, that the common law not only gives no definition of
fraud, but perhaps asserts as a principle, that there shall be no definition of it. It is of the very nature and essence of fraud to elude
all laws, and violate them in fact, without appearing to break them
in form; and if there were a technical definition of fraud, and
everything must come within the scope of its words before the law
could deal with it as fraud, the very definition would give to the
crafty just what they wanted, for it would tell them precisely how
to avoid the grasp of the law. Whenever, therefore, any court has
before it a case in which one has injured another, directly or indirectly, by falsehood or artifice, it is for the court to determine in
that case whether what was done amounts to cognizable fraud.
Still, this important question is not left to the arbitrary, or, as it
might be, accidental decision of each court in each case; for all
courts are governed, or at least directed, by certain rules and
precedents, which we will now consider. [Id. 263-64]

The discussions in Parsons' second volume of construction and
fraud were more elaborate and more serious than anything in the
first. They suggest a dawning consciousness of a terrible problem. Classical objectivism was a response to this change in awareness. For example, in the first volume, Parsons' brief chapter on
"Assent of the Parties" is wholly innocent of the existence of an
issue of objectivity in the law of offer and acceptance. For example on the issue of the length of time an offer remains open for
acceptance, Parsons adopted his typical framework of "implied
intent." He first enunciated the usual rule that unless the offeror
fixes its duration, the offer may be accepted within a "reasonable"
time. He then fudged the issue of voluntariness:

> It may be said, that in either case, *the intention or understanding of
> the parties is to govern.* If the proposer fixes a time, he expresses his
> intention, and the other party knows precisely what it is. If no def-
> inite time is stated, then the inquiry as to a reasonable time
> resolves itself into an inquiry as to what time it is rational to sup-
> pose that the parties contemplated; and the *law will decide this to be
> that time which as rational men they ought to have understood each
> other to have in mind.* [Id. 405, my emphasis]

Proceeding to the "analogous and closely connected question" of   219
when the revocation of an offer becomes effective, Parsons again
obscured the issue objectivism brought to the fore. The problem
in this situation is as follows: The rule then and now is that the
revocation is effective only on receipt. The offeree can therefore
bind the offeror by putting an acceptance in the mail after the
offeror has changed his mind, but before he has gotten his message
through. Parsons handled the issue of the reality of the offeror's
intent to be bound as follows:

> We consider that an offer by letter is a continuing offer until the
> letter be received, and for a reasonable time thereafter, during
> which the party to whom it is addressed may accept the offer. We
> hold also that this offer may be withdrawn by the maker at any
> moment; and that it is withdrawn as soon as a notice of such with-
> drawal reaches the party to whom the offer is made, and not
> before. If, therefore, that party accepts the offer before such with-
> drawal, the bargain is completed; there is then a contract *founded
> upon mutual assent*. [Id., 406-07, my emphasis]

Parsons does not discuss at all the issue of unilateral mistake,
which was the key to the whole question of objectivism for both
Williston and Whittier. In the area of agency, he used the estoppel concept to justify the liability of the principal when an agent
acts within his apparent but in violation of his actual authority.
[Id. 38-39; 43; 44-46]

    It seems as clear as such things ever are that the first volume of
Parsons is much more representative than the second. Leake,
whose treatise of 1867 was the first to state the contract/quasi-
contract distinction as an important organizing principle, and who,
in a passage already quoted, claimed concern with general theory,
was probably the first to focus the issue.

> Agreement consists in two persons being of the same mind con-
> cerning the matter agreed upon. The state of mind or intention of
> a person, being impalpable to the senses, can be ascertained only
> by means of outward expressions, as words and acts. Accordingly,
> the law judges of the state of mind or intention of a person by out-

ward expressions only, and thus excludes all questions concerning intentions unexpressed. It imputes to a person a state of mind or intention corresponding to the rational and honest meaning of his words and actions; and where the conduct of a person towards another, judged by a reasonable standard, manifests an intention to agree in regard to some matter, that intention is established in law as a fact, whatever may be the real but unexpressed state of his mind on the matter. [Leake 8]

The first attempt to bring Leake's principles to bear systematically on the problem of the contract by correspondence was Langdell's (1871), although he had nothing to say about mistake or construction. At the end of a discussion that blends the issues in a way that is almost unintelligible today, he concluded that an acceptance must be received and read before a contract by correspondence can be formed. In other words, he thought that the mailbox rule was wrong because it was based on the faulty conception that the law was concerned with the meeting of the minds in itself rather than with its communication. In considering the arguments in favor of the mailbox rule, he said the following:

> 4. It has been claimed that the purposes of substantial justice, and the interests of contracting parties as understood by themselves, will be best served by holding that the contract is complete the moment the letter of acceptance is mailed; and cases have been put to show that the contrary view would produce not only unjust but absurd results. The true answer to this argument is, that it is irrelevant; but, assuming it to be relevant, it may be turned against those who use it without losing any of its strength. [L. 20-21]

Compare the following discussion of the revocation of offers, which is perhaps the clearest of all the early objectivist arguments:

> An opinion has prevailed, to some extent, that an offer is only evidence of the offerer's state of mind, and hence that it will be destroyed by any satisfactory evidence that the offerer has changed his mind since he made the offer; and this has been supposed to be a necessary consequence of the rule that, in order to make a contract, the minds of the contracting parties must concur

at the time of making it. But an offer is much more than evidence of the offerer's state of mind; otherwise, communication to the offeree would not be of its essence. It is, indeed, evidence of the offerer's state of mind, but it is not evidence which can be rebutted, except by showing that the offer has expired, or has been revoked. If an offer could be destroyed by evidence that the offerer has changed his mind, it could also be rehabilitated after it has expired by evidence that the offerer continued of the same mind. As to the rule that the wills of the contracting parties must concur, it only means that they must concur in legal contemplation, and this they do whenever an existing offer is accepted, no matter how much the offerer has changed his mind since he made the offer. In truth, mental acts or acts of the will are not the materials out of which promises are made; a physical act on the part of the promisor is indispensable; and when the required physical act has been done, only a physical act can undo it. An offer is a physical and a mental act combined, the mental act being in legal intendment embodied in, and represented by, and inseparable from, the physical act. [Id 243-44]

After Langdell, the discussions of offer and acceptance identified the issue of objectivism quite unambiguously, but the mode of formulation still varied widely. Pollock and Anson stated that parties were held from time to time against their will, but chose to put this in terms of a requirement of real assent modified by a "rule of evidence" under which "when men present all the phenomena of agreement they are not allowed to say they were not agreed." [Anson 3d p.9n.] The formula that won the day was rather that of Holland (1880). His mode of statement shows at how late a date the whole problem of objectivism in contract was unresolved:

Is it the case that a contract is not entered into unless the wills of the parties are really at one? Must there be, as Savigny puts it, "a union of several wills to a single, whole and undivided will?" Or should we not rather say that here, as elsewhere, the law looks, not at the will itself, but at the will as voluntarily manifested? When the law enforces contracts, it does so to prevent disappointment of well-founded expectations, which, though they usually arise from expressions truly representing intention, yet may occasionally arise otherwise.

If one of the parties to a contract enters into it, and induces the other party to enter into it, resolved all the while not to perform his part under it, the contract will surely be good nevertheless. Not only will the dishonest contractor be unable to set up his original dishonest intent as an excuse for non-performance, but should he, from any change of circumstances, become desirous of enforcing the agreement against the other party, the latter will never be heard to establish, even were he in a position to do so by irrefragable proof, that at the time when the agreement was made the parties to it were not really of one mind.

This view is put forward with some diffidence, opposed as it is to the current of authority from Javolenus to Mr. F. Pollock and Sir W. Anson, but when the question is once raised it is hard to see how it can be supposed that the true consensus of the parties is within the province of law, which must needs regard not the will itself but the will as expressed, taking care only that the expression of will exhibits all those characteristics of a true act which have already been enumerated. [Holland 2nd pp. 194-95]

Objectivism and the "Nature" of Contract

There remains the point that objectivism was not then, as it is today, conceived as posing no more than a series of issues of policy. In the passage from Parsons' discussion of construction quoted on page 215, *supra*, we find him claiming that the judge must disregard the subjective intent and act on the "real" meaning of the words used. There is a policy argument for this, but there is also a strong suggestion that it would be wrong and irrational rather than merely impolitic for the judge to proceed otherwise.

A similar contrast existed in the offer and acceptance discussions. On the one hand, there was the idea that in order to do substantial justice and achieve a measure of certainty, the court would disregard evidence of actual subjective intent and bind or discharge the parties objectively. The purpose was clearly to punish fraud or negligence and to enhance predictability. On the other

hand, writers like Holland at least suggested that there was some
sense in which objectivism was the result of the "logic" of law.
Leake derived his objectivism, at least apparently, as a deduction
from the fact that the inner state of mind is unknowable. The
reports are full of statements with an axiomatic, *a priori* ring, as for
example:

> All the plaintiff did was merely to determine in his own mind that
> he would accept the offer—for there was nothing whatever to
> indicate it by way of speech or other appropriate act. Plainly, this
> did not create any rights in his favor as against the defendants.
> From the very nature of a contract this must be so; and it there-
> fore seems superfluous to add that the universal doctrine is that an
> uncommunicated mental determination cannot create a binding
> contract. [69 N.H. 305 (1898); K&G 174]

The distinction between the two kinds of justification for objectivism was discussed in modern terms for the first time in an article by George Costigan published in 1907. He was commenting on
one of Walter Wheeler Cook's early polemical excursions, which
contained the following remark about the mailbox rule:

> "As yet no one has arisen to argue that, inasmuch as real assent on
> the part of A is lacking there has been no meeting of minds, and
> so that no contract has been made; that, therefore, the true expla-
> nation of A's liability is to be sought in estoppel —he has repre-
> sented to B that the offer is still open, B has changed his legal posi-
> tion in reliance on this representation, and A is therefore estopped
> to deny that a contract has been made."
>
> May be nobody has arisen to call such contracts ones by estop-
> pel; may be nobody will arise to do so. But certain it is that they
> are not, from the point of view of legal philosophy, contracts
> based on genuine mutual assent, though of course they are
> enforced as such contracts every day in the year. And why are
> they enforced as mutual assent contracts? Only because no name
> has been coined for them. It is only a short time since quasi-con-
> tracts were insisted upon as genuine implied contracts because
> assumpsit was the remedy on them; yet they never were genuine
> contracts and to-day bear the distinctive name quasi-contracts. In

THE RISE AND FALL OF CLASSICAL LEGAL THOUGHT

the same way, though we teachers in the law of contracts are, for the present, obliged to tell our students that the "meeting of minds" talked of in the contract cases is often a misnomer, —-that a meeting of the expressions of the parties in an offer of contract and a communicated acceptance is enough to make a mutual assent contract despite the fact that in an accurate sense of the words the minds of the parties never meet at one and the same moment of time; —-we do this because the poverty of legal phraseology so compels. [19 Green Bag 512, 513]

After proposing the name "constructive contract" for situations where objectivism prevails over the intent of parties, he added that it was "only fair to notice" that constructive contracts were "doubtless once regarded as literally what above are called consensual contracts." Objectivism was "born of practical necessity, or if one prefers, a fair rule of the game of making contracts." [Id. 516] "Yet in applauding [it] we must not go so far as to say that the absence of a consensus of minds is the same thing as its presence." [Id. 515] "[I]t is only confusing to treat the obligations of such an unwilling party as if they rested on the same kind of consent that obligations actually intended by all parties at the time they arise rest upon." [Id. 516]

If the Costigan analysis is accepted, it becomes reasonable to ask, as Whittier did in 1927, why we should use the inflexible and inherently deceptive technique of full contractual liability to achieve tort objectives. And the question of objectivism ceases to be a unified one, becoming an ad hoc investigation of pros and cons of policy in particular situations. This modern attitude is at a great distance both from the unintegrated pre-Classical treatment and from the Classical belief that objectivism was part of the science of law. Here is a sample from a judicial opinion of 1947:

It is true that there is much room for interpretation once the parties are inside the framework of a contract, but it seems that there is less in the field of offer and acceptance. Greater precision of expression may be required, and less help from the court given, when the parties are merely at the threshold of a contract. If a court should undertake to resolve ambiguities in the negotiations between parties, disregard clerical errors, and rearrange words, leaving out some and putting in others, it is hard to see where the line of demarcation could be drawn and the general effect would inevitably be a condition of chaos and uncertainty. [75 F. Supp. 137; K&G 187-88]

Autonomy

The issue of autonomy vs. community is at least as pervasive within contract law as that of formality vs. informality, but it is less visible. Indeed, there exists, to my knowledge, no general discussion of it at all in the legal literature. The closest thing to it is contained in Prof. Gilmore's book on what he calls the "classical" contract theory of Langdell, Holmes and Williston.

The book contains fragmentary references to a theory of "absolute liability," meaning the constriction to extreme cases of doctrines nullifying contracts in case of impossibility, frustration or mistake. Gilmore associated this position with the ideas that third party beneficiaries have no rights, that there can be no suit for breach until performance has become impossible, and that plaintiffs in default can never recover. He added the idea that there should be the widest possible scope for pre-contractual maneuver and puffing, with no liability for ensuing damages if the contract falls through, and the idea that the law of fraud should impose only the most minimal duties on sellers.

What links these doctrines is that they all deal with parties within or just outside of contractual relationships who suffer losses or reap benefits that are neither clearly attributable to negligence nor bargained over in advance. The judge must devise rules allocating the gains and losses, ranging from letting them lie where they fall, to imposing them on someone, to splitting them equitably. I call "autonomist" solutions to this dilemma that insist that one party to the relationship has no obligation to share the other's losses or his own gains. Autonomism also means a preference for sets of rules that leave each party free to *increase* the other's losses in pursuit of his own gain.

Autonomy in contract is thus closely analogous to autonomy in property law. The cutting off of the easements that forced an

226   owner to look after his neighbor's interests corresponds to the doctrines that reduced the interdependence of contractual parties when unexpected losses occur. Since there is no theoretical literature on the issue as it arises in contract, and to trace the dilemma through each doctrinal area would take too much space, I will restrict the discussion to the crucial instances of the theory of conditions, and the problem of extra-contractual reliance.

The issue of autonomy arises in the area of conditions as follows: Suppose two parties, A and B, each of whom has promised a performance to the other. Further suppose that A is scheduled to perform before B, but is unable to do so. B then must decide whether to go ahead and do his part, seeking some compensation for A's breach, or to drop the whole contract. If the law says that he must go ahead, and sue A for whatever damages his breach may have caused, then we call the promises of A and B "independent covenants." If, on the other hand, A's default allows B to drop the whole deal, then performance by A is a "condition precedent" to B's duty.

The testing case for autonomy arises where A's breach is minor, but the losses to A if B drops the deal will be major. If the law is willing to say to B that he must look to A's large loss, compared to his risk of a small one if A refuses to compensate for his breach, and go through with his part, then it is communitarian. If the tendency is to avoid any situation in which we compare the respective losses, and if instead we give B the power to drop A for a slight default even if A will be ruined, then we are after autonomy.

Kent's treatment of this issue as it arose in deeds gives the flavor of the "liberal" strand in the pre-Classical approach:

> If it be doubtful whether a clause in a deed be a covenant or a condition, the courts will incline against the latter construction; for a covenant is far preferable to the tenant. If a condition be broken, the landlord may indulge his caprice, and even malice, against the tenant, without any certain relief; but equity will not enforce a covenant embracing a hard bargain; and, at law, there can be no damages without an injury.... The intention of the party to the instrument, when clearly ascertained, is of controlling efficacy;

though conditions and limitations are not readily to be raised by mere inference and argument. The distinctions on this subject are extremely subtle and artificial; and the construction of a deed, as to its operation and effect, will after all depend less upon artificial rules than upon the application of good sense and sound equity to the object and spirit of the contract in the given case. [IV, 136-37]

In *Norrington v. Wright* (1885), the U.S. Supreme Court held that a seller of goods must make a "perfect tender," complying with *all* the terms of the contract, or the buyer can reject the goods, even if the breach is utterly trivial and the buyer's motive is to get out of what has turned up as a losing bargain. The court was unwilling to initiate a calculus of the degree of breach and the degree of loss to the seller, preferring to give the buyer an absolute power which he could exercise in his own interests without regard to those of his partner. In an historical note to this case, Kessler and Gilmore pointed out that:

> The first American treatise on sales law suggests that, half a century earlier, the tender rule had been quite different: except for serious defects in the goods, the buyer had to accept the tender and sue in damages for breach; he did not have the privilege of rejection. See Story on Sales S.448 (1847). Thus, aspects of the sales contract which had been "independent covenants" in the first half of the century had become true "conditions precedent" by 1890. [Kessler & Gilmore p. 833]

The law of conditions deals with the problem of interdependence within an established contractual relationship. The problem of autonomy vs. community also arises regularly when one party relies to his detriment on non-fraudulent and non-negligent representations that don't become contractual obligations, or become contractual and are then voided by mistake or the like. When the events promised or foretold do not come to pass, the relying party sues for damages. The judge must decide whether to set rules that will oblige the party responsible to share the loss, or to declare that although there may be a moral obligation, there has been no breach of legal duty.

The strategy of autonomy here consists in maintaining a

228   vivid contrast between two states. Before a formal contract is signed, the parties are "at arms length," unless the relationship is fiduciary. Their only duties toward one another are those that apply even between strangers, though in fact they may be intimately involved. After the contract has been signed, this changes utterly, and each must perform his obligations even if ruined.

The doctrinal vehicles for the playing out of the conflict of autonomy and community are the consideration doctrine, with its counter rule of promissory estoppel, and the concept of "quantum meruit," a survival from the days before quasi-contract, through which the courts *sometimes* protect reliance outside of formal contracts. The story of the rise of counterrules in response to the theoretical dominance of the strategy of autonomy after the Civil War has been well told elsewhere. The outcome has been that we are now aware of the pervasive problem of protecting extra-contractual reliance, but have no coherent theory to explain either when during negotiations duties begin, or to what *extent* the parties accept responsibility for each other's welfare once that point is passed.

∾ 5 ∾

The Classical Theory of Torts

The Classical theory of torts has a clear cut internal structure much easier to describe than that of Classical contract law. It can be summed up as follows:

(a) The emergence of will theory was reflected in the tripartite division of the field into:

    (i) *intentional torts,* where liability was based on willful violation of a command of the sovereign, so that will figured both as the source of duty and as the criterion of its violation.

    (ii) *negligence,* where liability was based on the will of

the sovereign acting in response to a defect in the will of the defendant.

(iii) *liability without fault*, based on the will of the sovereign concerning the equitable or otherwise socially desirable redistribution of losses that would otherwise lie where they fell.

(b) Autonomy was expressed in the slogan of no liability without fault, which reversed the earlier presumption of liability wherever there was damage (in the absence of "inevitable accident"), and represented a constriction of the legal bonds obligating actors to take account of the effects of their activities on the welfare of others.

(c) Objectivism was reflected in the development of the reasonable man standard of liability into a prominent instrument of analysis, with an ambiguity, as in contract objectivism, as to whether it was policy or the internal logic of legal science that required the random imposition of liability without moral fault in a system that claimed to embody moral notions.

Legal historians seem to be in virtually universal agreement that such was the self-conscious, formal organization of the theory of torts at the end of the nineteenth century. It is impossible to determine to what extent this description would apply meaningfully to the total pattern of actual results, but it was tolerably overt in treatises, articles and leading cases. The main problem for us is to determine more specifically than has been done in the past the sequence of events. My contention is that, as with contract law, the new synthesis emerged only between 1870 and 1880, rather than, as the conventional wisdom would have it, in the 1850's. My second point is unlikely to be controversial and I will do no more than state it. The modern dilemmas of tort law, which have to do with the tensions between fault and compulsory insurance and between expensive systems ensuring full compensation and cheap ones that allow leeways for the arbitrary imposition of uncompensated damage, are altogether absent from pre-Classical legal thought.

The Will Theory and Autonomy

The event that has attracted the attention of modern historians of tort law is that between 1850 and 1855, beginning with the Massachusetts case of Brown v. Kendall, there appeared a spate of judicial opinions declaring that it was a general principle that a person acting with due care in a course of conduct not illegal in itself was not liable for damages accidentally caused to the persons or property of others. These opinions are supposed to mark the "triumph of negligence" over liability without fault. Prior to 1850, the argument goes, negligence (hence fault) was a requirement only in the action on the case. Liability in trespass was based on the fact of injury rather than any particular mental element, except for cases of "inevitable accident." These were cases in which the defendant was conceived as not having acted at all, since the injury could not have been prevented no matter what he did.

After 1850, the argument goes, any injury that happened in spite of the defendant's exercise of due care came to be defined as an inevitable accident. We began with a narrow exception to a general notion that, for the class of acts called trespasses to the person, damage led to liability. We ended with the idea that negligent acts were exceptions to the general proposition that damages from accidents should lie where they fall. Since negligence had all along been necessary in the action on the case, the events of 1850-1855 eliminated liability without fault from the law of injuries to the person.

Professor Horwitz has suggested two reservations with respect to this thesis. First, there were at least four opinions during the 1830's and 1840's, all from New York, that enunciated with perfect clarity the distinctions and the general principle for which *Brown v. Kendall* and the year 1850 are famous. Second, the action on the case had not developed a clear theory of liability based on negligence long before the corresponding change in trespass. Rather, there was a generalized emergence of negligence across the board, with 1850 an especially important year, but not a year of conceptional revolution. With these emendations, I have found nothing that contradicts the conventional theory, as far as it goes.

The difficulty arises when we attempt to pin down the meaning
of the language in which the judges phrased their new general
principle. Here is an example from New York in 1832:

> In most of the cases referred to, the question chiefly discussed was
> whether the action should be trespass or trespass on the case. But
> the general principle which I have stated, in relation to the liabili-
> ty of a defendant, is to be fairly deduced from them. When we
> speak of an unavoidable accident, in legal phraseology, we do not
> mean an accident which it was physically impossible in the nature
> of things for the defendant to have prevented; all that is meant is,
> that it was not occassioned, in any degree either remotely or
> directly, by the want of such care and skill as the law holds every
> man bound to exercise. [Dygert v. Bradley, 8 Wend. 469, 472-73]

The famous language of *Brown v. Kendall* (1859) is as follows:

> We think, as a result of all the authorities, the rule is correctly stat-
> ed by Mr. Greenleaf, that the plaintiff must come prepared with
> evidence to show either that the *intention* was unlawful, or that the
> defendant was *in fault*; for if the injury was unavoidable, and the
> conduct of the defendant was free from blame, he will not be
> liable. ...If, in the prosecution of a lawful act, a casualty purely
> accidental arises, no action can be supported for an injury arising
> therefrom. [6 Cush. 292, 295-96]

The evidence as a whole suggests the following ill-assorted conclusions about the meaning of these words:

(a) The judges in question saw themselves as stating a rule
    whose scope was
    (i) wider than any particular form of action (their think
    ing was liberated from primitive proceduralism); and
    (ii) wider than the injuries covered by the writs of case
    and trespass to the person.
(b) But they did not conceive of themselves as generalizing
    about a field of "tort law" representing the total residu-
    um of the law of wrongs after subtracting breach of
    contract, quasi-contractual obligation, and status.
(c) Insomuch as they spoke of wrongs not included in tres-

pass to the person and case, they misstated the law, since liability without fault was then and remained the rule in at least the following areas:

- (i) trespass to real property
- (ii) battery
- (iii) nuisance
- (iv) respondeat superior
- (v) responsibility of bailees such as innkeepers and common carriers.

(d) But while torts as we currently conceive it contained many areas of absolute liability, the slogan of no liability without fault was that of a powerful reforming elite with a real chance of substantially remodeling the law to correspond to its emerging vision of justice and policy.

What it is hard to imagine is the inchoacy of torts between 1850 and 1870. The initial assertion of the general principle of no liability without fault was made not *within* the context of a developed theory of the field, but as one of the incidents in its creation. The slogan helped bring into existence the context in which we now know exactly what it means. When it was first put forward, its meaning was relatively indeterminate.

In the Classical view, there were two kinds of liability: "with fault" meant there must be a showing of intent or of a degree of negligence; "without fault" meant you were liable even if you exercised due care. In the Classical view, a "general" principle was one that applied to all of torts, and torts included all of the cases of liability without fault listed above. It followed from this set of definitions, applied to the legal rules, that torts was a battleground. On one side were those favoring liability based on the sovereign's redistributive will carried out regardless of fault. On the other were those who would recognize the autonomy of legal actors within the sphere bounded by intentional wrongdoing and negligence.

The *pre*-Classical vision of the subject, *circa* 1850, already included the "no liability without fault" slogan. The evidence that the pre-Classical view was nonetheless indeterminate, rather than Classical, is as follows:

First. The treatises published between 1859 and 1880 did not put forward "no liability without fault" as an integrating generalization in the manner of the cases. They did not even organize the new field in these terms. Rather, they looked for categories that would fudge the distinction (e.g., sic utere tuo ut alienum non loedas) and preserve the all-inclusiveness of torts as a subject.

Second. In the early 1870's, Holmes wrote a series of reviews and articles that included liability without fault as an obviously important part of torts; during this period he, and Markby as well, tended to deny that negligence really involved fault at all, given the enormous discretion of juries to give it the meaning that seemed best to them.

Third. In the period 1872-75, several American Courts took up the question of whether to "receive" the doctrine of *Rylands v. Fletcher*, imposing liability without fault on landowners using their land in "unnatural" ways. Rylands rested on general principles, rather than on reference to existing pleading categories such as trespass or nuisance. The American courts treated the question of whether there could *ever* be liability without fault as open, and then decided it in the negative. In a case involving an accidental explosion, the Supreme Court, per Field, J., for the first time declared its allegiance to the slogan of *Brown v. Kendall*.

Fourth. In the 1850's, numerous legislatures passed statutes imposing liability without fault on railroads for fires caused by sparks from locomotives. When these were challenged as violations of due process, the state Supreme Courts affirmed them. In the 1870's, the same legislatures imposed liability without fault for cattle killed in various kinds of accidental encounters with trains. The state courts began to strike these down on the ground that liability without fault violated fundamental constitutional principles. Supreme Courts upholding the legislation argued that it did not in fact attempt to eliminate fault, rather than that the legislature could do so if it pleased.

Fifth. Beginning only with Bigelow's Treatise of 1878, there was a gradual movement toward the organization of the subject as Intentional Torts, Negligence and Liability Without Fault, but this organization was not clearly present in any book before

234   Pollock's of 1886. Cooley's famous treatise of 1879 reiterated the doctrine of *Brown v. Kendall,* but also contained a number of statements to the effect that there is "no anomaly in compelling one who is not chargeable with wrong intent to make compensation for an injury committed by him; for, as is said in an early case, the reason is, because he that is damaged ought to be compensated." [99]

    Sixth. In *The Common Law* (1880), Holmes revised his earlier position, and adopted the view that there should be no liability without fault, though "fault" meant conformity to an external standard rather than "actual" moral blameworthiness. He asserted the theoretical unity of tort law with criminal law, thereby accepting the essential features of Shaw's position of 1850. [See also II Howe, Ch.7]

    Given this evidence, we should place the emergence of the Classical/modern framework of tort law in the decade 1870-80. The beginning of the transition is the debate about *Rylands v. Fletcher,* 1872-75. The transition was complete with Holmes' lectures in 1880. Pollock's treatise of 1886 collected and systematized the elements of the new ordering, as Holmes acknowledged ten years afterward in his "Path of the Law" lecture.

Objectivism

The emergence of objectivism is as easy to deal with in torts as it is difficult in contracts. The leading case was English, *Blyth v. Birmingham,* decided in 1847. Treatise and opinion writers quoted it endlessly to the effect that:

> "Negligence," is the omission to do something which a reasonable man, guided upon those considerations which ordinarily regulate the conduct of human affairs, would do, or doing something which a prudent and reasonable man would not do.

In the statements before Holmes wrote *The Common Law,* there was not the slightest indication of awareness that the reasonable man standard conflicted with the idea that culpability was the foundation of liability. The choice of standard was founded on

policy, as in *Blyth*, but it was a policy not articulately opposed by   235
morality. One might attribute to a dawning awareness of inconsistency Cooley's attempt to blur the issue in his 1879 treatise:

> [N]egligence in a legal sense is no more nor less than this: the fail-
> ure to observe, for the protection of the interests of another per-
> son, that degree of care, precaution, and vigilance which the cir-
> cumstances justly demand, whereby such other person suffers
> injury....
>
> But in a very large proportion of the cases in which negligence
> is counted upon, the facts are of that ambiguous quality, or the
> proper conclusion so doubtful, that different minds would be
> unable to agree concerning the existence of fault, or the responsi-
> bility for it. The question will often be, does the defendant appear
> to have exercised the degree of care which a reasonable man
> would be expected to exercise under like circumstances? [Cooley,
> Torts, 630; 668]

Cooley here exemplified that pre-Classical fuzziness the Classics
most abhorred. Holmes gave the answer a year later:

> Notwithstanding the fact that the grounds of legal liability are
> moral to the extent above explained, it must be borne in mind that
> law only works within the sphere of the senses. If the external
> phenomena, the manifest acts and omissions, are such as it
> requires, it is wholly indifferent to the internal phenomena of con-
> science. A man may have as bad a heart as he chooses, if his con-
> duct is within the rules. In other words, the standards of the law
> are external standards, and, however much it may take moral con-
> siderations into account, it does so only for the purpose of draw-
> ing a line between such bodily motions and rests as it permits, and
> such as it does not. What the law really forbids, and the only thing
> it forbids, is the act on the wrong side of the line, be that act
> blameworthy or otherwise. [Holmes, *The Common Law*, 88]

After *The Common Law*, the treatise writers made no effort to dis-
guise the character of the standard; but they also felt no need to
offer any explanation of its consistency with the slogan of no liability without fault. They seemed to suffer from the same uncon-

236   sciousness of the issue as characterized the contract theorists who
treated as "true contracts" those that Costigan saw as merely
"constructive." This is the puzzle of objectivism in a period that
exalted private will and believed in the meaningfulness of the concept of individual culpability.

∾ 6 ∾

In the next chapter, I will argue that once we add the theory of the
judicial role to will theory, autonomy and objectivism, we can see
that Classical legal thought was an entity with an internal logic. It
may be helpful, as a preliminary, to end this chapter with a sketch
of the way the notion of "internal logic" can help in understanding anomalies like that of objectivism in a fault-oriented system.

Mark Howe has suggested that Holmes' position in favor of
liability only for fault, but fault objectively determined, represented a "compromise" between an American trend in favor of,
and an English trend against culpability as a determinant of
responsibility. He also suggested that the explanation for Holmes'
choice of the reasonable man standard was a reformer's urge to
make the law more socially useful by making it more certain. On
the other hand, it has been common to attack the late 19th Century
tort rules as a covert subsidy to big business, and to defend them
as the embodiment of a program of economically efficient judge-
made law that left questions of distribution to the legislatures.

It seems to me very hard to argue that any particular pattern of
outcomes is implicit in the reasonable man test. Too much
depends on the choices made along the road about causation,
about the definition of an act, and about the sources of "reasonable" behavior. The accomplishment of modernist analysis has
been to show that the ambiguities in the treatment of these issues
amounted to a veritable quicksand of counter rules and illusory
distinctions lying across the straight path of principle. Judges so
minded had no need to reject the Classical rhetoric even when
they sought unclassical results.

Howe's suggestion may be more useful, especially if we keep
in mind that quasi-contract is to objective contract as liability

without fault is to objective fault. In each area the Classics adopted the latter form of liability while restricting the former to special cases seen as vestigial. In each area, the moderns strengthened their argument against the logical necessity of the Classical conclusions by pointing this out. But in each case, there was a real though unarticulated difference.

The judge making rules of quasi-contractual liability or defining categories of tort liability without fault was obeying no will but his own. When there was no statute governing the matter and, ex hypothesis, no identifiable aspect of the will of the parties on which to hang the decision, the judge had to refer directly to morality and policy, the two ultimate sources of rules in all periods of common law history. In other words, the judge had to step into the role he usually at least pretended to reserve for the willing actors in the system.

This may be more obvious in the case of absolute liability than in that of quasi-contract. After all, we have seen the Classics insisting on the importance of a cause of action for restitution in the general scheme of private law, while the pre-Classics gave it only indirect recognition. Moreover, the emergence of quasi-contract as a distinct doctrinal category is often treated as of merely formal significance. It did away with conceptual confusion, in this view, but had no significance for outcomes. This view is incorrect. The distinction between a contractual cause of action for expectation or reliance damages and a restitutionary cause of action for restoral of benefits conferred did affect results. Specifically, it eliminated, in theory but not altogether in practice, the granting of reliance damages in situations where the parties had a relationship falling short of an enforceable contract. [Perillo, 73 Col. L. Rev.]

Before the creation of the sharp contrast between contract and restitution, courts had routinely granted reliance damages in implied contract actions on the "common counts." The characteristic pre-Classical imprecision as to whether the will in question was that of contracting parties or of a redistributively minded sovereign had camouflaged the issue. When it was brought to the fore by writers like Keener in the 1890's, Classical courts tended to hold that there was no legal basis for shifting losses or gains

238   between the parties where there was neither contract nor benefit
conferred.

   Boone v. Coe, decided in 1913, illustrates the point. The plaintiffs had moved with their household effects from Kentucky to
Texas in reliance on an uncle's oral promise of a farm lease. When
he went back on his promise, they returned to Kentucky and sued
him. There was no claim on the contract, because oral leases are
void under the statute of frauds. But twenty years before, the
court had held that parties in the position of the plaintiffs could
recover on an "implied contract," distinct from the invalid express
contract, for their reliance expenditures. In *Boone*, they overruled
that earlier decision, on the ground that the only recovery "off the
contract" would be of restitution damages, and here there had
been no benefit conferred on the defendant. [153 Ky. 233] Similar
problems arose when the plaintiff had relied during negotiations,
or when a contract turned out to be void because of mistake or
impossibility.

   Boone v. Coe was a typical instance of the Classical strategies of
objectivism and autonomy. The courts constricted the number of
situations in which the parties had to share gains and losses. They
did so through the distinction between restitution, a *relatively* concrete doctrine about the disgorgement of ill gotten gains, and
reliance. Reliance is hard to measure at best, and at worst poses
horrid evidentiary problems.

   More important, there are no obvious limits that can be set to
the idea of compensation for such losses. By definition, the obligation of one party to the other cannot be defined through will
(contract) or fault (tort). If there is a recovery, it must be based on
a notion of community that is more fundamental than either. But
if we recognize a duty to share based on relationship alone we will
be drawn into questions like: How much involvement, beyond
common membership in the human race, generates a legal obligation to share? Given an obligation, how is the judge to apportion
gains and losses?

   Quasi-contract, restricted to cases of benefits conferred,
ressembles liability without fault, restricted to the traditional
"exceptions" of respondeat superior and common carrier liability

as an insurer. In each case, a doctrine whose implications are "rev- olutionary," in the sense of representing the ideals of community and informality, was accepted into the legal order, but cabinned so as to pose no threat to a whole animated by ideals of autonomy and formality. [cf. Dawson, *Restitution*, Ch. 1]

We can also define a relationship between restitution and absolute liability, taken as a unit, and objectivism in tort and contract law. Contract objectivism *functioned* to protect reliance outside of relationships of real assent. The promisee who had taken action on the basis of action by his partner that *looked* contractual could recover in spite of the fact that the partner never intended to be bound. Likewise in tort law, objectivism functioned to redress injuries inflicted by blameless defendants.

Objectivism therefore involved an appeal to and accomodation of autonomy and community. But it crystalized the issue in an abstract principle, a general formula without overt social or political content, which could be followed out, once adopted, according to an impersonal judicial method. Objectivism was therefore consistent with the Classical theory of the separation of powers.

Objectivism was tied, on the one hand, to the will it was supposed, however clumsily, to mirror. On the other, it was constrained, in theory, to the pseudo-scientific determination of actual patterns of behavior. By contrast, quasi-contract and liability without fault brought the judge face to face with the problem of autonomy vs. community. They demanded an *ad hoc* judgment based on all the aspects of the case, about the extent to which the members of society should be obliged to look after each other's interests.

This explanation of why objectivism was more acceptable than quasi-contract and liability without fault also helps in understanding the function of objectivism within the sytem. It rendered the will theory plausible as a basis for the claim of judicial neutrality. It made it possible to claim for the legal order the moral legitimacy of rules based on consent or fault, without requiring the descent into an evidentiary morass that was implicit in genuine subjectivism. And objectivism once adopted, there appeared numerous leeways in the definition of the reasonable man that

240 allowed the injection of the policies ostensibly banished at the moment of the judge's submission to the wills of others. In short, objectivism served, in Classical legal thought, as a mediator of the contradiction of morality and policy; its function was not unlike that of implied intent in the consciousness of the antebellum period.

There is a difference between mediation and compromise, and that is the shortcoming of Howe's approach. *Today*, objectivism, as a way to reduce the tension caused by the conflict of the ideal of individualized justice with that of social efficiency, is implausible. The Moderns have taught us from the first month of law school that there is little or no difference between an open textured reasonable man test and an open textured program of enterprise liability or of judicial regulation of consumer contracts. But, like implied intent for their predecessors, objectivism was much more to the Classics than a name for one approach to one branch of this general problem.

The passages from their writings that I have already quoted suggest strongly that, for them, objectivism actually made the problem go away. "No one arose" to argue that constructive contracts were not "real" contracts, until 1907. After Holmes' sharply etched portrayal of the fundamentally amoral character of external standards, the treatise writers continued for 30 years to repeat the reasonable man standard and the principle of no liability without fault practically in the same breath. There was a crucial distinction between the working out of the logical implications of an apparently neutral abstraction, and ad hoc enforcement of the moral bond that does or should exist among men independently of contract or in spite of it. Issues arising on different sides of that chasm simply did not come to mind as instances of the same thing; it followed that there was no requirement that they be treated consistently.

We are now in a position to give content to the notion that the structure of Classical private law thinking mediated the contradictions of private law theory. This it did, as I said in the last chapter, by organizing private law in terms of a core of self-determination, facilitation, autonomy and formality, surrounded by a periphery of paternalism, regulation, community and informality.

The diagram below uses the image of core and periphery in 241
arranging the subject matters involved in the disintegration and
reconstitution of the pre-Classical law of contracts.

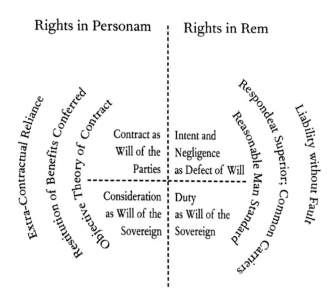

CORE AND PERIPHERY
IN CLASSICAL LEGAL THOUGHT

CHAPTER V

The Integration of Classical Legal Thought

IN THE LAST THREE CHAPTERS, we have examined the conceptual structure of the horizontal dimension of Classical legal thought. My purpose has been to show that that structure changed through the middle decades of the century so that by the 1870's both public and private law were coming to share a number of significant characteristics. All legal rules were more and more cast in terms of areas of autonomy for the wills of legal actors, whether those were private individuals, state legislatures or the federal Congress. The rules required the judge to identify the relevant will objectively, by reference to a formal, external language, rather than attempt to get at "real" or subjective intent.

This conceptual parallelism of all legal rules was one of three kinds of integration achieved by Classical legal thought. This chapter describes in an abstract and schematic fashion the second and third of these. It is a first attempt at a picture of Classical legal thought as a structured whole with a great deal of internal consistency and a powerful internal logic through which it could assimilate new matter.

The only major structural element in this whole that we have not yet addressed directly is the theory of the judicial role. The

next section remedies this deficiency, using what should by now   243
be the familiar model of consciousness as a mediator of the contradictions of experience.

∾ 1 ∾

The constant theme of the theory of the separation of powers, in
pre-Classical, Classical and modern legal thought is that the activity of the judges is an objective, rational one, while that of the legislature is political and, if not arbitrary, at least arational and contingent. It is a striking fact that during the pre-Classical period, a
belief in objectivity and rationality as the hallmarks of the judicial
role was consistent with a general indifference to the problem of
judicial method. Moreover, the sense of acting objectively was
consistent with methodological eclecticism in practice.

As we have seen already many times, pre-Classical judges
unhesitatingly mingled direct appeals to natural rights, morality,
sovereignty, policy and implied intent. These coexisted with arguments from precedent and deductions from legal conceptions
without any apparent tension. By contrast, in Classical and modern legal thought, the requirement of objectivity appears to have
as corollaries both a near obsessive concern with defining and
defending what judges do, and the belief that there is only one
judicial method, applicable to all legal problems.

In both Classical and modern legal thought, the basic strategy
in defense of the objectivity of legal reasoning has been to assert
that judges make new rules by developing the implications of legal
principles that pre-exist them. In both periods, there have been
two main sources for such principles: natural rights and morality;
and the idea of the maximization of social welfare. The difference
between the periods is that the Classical theorists proclaimed the
creed of principle with confidence, enthusiasm, and aggressiveness, while the moderns consider it to be problematic.

Modern theorists preoccupy themselves with attempting to
show that there is some sense in which it is meaningful to describe
the process of legal reasoning as bounded and determinate, and
with attacking as inadequate all the solutions previously put for-

244   ward by other theorists. The main difficulties that each new
knight must confront in his quest are the following:

(1) The general belief in the incompatibility of natural
rights/morality as a premise with social welfare maximization as a premise. When the implications conflict,
the judges must have a way to choose between them, or
he is not bound.

(2) The general belief that there are conflicting *sets* of principles both of morality and right and of social welfare
maximization. These sets have radically different implications for the design of particular rules. If the judge is
free to choose between the conflicting sets, he is not
bound.

(3) The general belief that the federal Constitution does not
unequivocally direct the judge in making choices
between or within the conflicting traditions. Since the
basic public law source of authority points in all directions at once, the judge can justify *any* choice he may
want to make.

(4) The general belief that there is no neutral, objective way
to generate a ratio decidendi from a case. It follows that
the system of precedent only very rarely determines
either the choice among conflicting sets of principles or
the outcome of particular cases.

(5) The general belief that even where, in a particular jurisdiction, a particular principle has been adopted, there is
no such thing as an objective process of derivation of
particular rules for new situations. Both the passage from
principle to rule and that from the mass of raw facts to
the legally operative facts are inescapably open to influence by factors other than the principle itself. ("No rule
can determine the scope of its own application.")

[Consult Holmes, Hohfeld, Pound, Dewey, M. Cohen, F.S.
Cohen, Cardozo, Llewellyn, Walton Hamilton, Fuller, H.L.A.
Hart, Wechsler, Henry Hart, Dworkin, Wasserstrom, Deutsch,
Berman, Wellington.]

The upshot of all the critical and constructive efforts of the modern theorists has been that the only rational decision process consists in a detailed, ad hoc weighing of all the "interests," or "values," or "utilities" that will be affected by adopting one rule or another. This methodological conclusion applies regardless of one's choices between or within the traditions of natural rights/morality and social welfare maximization. The point is that wherever one gets one's criteria, it is impermissible to erect them into principles.

This outcome is the exact reverse of that sought by those who brought it to pass. Each of them proposed some formulation that would distinguish the judicial from the legislative role, while attacking previous formulations. The misfortune has been that the attacks have been cumulatively successful, and none of the suggestions of why judges differ from legislatures, in their *reasoning process*, has survived them.

It is important to keep in mind that we are speaking of judicial methods for elaborating new rules to fill gaps. It is not uncommon to believe that this is an exceptional function, and that in some high percentage of cases (say, 90%) the judge is confronted with a situation in which there is only one possible decision. A variant is to argue that although the mere fact of a lawsuit is some evidence of leeway to choose, the overwhelming number of transactions are completed without litigation, indicating that gaps in the system are relatively infrequent. There is a counter-position to the effect that only a small percentage of the cases that *could* be litigated are litigated, and only a small percentage of these can be decided by an unproblematic application of rules to facts; the absence of a satisfactory theory of judicial reasoning is consequently an extremely important piece of information about the legal system. This dispute is not important, for the moment, since both sides to it concede the existence of the problems of legal reasoning I have just referred to.

The Classics conceded the first two (the incompatibility of natural right/morality with social welfare maximization and the existence of alternative sets of premises within each of the two traditions). But they believed that the Constitution and the com-

246   mon law embodied definite choices, at a very high level of abstraction, among the conflicting premises available. It was possible to induce these from the cases and the sacred text. Moreover, the set of principles chosen was internally consistent, or at least in the process of becoming so, through a natural, organic, incremental evolution. Finally, they believed in the possibility of deducing rules from these principles, so that new cases could be decided in accordance with the pre-existing scheme.

Pollock, in his seminal book on Torts (1886), began by stating that:

> If the collection of rules we call the law of torts is founded on any general principles of duty and liability, those principles have nowhere been stated with authority. [4]

He then induces a general principle:

> Liability for delict, or civil wrong in the strict sense, is the result either of wilful injury to others, or wanton disregard of what is due to them (*dolus*), or of a failure to observe due care and caution which has similar though not intended or expected consequences (*culpa*). [13]

From this it followed that the rules of liability without fault for interference with property were "extraneous matter," [12] "accounted for by historical accident," [13] a "special case." [15] This conclusion was the result of a "scientific" [vi] and "rational" [12] exposition of the subject.

A few pages later, Pollock laid down, in passing, another fundamental idea: "It is not only certain favored kinds of agreements that are protected, but all agreements that satisfy certain general conditions are valid and binding, subject to exceptions which are themselves assignable to general principles of justice and policy." [16] As we have seen already the "general conditions" he refers to concern voluntariness (will theory), and the objective manifestation of assent.

The "exceptions" to the principle of enforcement meant mainly the requirement of consideration, which Classical thinkers used as the principle device for what policing of contracts seemed appropriate to them. They conceived the doctrine as the rational working out of a general idea. The definition of consideration was "detriment to the promisee bargained for or given in exchange for the promise." It followed as a matter of "logic" that the discharge of a debt in exchange for part payment was an unenforceable agreement.

The belief that judicial rulemaking in torts and contracts could proceed by deduction from scientifically induced general principles corresponded to an across-the-board rise in the possible level of abstraction of operative legal concepts. This phenomenon may be crudely but suggestively represented through the notion of a tree of legal rules and principles analogous to a family tree. Let us suppose that the Constitution positively mandates three different rules, which can be arranged as follows:

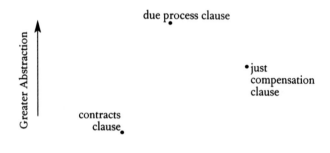

The idea of operativeness is that a number of more concrete subrules are somehow implicit in a legal principle or concept. It is possible to infer the exisitence of the more abstract whole from the concrete part and the concrete part from the more abstract whole. Supposing that a dotted horizontal line represents the level beyond which concepts are inoperative, we can represent the situation: Supposing that rules or principles above the line are considered

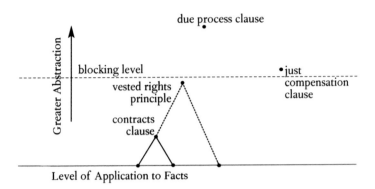

mere catchalls rather than operative catagories, it will follow that
neither due process nor just compensation can be applied by the
judiciary except by the relatively indeterminate and open-ended
processes, such as appeals to morality or natural rights or utility,
that were typical of pre-Classical legal thought. The Contracts
Clause, in our example, is altogether different: it has rules implicit in it, represented here by solid lines (e. g., the rule of the
Dartmouth College Case and that of *Ogden v. Saunders*); and if it
has been once enacted, then the whole of which it is an inseperable
part has also been enacted. The dotted lines running up from
it represent the influence of the existence of a more abstract rule
not expressly written into the Constitution, e. g., the principle that
once a private right "vests" the state may not interfere with it. The
dotted lines running downward represent the idea that a court can,
objectively, infer concrete subrules from an abstraction whose
presence in the Constitution is itself an inference from explicitly
enacted provisions, e. g., *Gelpcke v. Dubuque*. In this figure, the 5th
Amendment requirement of just compensation when private
property is taken for a public use is too abstract to be the basis of
more concrete subrules objectively derived. Of course, the Court
must still enforce it, using its moral intuition, interest-balancing,
or whatever other technique it can devise.

Now suppose that the level of abstraction at which operativeness ceases moves upward:
The raising of the level of abstraction makes it possible to demon-

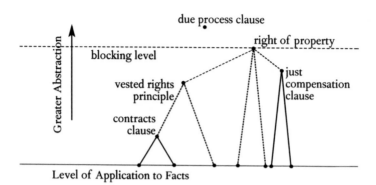

strate that rules previously thought applicable only through subjective processes have objective implications; that several rules previously thought isolated and distinct are implied in a single principle; that the more abstract unifying principle is part of the Constitution; and that previously unknown concrete subrules can be derived from the new abstraction.

What was disruptive about the increasing potency of the method of deduction based on abstract operative concepts was that the method's claims to determine results were inconsistent with the continued viability of the other pre-Classical approaches to judicial reasoning. The claim to objectively determine results was consistent with other methods so long as it applied only to clauses like the ban on titles of nobility. This left all the hard questions to be disposed of through the complex and eclectic arguments of rights and utility. When deduction laid claim to the administration of the due process clause, there was a problem. If the bare language of the Constitution compelled a result in *these* cases, there were simply no questions left to which the method of philosophy could be applied.

This result is implicit in the concept of operativeness itself: it refers to the experience of being bound. The process of deriving subrules from operative concepts is experienced as compulsory. Disagreement can reflect only bad faith or error on one side or the other. It follows that if other methods lead to results different from those of the process of derivation of subrules from rules,

250   then either the premises of the deductive method are wrong, or we must scrap the other methods. In Classical legal thought, the claim was that the judges could use the clauses of the Constitution and the most abstract common law maxims as operative premises. It followed that the judge had no choice but to abandon appeals to right, morality, utility or practicality where they conflicted with the results of deduction.

The gradually increasing importance of the method of induction and deduction in all the different areas of law amounted to a second kind of integration exactly analogous to the first. Scientific method created a parallelism of all the judge's actions in the vertical dimension, as will theory, autonomy and objectivism established parallelism in the horizontal. The steps of the process were also somewhat similar, as we will see in the next chapter. Scientific method appeared first in the law of federalism, and specifically in Marshall's famous opinions on the Commerce Clause. It also began to predominate in opinions on property law in the decade before the Civil War. After the War, it spread to the body of private law; only in the 1890's did it finally become commonplace in the field of rights against the state.

There were at least two senses in which the increasing breadth of horizontal integration was causally interrelated with increasing tightness in the vertical. One of these we might call the snowball effect. The concepts of will, autonomy and objectivism were among those discovered to have important particular implications. Their amenability to the new method was a strong argument in its favor. But their very existence as operative elements in the system was in part the outcome of the inductive side of the method. Classical thinkers discovered them everywhere; each discovery confirmed both their reality and the validity of the method that brought them to light.

The irony was that the very success of the enterprise of subsuming all legal relationships under a single small set of concepts eventually destroyed belief that it was the concepts themselves that determined the outcomes of their application. When the abstractions had performed their task of integrating legal thought, it became apparent that while pre-Classical particularity had been irrational, the new unity was merely linguistic—a verbal trick—rather than a substantive reconstruction. We came gradually to see that there were an infinity of possible results that might all plausibly find expression in the new conceptual language, and, what was worse, might all claim to be derivations of the abstract governing principles. The concepts, then, could be nothing more than a vocabulary for categorizing, describing and comparing, rather than the elements in a method for deriving outcomes. The famous principles, taken together, appeared either self-contradictory or so vague as to be worthless as guides to particular decisions.

It was only for a relatively brief moment, that during which the process of abstraction and unification was proceeding apace but had not yet achieved its disillusioning total triumph, that it was possible to believe in the objectivity of the new method. But it does not follow that the emergence of the new language was without long range influence on results. The work of destruction was in itself of massive impact on what could be thought about the legal order. Because the old way of thought was swallowed whole and digested by Classicism, we are without anything more than an indirect, quasi-antiquarian access to it. We attempt the construction of operative categories and integrating schemes in a world dominated by the death of the Classical organism, rather than in the naively pluralist world in which Classicism itself arose.

∾ 2 ∾

The second kind of causal interaction between the elements of the horizontal and vertical dimensions of Classical legal thought is more obscure. To modern eyes, the elements of the horizontal dimension all embody choices among the contradictory positions available within private and public law theory. Moreover, the choices made were by no means obviously harmonious. Objectivism means the sacrifice of an individual will in favor of a generalized social entity (the reasonable man) whose definition seems to us inherently arbitrary. The will theory implies that the will of the parties cannot extend to putting the judge in any role smacking of the arbitral, even where this limitation inevitably

252 leads to sanctioning arbitrariness. The strategy of autonomy means rejecting the direct enforcement of communal obligations without any more than a hope of achieving these objectives indirectly and "over the long run."

Likewise, in the vertical dimension we tend to regard the "scientific" character of the Classical theory of legal reasoning as illusory. To begin with, we doubt that *any* consistent set of principles can be induced from the relevant sources. Second, we do not believe in the deductive derivation of rule from principle. Where they claimed objectivity, we charge the vice of being "mechanical." Where they saw certainty, we see "formalism." Holmes' propositions, that the Constitution does not enact a social philosophy, and that, even if it did, general principles don't decide particular cases, have carried the day.

It is important to understand the precise point of disagreement. They admitted freely that legal rules were based on judgments of a political, moral and economic character. The right to contract was based on the political/moral/economic ideal of freedom; the limitation of the sphere of contract by consideration doctrine was based on reasons of policy and morality. The right to collect compensation for injuries was based on moral/economic ideals, limited by the moral notion that a person should not be held liable unless his conduct was morally or socially reprehensible. But they claimed that these foundations were plain for everyone to see: they were highly abstract and strikingly uncontroversial statements like *pacta sunt servanda*, or that a system of entails is inconsistent with political and social democracy, and they had been authoritatively established alike by popular acceptance, common law, and Constitution.

A basic question posed in this book is: How could Classical legal thinkers have believed in such a system? The question can be answered only by putting the system into a much larger context of moral, political and economic belief. The ideas of will theory, autonomy, objectivism and scientific method appeared both meaningful, neutral, and mutually consistent because of their places in a larger body of ideas that, as a whole, suppressed the contradictions of modern legal thought. This relation between

Classical legal thought and late nineteenth century thought in general might be called the external dialectic. The second part of this book will describe it in detail. It must be distinguished from the internal dialectic.

My premise is that although Classical legal thought is unintelligible except in relation to thought as a whole, it was nonetheless an entity. It was not a mere reflection upon law of extra-legal ideas. It had elements of internal coherence and a logic of its own that made it partially autonomous. The notion of the internal dialectic is to describe this autonomous systemic character. What this means is that we can give a partial explanation of the credibility of will theory, autonomy, objectivism and scientific method in terms of the internal needs of Classical legal thought. The explanation is that this group of ideas made possible the harmonious integration of the court-legislature relationship into the general schema.

Judges, like everyone else in the Classical system, had their sphere of absolute power. It was the power to decide "judicial questions," which meant the power to "apply" (as opposed to "make") the law. But the judges differed from all other actors in the system in that they were not *exercising* "will," but merely carrying out the wills of others. The impersonal, neutral character of the judicial function was what differentiated it from the legislative, and what justified the enormous power of judges in an otherwise democratic political system.

Each of the salient characteristics of Classical law was an indispensable element in the case for an impersonal, neutral judicial role. The casting of all legal rules in terms of the wills of legal actors meant that the judge could always claim that he was acting in subordination to an external compulsion. The parties to the contract, or the sovereign, decided everything; he decided nothing. He simple executed.

Autonomy and objectivism were protections against the danger that the judge would carry out his own will behind a smokescreen of interpretation. If the law prescribed only a minimum of duties of solidarity, it withdrew from the judge any right to appeal to the uncertain and fluctuating standards of his own particular morality

254   of aspiration. If boundary lines were defined by the literal meanings of words or the behavior of the reasonable man, the judge lost the chance to import his prejudices by way of an inquiry into subjective intention.

Both autonomy and objectivism implied, perhaps, a willingness to frustrate the expectations of the parties. But random disappointment of expectations in the application of a rigid standard meant judicial subordination. The parties *could* control the judge by mastering the formalities. Communal standards and subjectivism might secure their real will in a few cases, but only at the expense of institutionalizing judicial discretion.

Deduction from a small number of abstract first principles did for judicial rule formulation what autonomy and objectivism did for rule application. Since the process of derivation was neutral and impersonal, it could not be said to involve will of the kind legislatures exercised. And to put the judges above politics was therefore not inconsistent with democracy.

Given these characteristics, the role of the judiciary was as different as possible from that of the legislature. To begin with, the legislature was the proprietor, or master, or guardian of the public sphere of social and economic life. With respect to the management of the Army, the regulation of railroads and other activities "affected with a public interest," the printing of money, or the administration of public lands, the legislature was a legal power holder able to command absolute obedience to its will objectively construed. There was a strong, conscious analogy between the state and private economic actors so far as their relationship to the judiciary was concerned.

But there was a second legislative function that created a much more problematical relationship with the judges. In the exercise of the police power, the legislature had unquestionable jurisdiction to modify the common law rules laid down by the courts. The great battleground of Classical legal thought was the question of the exact nature of this jurisdiction. The dispute over "strict construction of statutes in derogation of the common law" was one incident in the larger struggle.

The details are not important for present purposes. It is enough to point out that even those who advocated codification of private law saw themselves as attempting to simplify, clarify and purify the existing body of judge made doctrine. Furthermore, their program required them to argue just as vociferously as their opponents that there existed an impersonal judicial role radically distinct from that of the legislator.

At the other extreme, those most hostile to legislation acknowledged that the very mechanisms that made judicial rule making neutral and impersonal—namely deductive method and adherence to precedent—also created rigidities. If judges were to be "bound," then there must be some mechanism to undo mistakes. Rapid changes in the conditions to which judges applied the general principles made prospective modifications of the rules desirable in at least a few cases. And there were cases where an arbitrary rule—the fixing of a statute of limitations, designation of which contracts must be in writing—was positively desirable. If judicial action was in its very nature rational rather than arbitrary, legislation was a necessity.

Given consensus on the sharp distinction between legislative and judicial functions, the theory of the separation of powers fitted neatly into the larger schema of Classical legal thought. The two institutions were powers absolute within their spheres. Judicial legislation was as reprehensible as legislative adjudication. But because of the peculiarity that it never asserted its own will, but only those of other actors in the system, the judiciary could be outside the schema as well as within it. Judges could define the limits of everyone else's powers/rights, without usurping sovereignty, because those limits were always implicit in the general principles they merely interpreted and applied.

∿ 3 ∾

The third form of integration of Classical legal thought had its origin in the descriptive generalization that legal rules involved will theory, autonomy and objectivism, and that the judicial role consisted of induction and deduction. The third integration transformed these empirical statements into necessary implications of

256   the "very nature" of fundamental legal concepts. For example, the Classics argued that it was implicit in the "very nature" of judging to proceed by induction and deduction. Since the various constitutions allocated only the judicial power to the judge, it would be a usurpation for him to proceed otherwise than scientifically.

We can describe the two steps of this process of integration schematically. First, there is the establishment of formal analogy:

The judicial power is to the private-private
relation as
the judicial power is to the private-legislature
relation as
the judicial power is to the state-state
relation as
the judicial power is to the state-federal
relation.

The second step is the assertion of the *unity* of the judicial power:

private-private		private-legislature
	judicial power	
state-state		state-federal

It is essential to remember that what occurs here is the result of abstraction. The particularity of the different relationships of legal actors to the judiciary is a primary fact: the judge develops and applies contract law between private parties, but constitutional law between individual and legislature. He does "the same thing" in the two situations only when through an analytic effort we bring into mental existence a concept that transcends this particularity. In this case, it is the complex concept of the judicial role as characterized by induction and deduction within the context of will theory, autonomy and objectivism.

During the classical period, a similar process of abstraction was at work on each of the other crucial legal concepts. Individuals have property rights among themselves and also property rights against the state. States have sovereign powers with respect to individuals and sovereign powers with respect to other states and the federal government. The content of these rights and powers varies from relation to relation, according to the identities of the actors involved, the sources of rule, and the modes of administering them. But the Classics conceived the property right as "the same thing" whether exercised against a neighbor or against the state, and sovereignty as the same thing whether its object was the citizen or another government.

We can distinguish three important phases in this process of fusion. The first, and easiest to grasp, concerns words like "property" in the just compensation clause and "contract" in the contracts clause of the federal constitution. Before the Civil War, there was only a limited tendency to identify the constitutional law meanings of these words with their common law meanings. After the Civil War, there was a striking tendency to argue that "property" is "property," whether we are talking about state takings or about neighborly violations of easements.

The second form of identification involved the phrase "police power." The police power was a crucial concept in the law of federalism. We have already seen that it came after the Civil War to be conceived as the countervailing entity to the federal commerce power. The two were formally identical but factually antagonistic. But the police power also figured in the law of rights against the state. In the 1880's, it became common to treat it in this context as the countervailing entity to individual rights to substantive autonomy. Its two aspects finally fused into a single more abstract entity whose nature was unitary, and whose implications could be worked out deductively in the different contexts of public law.

Finally, individual rights inter se came to be more than analogues of rights against the state. They came to *define* those rights. The rules of property and contract law were thought of as derived from abstract principles of property and contract that the people had enacted constitutionally in the due process clauses. The particular common law rules thus derived were no more subject to legislative change than the text itself. The rules constituted the body of substantive private economic rights. It was the function of the judges to police the boundary between individual and legislature exactly as they policed that between individual and individual.

258   Once again, we can begin with the formal analogies:

Private rights are to private rights

as

Private rights are to sovereign legislative powers

as

Sovereign state legislative powers are to
sovereign state legislative powers

as

Sovereign state legislative powers are to
sovereign federal legislative powers.

The second step is the identification of the private or public
right/power in one relation with that in the other.

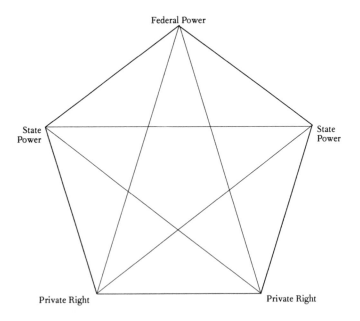

Finally, we can add the judicial power, which was identical with respect to each of the relationships in the structure, and also central to the whole, as the representative of the overarching constitutional scheme.

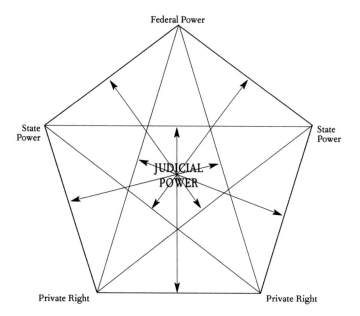

The third systemic characteristic of Classical legal thought was the assimilation of all of law to the highly integrated structure just described. The process of abstraction went beyond the creation of analogies, to the constitution of fused legal entities corresponding to the institutional actors in the system. The result was an interlocking pattern that was a kind of legal mirror image of the real world of political and economic action.

The abstractions that composed this system (e.g., judicial power, property, sovereignty) were fully *operative*. The property right was an entity from which both private and public law rights followed as deductions or implications. In itself, it was neither

260   public nor private: it was the more abstract notion of absolute dominion within a judicially delimited sphere. It was possible to speak of the various bodies of subrules, for example the law of easements, as "essential aspects" of the "very nature" of this concept. This meant that the whole system was as fully integrated in the vertical as in the horizontal dimension. In other words, the abstract concepts that fitted all legal relationships together in a pattern also provided the source of all particular legal rules.

When we add that all of the operative abstractions could be found in the federal Constitution, then we can close the system, in the sense of making it self- perpetuating through time. The constitutionalization of the first principles put the whole beyond the danger of subversion through the aggressiveness of any of its parts. The judiciary, as interpreter of the Constitution, became the custodian of the orderliness of the structure, and the judiciary had no particular "will" of its own. As long as the judges, according to the "nature" of the judicial power, operated always in the context of will theory, absoluteness, objectivism and deduction constrained by precedent, the will controlling the whole would be that of the People.

This brings us to a final point about the relationship between public and private law in Classical legal thought: the use of the common law rules to provide a meaning for concepts like property, liberty, contract, and so forth, reenforced the judges' claim to a neutral, apolitical method of public law adjudication. The process of abstraction made the unquestionable legality of private law available as a structure for public law rights that would otherwise have seemed too dangerously undefined for judicial administration. This is the "parasitism hypothesis." It suggests that there was something more to the process of abstraction by which we acquired fused notions of property, contract, etc., than the autonomous systematizing impulse. The type of abstraction that occurred served to further integrate the system, to further elaborate its "logic." It gave the theorists of the relatively weak public law sector access to the strength of the private law sector.

I mean to suggest a property of the system here, rather than a causal hypothesis. There is a parallel with the emergence of will theory, absoluteness and objectivism. These *functioned* to support

the judges' claim to act in a neutral and apolitical fashion.
Likewise, the use of common law rules, supposedly implicit in
operative constitutional abstractions like liberty and property,
functioned to make rights against the state seem legal rather than
political. If freedom of contract was part of the liberty guaranteed
against state action by the Fourteenth Amendment, and if the
common law provided *the* definition of contract, then there was a
neutral, apolitical basis for judicial review of social legislation.

At that point the "logic of the system" created intense jeopardy
for the theory of private law. Feeding on the felt operativeness of
common law concepts, the legal elite made radical claims about
judicial power under the due process clause. A basic objective of
sociological jurisprudence and then of legal realism came to be to
undermine the basis for this judicial activism. And beginning
around the turn of the century, it was clear that the system was so
fully integrated that an attack on a part was an attack on the whole.
One of the most effective tactics proved to be the demonstration
that the supposed operativeness of the private law concepts was
illusory. Public law issues thus drew the attention of liberals and
progressives to the critique of private law.

∾ 4 ∾

The famous 1933 case of *Home Building & Loan Association v.
Blaisdell* may serve as an illustration of each of the preceding
points about Classical legal thought. Wisconsin had passed a
mortgage moratorium, temporarily allowing debtors to avoid
foreclosure in spite of their inability to make scheduled payments.
The question was whether this law violated the constitutional provision against impairment of the obligation of contracts. For
Justice Sutherland dissenting, the "obligation" consisted of the
common law rights of the creditor as defined by the parties in the
mortgage agreement:

> The phrase, "obligation of a contract," in the constitutional sense
> imports a legal duty to perform the specified obligation of that
> contract, not to substitute and perform, against the will of the par-
> ties, a different, albeit equally valuable, obligation. And a state,

under the contract impairment clause, has no more power to accomplish such a substitution than has one of the parties to the contract against the will of the other. [482]

In this view of the matter, the public law right against impairment of the obligation of contract was defined by the private law rules of contract. To discover just what entity it was that the legislature must leave alone, we consult the common law rules about what the contract creditor is entitled to receive from the debtor. If the legislature is changing those rules after the fact then it is impairing the obligation. The judge resisting a legislative interference with the contract is performing exactly the same function as the judge who orders specific performance or damages for a private breach.

What this view suppressed was the similarity between legislative regulations of existing contracts and common law judicial rule making by the case method. Sutherland's way of putting it suggested that the private law rules were simply facilitative of the will of the parties, rather than inherently regulatory in their own right. What he dropped out was the "will" of the judges, who, in the modern view, had from the beginning defined just what kind of enforcement mortgages were to receive.

The importance of the suppression of the "legislative" regulatory character of the common law rules was that it allowed Sutherland to claim that the moratorium obviously impaired the mortgage obligation. He saw that obligation as fixed by the parties; the legislature was interfering; ergo it was impairing. In the modern view, however, to show interference is not enough. There is a need to show that the statute in question is *more* of an interference than the common law rules, so that it does, although the common law rules do not, impair the obligation of contract.

Justice Hughes based his majority opinion in part on the proposition that no such distinction was possible. The State, through its judges had all along been impairing or regulating contract rights. It followed that the Contracts clause had never protected an "absolute" obligation, but rather an obligation subject to "reasonable" limits on individual autonomy. Judged by this standard, the statute was acceptable:

In the absence of legislation, courts of equity have exercised jurisdiction in suits for the foreclosure of mortgages to fix the time and terms of sale and to refuse to confirm sales upon equitable grounds where they were found to be unfair or inadequacy of price was so gross as to shock the conscience. The "equity of redemption" [which allows the debtor to avoid foreclosure by paying up even after he has violated his contract by falling in arrears] is the creature of equity. . . . This principle of equity was victorious against the strong opposition of the common law judges, who thought that by "the Growth of Equity on Equity the Heart of the Common Law is eaten out." The equitable principle became firmly established and its application could not be frustrated even by the engagement of the debtor entered into at the time of the mortgage, the courts applying the equitable maxim "once a mortgage, always a mortgage, and nothing but a mortgage." Although the courts would have no authority to alter a statutory period of redemption, the legislation in question permits the courts to extend that period, within limits and upon equitable terms, thus providing a procedure and relief which are cognate to the historic exercise of the equitable jurisdiction. If it be determined, as it must be, that the contract clause is not an absolute and utterly unqualified restriction of the State's protective power, this legislation is clearly so reasonable as to be within the legislative competency. [397-98]

In effect, Sutherland was claiming that the public law right was certain and judicially administrable because founded on highly legal, operative private law concepts. The critics set out to show that, on the contrary, the common law rules represented the policy and moral judgments of a corps of economic regulators. It followed that the constitutional references to property, contract, liberty, and so forth, could not provide operative bases for judicial review, and that the judges should defer to the legislatures. Unfortunately, the legitimacy of common law adjudication was exploded along with the public law edifice that had been built upon it.

Before we return to the investigation of the origins of this dilemma, we may pause on the ironies of generational conflict.

264   The spirit of Classicism, of writers like Holmes, Bishop, Gray, Smith, Brewer, Peckham, was that of post-Civil War disillusionment with an old ethos, and of willingness to try a Grand Scheme on problems the pre-Classical thinkers had preferred to duck. The spirit of the post-World War I modernism that laid that Grand Scheme low was not dissimilar. Henry James, who knew many of the participants in the making of Classicism, described the mood of his generation in words that apply *mutatis mutandis* to that which followed:

> Such was the bewildered sensation of that earlier and simpler generation of which I have spoken; their illusions were rudely dispelled, and they saw the best of all possible republics given over to fratricidal carnage. This affair had no place in their scheme, and nothing was left for them but to hang their heads and close their eyes. The subsidence of that great convulsion has left a different tone from the tone it found, and one may say that the Civil War marks an era in the history of the American mind. It introduced into the national consciousness a certain sense of proportion and relation, of the world being a more complicated place than it had hitherto seemed, the future more treacherous, success more difficult. At the rate at which things are going, it is obvious that good Americans will be more numerous than ever; but the good American, in days to come, will be a more critical person than his complacent and confident grandfather. [James, *Hawthorne*, 139-40]

He ends sententiously (but one can sympathize): "He has eaten of the tree of knowledge."

BIBLIOGRAPHY

Addison, Charles, *Wrongs and their Remedies: Being a Treatise on the Law of Torts* (London: V. & R. Stevens & Sons, 1860)

Amos, Sheldon, *The Science of Law* (New York: D. Appleton, 1878)

Anson, William, *Principles of the English Law of Contract* (Oxford: Clarendon Press, 1879)

Austin, John, *Lectures on Jurisprudence, or The Philosophy of Positive Law* (London: J. Murray, 1861)

Bigelow, Melville, *Leading Cases on the Law of Torts Determined by the Courts of America and England* (Boston: Little Brown, 1875)

Bigelow, Melville, *Elements of the Law of Torts, for the Use of Students* (Boston: Little Brown, 1878)

Bishop, Joel, *Commentaries on the Law of Marriage and Divorce and Evidence in Matrimonial Suits* (Boston: Little Brown, 1852)

Bishop, Joel, *New Commentaries on Marriage and Divorce and Separation* (Chicago: T.H. Flood, 1891)

Blackstone, William, *Commentaries on the Laws of England* (Oxford: Clarendon Press, 1765-69)

Bryce, James, *The American Commonwealth* (New York: Macmillan, 1888)

Cooley, Thomas, *A Treatise on the Constitutional Limitations which Rest upon the Legislative Power of the States of the American Union* (Boston: Little Brown, 1868)

266   Cooley, Thomas, *A Treatise on the Law of Torts: or the Wrongs which Arise Independent of Contract* (Chicago: Callaghan, 1879)

Corwin, Edward, The Doctrine of Due Process of Law Before the Civil War," 24 *Harv. L. Rev.* 366 (1910)

Corwin, Edward, The Basic Doctrine of American Constitutional Law, 12 *Mich. L. Rev.* 247 (1914)

Corwin, Edward, The Higher Law Background of American Constitutional Law, 42 *Harv. L. Rev.* 149 (1928)

Costigan, George, Constructive Contracts, 19 *The Green Bag* 512 (1907)

Dawson, John, *Restitution or Damages?* (Columbus: Ohio State University Press, 1959)

Gilmore, Grant, *The Death of Contract* (Columbus: Ohio State University Press, 1974)

Gray, John Chipman, *Restraints on the Alienation of Property* (Boston: C.C. Soule, 1883)

Hilliard, Francis, *The Law of Torts, or Private Wrongs* (Boston: Little Brown, 1859)

Holland, Thomas, *The Elements of Jurisprudence* (Oxford: Clarendon Press, 1889)

Holmes, Oliver Wendell, Codes, and the Arrangement of the Law, 5 *Am. L. Rev.* 1 (1870)

Holmes, Oliver Wendell, The Arrangement of the Law: Privity, 7 *Am. L. Rev.* 46 (1872)

Holmes, Oliver Wendell, The Theory of Torts, 7 *Am. L. Rev.* 652 (1873).

Holmes, Oliver Wendell, *The Common Law* (Boston: Little Brown, 1881)

Horwitz, Morton, *The Transformation of American Law* (Cambridge: Harvard Univ. Press, 1977)

Howe, Mark, Justice *Oliver Wendell Holmes: II. The Proving Years* (Cambridge: Harvard University Press, 1963)

Jaffe, Louis, *English and American Judges as Lawmakers* (Oxford: Clarendon Press, 1969)

James, Henry, *Hawthorne* (London: MacMillan & Co., 1879)

Keener, William, *A Treatise on the Law of Quasi-Contracts* (New York: Baker, Voorhis, 1893)

Kent, James, *Commentaries on American Law*, 12th ed., Oliver Wendell Holmes, ed. (Boston: Little Brown, 1873)

Kessler, Friedrich & Gilmore, Grant, *Contracts: Cases and Materials*, 2nd ed. (Boston: Little Brown, 1970)

Koegel, Otto, *Common Law Marriage and its Development in the United States* (Washington: J. Byrne & Co., 1922)

Langdell, Christopher Columbus, *A Summary of the Law of Contracts* (Boston: Little Brown, 1880)

Leake, Martin, *The Elements of the Law of Contracts* (London: Stevens, 1867)

Levi-Strauss, Claude, *The Savage Mind* (Chicago: University of Chicago Press, 1966)

Locke, John, *Two Treatises of Government*, Laslett, ed. (New York: New American Library, 1965)

Lukacs, Georg, Reification and the Consciousness of the Proletariat, in *History and Class Consciousness* (Cambridge: MIT Press, 1971)

Maine, Henry, *Ancient Law* (London: Murray, 1861)

Mannheim, Karl, *Ideology and Utopia* (New York: Harcourt Brace & World, 1936)

Markby, William, *Elements of Law Considered with Reference to Principles of General Jurisprudence* (Oxford: Clarendon, 1871)

268

Metcalf, Theron, *Principles of the Law of Contracts as Applied by Courts of Law* (New York: Hurd & Houghton, 1867)

Milsom, S.F.C., *Historical Foundations of the Common Law* (London: Butterworths, 1969)

Marcuse, Herbert, *Reason and Revolution: Hegel and the Rise of Social Theory* (New York: Oxford Univ. Press, 1941)

Parsons, Theophilus, *The Law of Contracts* (Boston: Little Brown, 1853-55)

Perillo, Joseph, Restitution in a Contractual Context, 73 *Colum. L. Rev.* 1208 (1973)

Piaget, Jean, *Play, Dreams and Imitation in Childhood* (New York: Norton, 1962)

Pollock, Frederick, *The Law of Torts: A Treatise on the Principles of Obligations arising from Civil Wrongs in the Common Law* (Philadelphia: Blackstone Pub. Co., 1887)

Pollock, Frederick, *Principles of Contract at Law and in Equity* (London: Stevens, 1876)

Pollock, Frederick & Maitland, William, *The History of English Law Before the Time of Edward I* (2nd ed., S.F.C. Milsom, ed., Cambridge: Cambridge Univ. Press, 1968)

Pound, Roscoe, The End of Law as Developed in Juristic Thought: II. The Nineteenth Century, 30 *Harv. L. Rev.* 201 (1917)

Pound, Roscoe, Consideration in Equity, 13 *Ill. L. Rev.* 667 (1919)

Reeve, Tapping, *The Law of Baron and Femme* (New Haven: Oliver Steele, 1816)

Salmond, John, *The First Principles of Jurisprudence* (London: Stevens & Haynes, 1893)

Story, William, *A Treatise on the Law of Contracts not under Seal* (Boston: Little Brown, 1844)

Terry, Henry, *The First Principles of Law* (Tokyo: Z.P. Maruya, 1878)   269

Tiedeman, Christopher, *The Unwritten Constitution of the United States* (New York: G.P. Putnam & Sons, 1890)

Von Jhering, Rudolph, *Geist des Romischen Rechts* (Leipzig: Breitkopf und Hartel, 1852-1865), French translation: *L'Esprit du Droit Romain* (O. de Meulenaire, trans., Paris: Chevalier-Maresq, 1887)

Whittier, Clarke, The Restatement of Contracts and Mutual Assent, 17 *Cal. L. Rev.* 441 (1929)

Wigmore, John, The Tripartite Division of Torts, 8 *Harv. L. Rev.* 200 (1894)

Williston, Samuel, Mutual Assent in the Formation of Contracts, 14 *Ill. L. Rev.* 525 (1919)

INDEX OF CASES AND NAMES

Cases

Adair v. U.S., 63

Blyth v. Birmingham, 234

Boone v. Coe, 238

Brown v. Bd. of Education, 49

Brown v. Kendall, 230, 231, 233, 234

Calder v. Bull, 51

Callendar v. Marsh, 115

Civil Rights cases, 91

Collector v. Day, 40

Corfield v. Coryell, 81

Dartmouth College case, 65

Dygert v. Bradley, 231

Gelpcke v. Dubuque, 248

Gibbons v. Ogden, 82

Grimley's Case, 203, 204

Hertzog v. Hertzog, 172-174

Home Bldg. & Loan Assoc. v. Blaisdell, 261-63

In re Debs, 17-20

Laidlaw v. Organ, 110

Loan Association v. Topeka, 52

Lochner v. New York, 8-16

McCulloch v. Maryland, 15-16

Moses v. Macpherlan, 159

Norrington v. Wright, 227

Ogden v. Saunders, 248

Pacific Steamship Co. v. Joliff, 173

Pumpelly v. Green Bay Co., 47

Reapportionment Cases, 49

Reagan v. Farmer's Loan & Trust, 62

Robertson v. State, 200

Rylands v. Fletcher, 233, 234

Slaughterhouse Cases, 50, 77-92

Swift v. Tyson, 114

Texas v. White, 35-38

Thurston v. Hancock, 153

Tyler v. Pomeroy, 203

U.S. v. DeWitt, 39

U.S. v. Bainbridge, 203

Yick Wo v. Hopkins, 49

Names

Addison, Charles, 176, 177

Amos, Sheldon, 182

Anson, William, 205, 206, 207, 221, 222

Austin, John, 173, 174, 187, 190, 193

Berman, Harold, 244

Bigelow, Melville, 179, 180

Bishop, Joel, 196, 197, 198, 200, 264

Blackstone, William, 32, 34. 114, 119, 120, 121, 139, 150, 160, 170, 172, 180, 185, 186, 189, 190

Bradley, Justice, 46, 84-90, 231

Brewer, Justice, 17, 46, 50, 84-91

Bryce, James, 36, 40, 41

Cardozo, Benjamin, 244

Chase, Chief Justice Salmond, 36, 39, 55, 57

Chase, Chief Justice Samuel, 51, 61

Clifford, Justice, 52, 54, 60, 81

Cohen, Felix, 244

Cohen, Morris, 244

Coke, Lord, 90

Cook, Walter Wheeler, 223

Cooley, Thomas, 33, 65-69, 86, 234, 235

Corbin, Arthur, 206

Corwin, Edward, 44, 60, 61, 65

Costigan, George, 223, 224, 236

Dawson, John, 239

Deutsch, Jan, 244

Dewey, John, 244

Dworkin, Ronald, 244

Field, Justice, 84-91, 207, 232

Fuller, Lon, 244

Gilmore, Grant, 225, 227

Gray, John Chipman, 148-152, 180, 264

Gray, Horace, 203

Hamilton, Alexander, 70

Hamilton, Walton, 244

Harlan, Justice, 9, 13, 15, 16, 51

Hart, H.L.A., 244

Hart, Henry, 244

Hilliard, Francis, 176, 177

Hohfeld, Wesley, 244

Holland, Thomas, 182, 190. 194, 207, 221, 222, 223

Holmes, Oliver Wendell, 9, 121, 138, 151, 152, 173, 174, 178, 179, 180, 181, 198, 207, 213, 214, 225, 233, 235, 226,

240, 244, 252, 264

Horwitz, Morton, 29, 153, 154, 230

Howe, Mark, 234, 236

Hughes, Chief Justice, 262

Iredell, Justice, 60

Jaffe, Louis, 71

James, Henry, 264

Keener, William, 174, 175, 237

Kent, James, 47, 115, 119-44, 150, 152, 158, 170, 180, 186, 195, 198, 215, 217

Kessler, Friedrich, 227

Koegel, Otto, 201

Langdell, Christopher Columbus, 207, 214, 220, 221, 225

Leake, Martin, 173, 207, 208, 219, 220, 223

Levi-Strauss, Claude, 29

Llewellyn, Karl, 244

Locke, John, 64

Lukacs, Georg, 29

Maine, Henry, 173, 180, 192, 193

Maitland, William, 29

Mannheim, Karl, 29

Mansfield, Lord, 126, 129, 158, 159

Marcuse, Herbert, 29

Markby, William, 177, 178, 180, 181, 207, 233

Metcalf, Joseph, 122, 186

Miller, Justice, 47, 52-55, 61, 79-91

Milsom, S.F.C., 42

Marcuse, Herbert, 29

Parsons, Theophilus, 110, 122, 138, 159-72, 207, 214-21, 222

Peckham, Justice, 8-14, 264

Perillo, Joseph, 237

Piaget, Jean, 29

Pollock, Frederick, 29, 207, 221, 222, 234, 246

Pound, Roscoe, 118, 167, 209, 212, 215, 244

Reeve, Tapping, 199

Salmond, John, 182

Smith, Adam, 86

Story, Justice, 195, 202, 204

Story, W. W., 122, 170, 186

Sutherland, Justice, 261, 263

Swayne, Justice, 86

Terry, Henry, 150, 182, 183, 191

Thayer, James Bradley, 180

Tiedeman, Christopher, 37

Von Jhering, Rudolph, 29

Wasserstrom, Richard, 244

Wechsler, Herbert, 244

Wellington, Harry, 244

Whittier, 211, 212, 219, 224

Wigmore, John, 183-84

Williston, Samuel, 174, 210-214, 219, 225